adriana's
SPICE
CARAVAN

Exciting cross-cultural recipes using over 100 easily obtainable, exotic herbs, spices, and blends

ADRIANA ZABARKES
AND ROCHELLE ZABARKES

A Storey Publishing Book

STOREY COMMUNICATIONS, INC.
SCHOOLHOUSE ROAD
POWNAL, VERMONT 05261

To my co-author:
There are no words that make me happier than
"This is my daughter, Adriana."

The mission of Storey Communications is to serve our customers by publishing practical information that encourages personal independence in harmony with the environment.

Editor: Pamela Lappies
Project Editor: Deri Reed
Designer: Eugenie Seidenberg Delaney
Production assistance: Erin Lincourt
Illustrator: Laura Tedeschi
Indexer: Word•a•bil•i•ty

Storey Publishing books are available for special premium and promotional uses and for customized editions. For further information, please call the Custom Publishing Department at 1-800-793-9396.

Printed in United States the United States by R. R. Donnelley
10 9 8 7 6 5 4 3 2 1

For permission to reprint copyright materials the publisher gratefully acknowledges the following:

Page 1: From *Herbs & the Earth* by Henry Beston. Reprinted by permission of David R. Godine, Publisher, Inc. Copyright ©1935 by Henry Beston. **Pages 6, 141, and 154:** Excerpted from *Sinkin Spells, Hot Flashes, Fits & Cravins,* copyright ©1988 by Ernest Matthew Mickler, with permission from Ten Speed Press, P. O. Box 7123, Berkeley, CA 94707. **Page 45:** Georgia Blend (adapted from) *The Cooking of the Eastern Mediterranean* by Paula Wolfert. Copyright © 1994 by Paula Wolfert. Reprinted by permission of HarperCollins Publishers, Inc. for additional territories: Lescher & Lescher, 67 Irving Place, New York, NY 1003. **Page 50:** From *London Fields* by Martin Amis. Reprinted by permission of Crown Publishers Inc. Copyright ©1990 by Martin Amis. **Page 55:** From *The Travels of Marco Polo* by Manuel Komroff. Copyright 1926 by Boni & Liverwright, Inc. renewed © 1958 by Manuel Komroff. Reprinted by permission of Liverwright Publishing Corporation. **Page 60:** From *Blue Highways* by William Least Heat Moon. Reprinted by permission of Little, Brown and Company. Copyright ©1983 by William Least Heat Moon. **Pages 95 and 176:** Copyright © 1994 by John Ferrone. Reprinted from *Love & Kisses & a Halo of Truffles: Letters to Helen Evans Brown* by James Beard, edited by John Ferrone, published by Arcade Publishing, Inc., New York, NY. **Page 158:** From *A Book of Middle Eastern Food* by Claudia Roden. Reprinted by permission of Alfred A. Knopf, Inc. Copyright ©1974 by Claudia Roden.

Library of Congress Cataloging-in-Publication Data

Zabarkes, Adriana, 1970-
   Adriana's spice caravan: cooking with spices, rubs, and blends from around the world/Adriana Zabarkes and Rochelle Zabarkes.
      p.   cm.
   Includes bibliographical references and index.
   ISBN 0-88266-987-7 (pb : alk. paper)
   1. Cookery (Spices) 2. Spices. I. Zabarkes, Rochelle, 1942-   . II. Title.   III. Title: Spice caravan.
   TX819.A1Z33   1997
   641.6'383—DC21
                                        97-16042
                                        CIP

Contents

Acknowledgments

Thanks to all of my family, friends, and associates who have been unfailingly supportive even though I'm going to make them pay for copies of the book.

Special thanks to Romy Dorotan, Jeff Loshinsky, Irene Khin Wong, and Rachel Yohannes for contributing their tantalizing recipes.

Additional thanks to Pamela Lappies, my editor at Storey, for calmly guiding me through the 5-Step Program of Authorship:

1. January 1 due date? Oh, Pamela, no problemo.

2. I'm writing the back of the book first; I'm sure it won't be a problem.

3. Can you explain again why you're so sure this book needs an introduction?

4. I won't allow you to cut that. It is absolutely my favorite paragraph in the *whole* book.

5. That was fun, when can we do another one?

More thanks to Deri Reed, my project editor, for wanting a good book as much as I do.

And, finally, many many thanks to David Weller, for an endless store of tolerance, good humor, friendship, and take-out food.

— R. Z.

DISCLAIMER

From ancient times to the present, superstitions and folk tales have risen about many of these spices and herbs. We have related some of these ancient beliefs and recipes for their historical interest only. None of these spices or herbs are proved to have any medicinal effect.

İntroduction

About 10,000 years ago, someone decided to throw some leaves, sticks, and seeds on her dinner — and changed the flavors of food forever. She may have lived in the Mediterranean basin, and used the herbs that grew around her — bay, dill, fennel, marjoram, oregano, and thyme.

Spices, most of which grow in tropical climates, would not appear on the Mediterranean scene for another 6,000 years. But when they arrived, these tiny little bits of dried bark, buds, flowers, berries, seeds, and roots managed to provoke wars, build empires, inspire poetry, evoke mythologies, induce madness, anoint bodies, and work miracles. Spices and herbs not only changed the flavors of food, they changed the history of the world, too.

The Egyptians were the first to crave great quantities of spices and herbs — anise, caraway, cassia, cardamom, fenugreek, and saffron. They used them for embalming and honoring their dead, anointing their bodies with perfumed oils, and sweetening the air in their homes.

Imagine the daring of the Phoenician spice traders who, in 1450 B.C., sailed down the Red Sea and out into the Indian Ocean, or westward through the Mediterranean into the Atlantic and around the Cape of Good Hope, looking for spices, known and unknown. The dangers they faced were both mythological and real. A many-headed sea serpent might have been waiting in the middle of those deep, black waters to swallow ship and crew whole. One sailor had to watch the horizon

A garden of herbs need be no larger than the shadow of a bush, yet within it, as in no other, a mood of the earth approaches and encounters the spirit of man. Beneath these ancestral leaves, these immemorial attendants of man, these servants of his magic and healers of his pain, the earth underfoot is the earth of poetry and the human spirit; in this small sun and shade flourishes a whole tradition of mankind. This flower is Athens, this tendril, Rome; a monk of the Dark Ages tended this green against the wall; with this scented leaf were kings welcomed in the morning of the world.

HERBS & THE EARTH,
HENRY BESTON, 1935

1

So in many other Things in Cookery, the great Cooks have such a high Way of expressing themselves that the poor Girls are at a Loss to know what they mean: And in all Receipt Books yet printed there are such an odd Jumble of Things as would quite spoil a good Dish; and indeed some Things so extravagant, that it would be almost a Shame to make Use of them, when a Dish can be made full as good, or better without them.

THE ART OF COOKERY MADE PLAIN & EASY,
MRS. HANNAH GLASSE, 1747

endlessly, to scream warning if the edge of the world suddenly came into view. More often, however, the end of the world appeared in the guise of storms, starvation, scurvy, disease, mutiny, or just getting lost.

The value of spices was made quite clear in the Bible, when the Queen of Sheba presented Solomon with gold, jewels, and spices to keep control of her trade routes, which were being threatened by the Phoenicians. Spice traders were commonplace: Joseph was sold by his brothers to spice merchants, the first traveling salesmen, for 20 pieces of silver.

Later, to satisfy the European demand for spices, the strategically located Arabs acted as middlemen in the spice trade with the Orient and Africa. They preserved their monopoly for centuries by keeping their sources a secret and concocting alarming, fantastical stories of fierce winged animals and poisonous snakes.

The Roman aristocracy exhibited an almost insatiable hunger for spices and strongly flavored food; whether this was spurred by their adventurous palates or by lead poisoning is unclear. Eventually, Roman mariners, sailing from India to Egypt, discovered the monsoon winds, which shortened their journeys to less than a year, and they broke the Arab hold on the spice trade. Ironically, the Romans drained their coffers of gold to buy black pepper and other spices, only to be compelled to pay a ransom of pepper to prevent the sacking of their city by the Goths.

During the Middle Ages there was very little spice trading. However, the desire for personal fame, the glory of God, and, not incidentally, a share in the wealth of the burgeoning spice trade ushered in the Age of Discovery in the 15th century. For the next 300 years the countries of Europe engaged in a reign of piracy and tyranny as each entered the water to seize a piece of the spice action.

Spice routes, silk roads, and saffron trails ribboned the world as explorers stirred up the waters and passions. Egypt, Arabia, Rome, Spain, Portugal, Italy, England, the Netherlands, and France all tried to take too much of the map. For one brief moment in time each country owned the world.

Fortunately, my own history is not nearly so tyrannical. When most cookbook authors reminisce about growing up, they paint pictures of fragrant kitchens and of grandmothers lovingly making food from the Old Country. My own memories are equally picturesque, but somewhat perverse. I remember my grandmother harboring a live carp in the bathtub and bludgeoning it to death just after I gave it a name. I'm sure the resulting gefilte fish was exquisitely flavored, but I couldn't touch it.

My mother learned to cook from her mother, but somehow the skill was never passed on to me. On one of the rare occasions when I was allowed in the kitchen, I shook cherry soda until it exploded and sticky droplets fell from the ceiling. I was also on the scene waiting for bacon to "crisp" in the pan and nearly set the house on fire.

I managed to make it to womanhood and marriage without a scrap of usable cooking knowledge. As a newlywed, my first attempt at lasagna contained two bulbs of garlic instead of two cloves — the aroma was staggering. Strangely, I was undaunted, and the marriage and my enthusiasm in the kitchen continued.

As my cooking skills evolved, the medieval cook's instruction to "smite them to pieces" and "hew them in gobbets" pretty much summed up my own approach to cooking, which can be described as cross-cultural casual.

Looking back, I see that knowing nothing was an advantage — I brought no cultural or familial food biases with me. I am living proof that all you need to know to cook great meals is how to read.

I put cooking and other household pleasures aside to be an audiovisual producer in New York. After 18 years in the biz, I decided that I needed to create something that no one had ever done, so that no one could tell me how to do it. I came up with the idea of a cook's store that would have hundreds of free international recipes, all of the ingredients necessary for those recipes, and ethnic kitchenware. One year later, I opened Adriana's Bazaar (named after my daughter and, now,

The only real stumbling block is fear of failure. In cooking you've got to have a what-the-hell attitude.

JULIA CHILD

my co-author) on the Upper West Side of Manhattan and became part of the amazing world of food.

The store has evolved into Adriana's Caravan — a mail-order catalog of every exotic food in the world and an eclectic catering company. I have found that this world of cookery is an extraordinary blend of nurturing and creativity. Now that I'm here I don't want to leave. I want to build my mail-order and catering businesses, but I also want to write books that give people the opportunity to explore new flavors and cuisines and to enjoy themselves in the kitchen. So here we go. But first, a few words about spices and what you'll need in the kitchen.

SPICE AND HERB CARE

After that arduous journey, the saga of passion and wars, spices have finally arrived in our kitchens. It is in the best interests of good cooks everywhere to treat them kindly.

Whenever possible, purchase and use fresh herbs (with roots still attached) instead of dried herbs. When making a sauce such as pesto, there's just no substitute for fresh basil. Whole herbs, loosely wrapped and stored in the refrigerator, will keep for 3 to 5 days. Chop leftover herbs and freeze in an ice cube tray with water. Simply pop a cube into soups and stews as needed.

Store dried herbs in tightly sealed glass jars away from heat and light. Dried herbs will remain potent for about 2 to 3 months.

Purchase whole spices whenever possible and dry-roast before using to heighten flavor. Grind spices using a mortar and pestle or an electric or manual coffee/spice grinder. Store spices in tightly sealed glass jars away from heat and light. Dried spices will remain potent for about 6 months.

EQUIPMENT

In addition to the usual pots and pans, I have a slightly eccentric short list of kitchen necessities.

MORTAR AND PESTLE — Use a mortar and pestle to pulverize small quantities of spices. Each country has its own version of this tool. In Mexico the *molcajete* is made from lava rock; in Thailand a large, smooth stone mortar is the implement of destruction. Japan has an elegant, ridged ceramic vessel, and the Italians use marble. All are available in specialty food markets and by mail.

COFFEE/SPICE GRINDER — For large quantities of spices use a manual or electric grinder. The most beautiful are the tall, slim brass and copper grinders from Turkey.

PROPANE TORCH — When I owned Adriana's Bazaar we topped our crème brûlées with sugar and browned them with a propane torch. This method offers much more control than the broiler, and is also very showy. Just stay away from the drapes.

CHINESE BAMBOO STEAMERS — I'm particularly fond of these tiered, woven steamers, because you can steam more than one food at a time, and the odors from one dish suffuse the others.

WOK — A 14-inch wok, equipped with a lid and a collar to support the wok, may become the most useful utensil in your kitchen. Use it for stir-frying, deep-frying, simmering, and steaming.

MUSTARD DISPENSERS — Once you've completed the cooking of the dish, it deserves a little plate decor. Buy a bunch of mustard or ketchup dispensers, and fill them with different sauces. Decorate the plates with names or words ("hot, hot, hot"). Draw something that vaguely represents the country of origin. Or drizzle on stripes, polka dots, or zigzags. You may have to snip off a bit of the top to let the sauces flow more freely.

HAIR DRYER — Nothing works better for drying a duck.

The other most important thing to remember in life was the total inadvisability of insulting the cook. What could be more misguided and reckless? When you thought of the power wielded by the cook, it was tantamount to taunting the driver on a hairpin bend.

THE 27TH KINGDOM,
ALICE THOMAS ELLIS, 1982

This book is about history, achievement, and enjoyment — yours and that of the people you cook for — with an emphasis on bold flavors.

If some unfamiliar spices are not available locally, you can get them from the mail-order sources in the back of the book. I encourage you to find these exotic ingredients and cook with them, but make substitutions if necessary — there are no spice police to tell you what or how to cook. Occasionally you may want to spend the whole day in the kitchen cooking and puttering. For those *other* days (and we all have them) a prepackaged product (roux, for example) will work as well as your own, and save you hours of work. My mother marinates one of the world's great shrimp dishes in Miracle Whip. Ask her for the recipe; she likes getting mail.

Today poetry and passion are inspired by things other than spices, and exploration occurs in the kitchen, not on the high seas. Chefs cross cultures instead of oceans as they blend the exotic flavors of other cuisines into their own domestic offerings. Every spice you stir into the broth carries with it a tiny fragment of history, and has links to the earliest kitchen in the world.

The techniques of cooking haven't changed all that much over the centuries. Sure, Mom or Dad is in the kitchen in cutoff jeans wearing a headset — you can hear the buzz of rap music — and waving a propane torch, but the basics are still the same. Read the ancient recipes in the sidebars with our contemporary offerings, and notice how similar some of them are to what you're making for dinner.

Now it's your turn to discover exotic spices, explore new cuisines, and expand your horizons. Cook boldly with herbs and spices. Create new flavors, because the world isn't flat anymore, and neither is food.

— ROCHELLE ZABARKES, 1997

An' you ladies out there, that works hard in your kitchens, I know I can depend on you to help me spot all that store-bought stuff and we'll throw it straight to the dawgs, where it belongs. Can you imagine seein' Mrs. Bridie duMac's delicious Shoe soles and Grits sittin' right next to a slice of some nasty frozen Pizza. Is that what we want our dinner affair to turn out to. No, It ain't!!

SINKIN SPELLS, HOT FLASHES,
FITS & CRAVINGS,
ERNEST MATTHEW MICKLER, 1988

Spice and Herb Guide

Spices have always enjoyed center stage. Read what the Bible, Shakespeare, Apicius, Gerard, and other notables, including Miss Piggy, have had to say about them. Enjoy the complexity and diversity of the following spices and herbs as we weave you a tale about their habitats, properties, flavors, and uses, as well as the fascinating lore surrounding them.

ALLSPICE

Thousands of years ago, the people of the Sun King, the Aztecs, were busily engaged in human sacrifice, but they also enjoyed the simple pleasures, like allspice in their frothy, hot, chocolate beverage.

Allspice, a versatile spice used in both sweet and savory dishes, flourished in subtropical America long before European explorers were presumptuous enough to call this continent the New World. The puzzling little allspice berry was overlooked completely by Columbus on his first voyage, and mistakenly called *pimienta,* or pepper, on the second trip — but what would you expect from a man who couldn't find China? The only spice to grow close to the colonies in North America, allspice was used exuberantly by the early settlers in pies and cakes. In the 19th century, allspice almost became an ex-spice, as Europeans and Americans displayed a taste for walking sticks made of young allspice shoots. Fortunately, this shortsighted fashion trend was forbidden in 1882, and allspice once again flourished.

Allspice, whose sweet flavor is suggestive of a mix of cloves, cinnamon, and nutmeg, is now enjoyed in almost every country in the world, though the cultivated trees thrive only on the beautiful island of Jamaica where they grow in groves called allspice walks.

Whole allspice berries flavor pickling liquids, spiced syrups, and mulled wine, or add intense flavor to poaching liquid for fish and marinades for game. Use ground allspice with ham, meat loaf, and lamb, or add to curries, sweet cakes, and puddings. Allspice adds a delicate sweetness to pilafs and rice dishes, and in Morocco it is essential in the irresistible spice blend Ras el Hanout, page 57. The Jamaicans add it lovingly to sweet potatoes, soups, stews, curries, and, of course, the inimitable jerk chicken. Try allspice, whole or ground, in Peanut and Sweet Potato Soup with Sweet Potato–Allspice Cream, page 81, and Allspice Pilaf Layered with Phyllo, page 170. An adequate substitute for 1 tablespoon of ground allspice is 1 teaspoon each of ground cloves, ground nutmeg, and ground cinnamon.

We found there a tree whose leaf has the finest smell of cloves that I have ever met with; it was like a laurel leaf but not so large; but I think it was a species of laurel. . . . We found other trees which I think bear nutmegs, because the bark tastes and smells like that spice, but at present there is no fruit on them.

DR. DIEGO CHAKA,
WITH COLUMBUS, 1493

Anise

The sweet yet sharp flavor of anise (like licorice with an edge) has been popular through the ages. The pharaohs prized it so highly that anise accompanied them in their tombs. The Romans added anise seed to after-dinner cakes, as if these seeds could combat the effects of the preceding gargantuan banquet. Early colonists brought the seed to the New World, where Shakers grew it as a medicinal crop.

Whole or ground anise seeds, which are used far more often than the leaves, can be used in soups, curries, and breads. Their special affinity with garlic lends them to Mediterranean fish stews, sausages, and marinades. Cookies and biscotti would be severely compromised without them. Try anise in Anise-Flavored Beet and Onion Salad with Pink Peppercorn Mayonnaise, page 178. When the anise cupboard is bare, use fennel. Dill, which is milder and not as sweet, will also work.

Annatto

A small sailing ship from Europe makes its way across thousands of miles of rough seas, it's crew suffering through disease and starvation. Finally, the ship lands, and the survivors staggers to the beach. The first humans encountered have skin the color of cooked lobsters — skin that has been dyed with the pulp from the annatto tree. Is it any wonder the early explorers called these people Red Indians or Red Skins?

Ancient Mayans in Guatemala and the Carib Indians were the first to use annatto to paint their bodies. Today, the seeds from the tree, also called achiote, dragon's blood, or lipstick tree seeds, add their color and subtle, musky, paprikalike flavor to rice, cakes, soups, and chicken dishes. To brighten your day and your food, see Lemon Pepper Bluefish with Chipotle Chile Cream, page 88. But be careful: Annatto can brighten carpets, clothing, and children, too. A substitute for the taste of annatto is paprika; turmeric can supply the color.

HISTORICAL RECIPE:
ANISE SEED CHICKEN

Throw into a mortar aniseed, dried mint, and laser root. Moisten with vinegar. Add dates, pour in stock, a little mustard and olive oil, and boiled wine. Blend, and then serve with boiled chicken.

OF CULINARY MATTERS,
MARCUS GARVIUS APICIUS, 14 A.D.

MARCUS GARVIUS APICIUS

Marcus Garvius Apicius, a Roman gourmand living during the 1st century A.D., was one of the earliest authors of books on cookery and was as well known for his penchant for excess as for his knowledge. He reportedly poisoned himself when he awoke from a drunken stupor one morning to discover that he had spent most of his fortune and would be unable to sustain his current standard of living. Pliny called Apicius *"altissimus gurges,"* or "sublime gullet."

ASAFETIDA

How does one wax poetic about a seasoning whose aliases are devil's dung and stinking gum? Quite simply, one does not. Asafetida was an extremely popular ingredient in Roman cuisine. In medieval times, its fetid, garlicky smell was said to ward off witches and the plague. Today it will usually get you a seat on a crowded bus.

Native to Afghanistan and Persia, this huge, evil-smelling perennial with yellow flowers grows to a height of 12 feet. When the stems of these plants are cut, a milky juice oozes out and dries into the solid resinlike mass that we know as asafetida. For reasons yet unfathomed, it is sublime when used sparingly in curries, thick soups, and other highly seasoned foods. It is particularly agreeable with fish.

The Romans weren't completely crazy. Asafetida was one of the few spices able to penetrate their lead-dimmed brains. You absolutely must try it. Guest will say, "What is that remarkable flavor?" and you will answer, "Oh (yawn) — asafetida." Use it in Fragrant Shrimp with Ethiopian Spiced Butter, page 106. There is no adequate substitute.

BASIL

In ancient India, land of exotic herbs and spices, sacred basil was dedicated to Krishna. This herb of kings was planted near temples and laid on the breasts of the dead as a powerful protection. However, it was seen in quite a different light in Greece, where it represented misery and misfortune. In the Middle Ages, it was believed that if basil was sandwiched between two rocks, it would turn into a scorpion by morning.

Nobody loves "kiss me, Nicholas" (another name for basil) as much as the Italians, who have glorified it by creating pesto, that wonderful, garlicky pasta sauce. Holy or Thai basil, an intense variety, is used in Southeast Asian cooking. Handle this assertive, sweet herb with care — it prefers to be torn, not cut. Use basil in its fresh form in salads and dried in Lobster Fra Diavolo, page 109.

Bay

The noblest of seasonings, bay, or laurel as it is also called, is said to have originated in Asia Minor, but it has been established in the Mediterranean since antiquity. The oracle at Delphi spoke her prophecies with a bay leaf held between her lips, its narcotic properties clearly responsible for her trancelike state. In Greek mythology, the nymph Daphne was changed into a laurel tree to preserve her purity, and Apollo, who pursued her, eternally adorned his hair with laurel leaves. In ancient Greece and Rome, a crown of laurel leaves was the symbol of wisdom and glory, worn by victors, emperors, and poets, who were called "poets laureate," a term still in use today. In the 16th century, bay was used as a purifying herb; it was burned in public places in the hope that its fragrance would guard against the plague. Throughout history, bay has been our guardian against lightning, witchcraft, and evil.

Bay leaves taste slightly bitter when fresh, but sweeten as they dry. They are an essential part of a bouquet garni and appear in soups, marinades, and tomato sauces. A constant in pickling marinades, their pungent flavor is also welcome in all kinds of seafood dishes. A bay leaf is sometimes found in sweet or savory milk-based sauces. Once a bay leaf has contributed its flavor, it should be removed from the cooking pot. Be a poet in your own kitchen; exhibit an ancient wisdom. Wear a wreath of laurel leaves and use them, whole or ground, as suggested in Marinated Shrimp and Onions in Rémoulade Sauce, page 69, and Magnificent Spice-filled Meat Loaf, page 142.

HOUSEHOLD USE:
BAY

A bay leaf in a canister of rice may keep weevils away.

BAY FOOTBATH

1 cup dried bay leaves
1 tablespoon coarse sea salt

Place the bay and salt in a large bowl. Add boiling water. Cool and use as a footbath.

Capers

There's an inherent nobility in this ancient, ragged little plant. Capers flavored the oil of that other old Mediterranean fruit, the olive, over 3,000 years ago. Apicius, that gluttonous gourmand and cookbook author in the 1st century A.D., added capers, finely chopped,

CAPER BERRIES

If caper buds are left on the bush to mature, they will eventually become fragrant white flowers, and then an olivelike fruit called a caper berry. Pickled caper berries are eaten like olives, added to martinis by those in the know, or chopped into pâtés and salads.

to a cheese, chicken liver, and cucumber mélange. In the 16th century, salted capers were served at magnificent banquets to "stimulate the appetite and to incite much drinking." An early American cookbook calls for "two spoonfuls of capers" for a stewed rump of beef.

The persistent little caper shrub grows like a weed in unwelcoming rocky places. It can be found throughout the Mediterranean, tenaciously holding plant and soil together as it pushes through cracks of ancient pavement. The unripened buds are cured and packed in salt or brine.

The smaller French variety of capers accompanies thinly sliced smoked salmon and other fish dishes. Italians love capers and add them to antipasti and tomato sauces. For a zesty and unexpected kick, use these tiniest of pickles in Halibut Puttanesca, page 93.

CARAWAY

This plain-looking, hardworking spice has taken care of our tummies and hearts for over 5,000 years. It's the "mom" of spices. Apicius, the ancient Roman bon vivant and writer, offered a recipe for lobster sauce with caraway and wine. Medieval cooks added caraway to soups and cabbage dishes. Although it fell out of favor for a century or two, it regained popularity in the 19th century.

In Northern Europe, caraway seeds are best known as a flavoring for breads and pastries. Caraway leaves, which are pleasantly mild and taste vaguely like parsley, are used in salads and in dips. Like a good mom, caraway is especially comforting on cold nights. We ask that you use it in all seasons, in Portuguese Pork and Shellfish Stew with Avocado Cream, page 154, and Spice-Rubbed Sea Bass with Stuffed Dates and Fiery Cucumber Salsa, page 96. If caraway seeds are not available, use cumin seeds, for a slightly different, but acceptable, flavor.

Cardamom

Breezes waft from the rain forests, carrying a mysterious fragrance so intriguing it casts a spell over all it touches.

Caravans traveled the route from India to Europe laden with trunks of goods as well as sacks of cardamom. The Romans used cardamom in perfume as well as in food. The Vikings carried the pods to Scandinavia, where the spice was wholeheartedly embraced.

This jewel of a spice grows with wild abandon in India and Sri Lanka. Green cardamom pods hold tiny, dark, aromatic seeds that have a lemony flavor. White cardamom pods — green pods that have been bleached by the sun or chemicals — are not recommended. Brown cardamom pods are rough hewn with an intense flavor. Use the green pods in subtle offerings, with fish and vegetables, and in desserts. Add the brown pods to hearty meat dishes or assertive vegetables. Dry-roast the seeds before using. Weave a web of fragrance and enchantment with Sautéed Spinach and Onions with Cardamom and Fennel Seeds, page 160. There is no adequate substitute.

Celery Seeds

There once grew in the swampy salt marshes of Europe a wild herb called smallage. Beloved by the Romans, it was used it as a medicine, an aphrodisiac, and a flavoring. Italian gardeners decided the ancient Romans drank too much wine and were misguided in their affection for this bitter herb. They allowed smallage to fade, and instead created the similar, but less interesting, celery plant we now cultivate as a vegetable and allow to rot in the bottom of our refrigerators.

The tiny brown seeds taste like an aromatic, slightly bitter version of the plant. Added to butter, they give a fresh flavor to breads; they are sublime in salads, cooked vegetables, and oyster stews. Call it smallage, celery, or swell, but use it. Celery stalks or tops are an adequate substitute.

CARDAMOM LORE

To induce the return of an errant husband, place a mixture of cardamom, cinnamon, and cloves in a bowl; read a prayer backward 7 times; fill the bowl with rosewater; immerse a shirt belonging to the absent husband, and a paper containing his name and that of 4 angels. Put the jar over a fire, and as soon as the boiling begins the husband is on his way home.

CELERY LORE

Medieval magicians put celery seeds in their shoes, believing that this could make them fly. (Don't you wish you could have been there to see this?)

MORE THAN ONE WAY TO SKIN A CHILI

Peeling a fresh chili is easy, once you've done one of the following:

1. Charring: Hold a chili with tongs over a gas flame or propane torch, turning frequently until evenly blackened.

2. Roasting: Preheat the oven to 400°F. Rub the chilies with oil and place on an oven rack. Roast, turning occasionally, for 15 minutes, or until soft and charred on all sides. Place in a paper bag and let them steam for 5 minutes, or until the skin slips away easily.

3. Frying: Heat ½ inch of vegetable oil in a saucepan until hot but not smoking. Holding the chili with tongs, deep-fry for 5 seconds.

4. Dry-roasting: Heat a cast-iron skillet over medium heat. Add the chilies and press down with a metal spatula until they soften. Turn over and dry-roast the other side.

5. Broiling: Place the chilies on the rack of the broiler 4 inches from flame. Broil, turning frequently, for 8 minutes, or until blistered and charred all over.

CHILI PEPPERS

When humans arrived in the Americas 10,000 years ago, 25 species of capsicum (peppers) were waiting for them. Worshipped by the Incas, chiles were abundantly represented in paintings and textiles. The pre-Columbian tribes of Panama used chiles in combination with other plants to induce hallucinations. The Aztecs added chile peppers to every dish they prepared, including hot chocolate. Christopher Columbus brought chiles back with him to Europe in 1493. The Portuguese introduced them into the East Indies, Asia, and Africa, where mustard seed had been the hottest flavoring available. Traveling full circle, these pungent pods came to North America with the European settlers, and the taste of food was changed forever.

Dozens of people are crowded into a room. Some are clutching their throats; others are holding their heads. The coughing and sneezing is interrupted by gasps, wheezes, and occasional whimpers or yelps of pain. One woman stands alone in the corner, tears streaming down her face. This is not a hospital emergency room, but rather the scene of a hot-sauce tasting in a spice and gourmet shop in Manhattan. And these people are enjoying themselves! Hundreds of varieties of capsicum have inspired chili clubs, chili tastings, posters, Web sites, a magazine, books, and T-shirts. There are even stores dedicated to selling only chili-based hot sauces with frightening names like Vampfire, Bat's Brew, Satan's Revenge, Voo Doo Jerk Slather, and Endorphin Rush.

Chilies can be as small as a pea, or as large as an eggplant, in hues of cream, yellow, orange, red, and green. Their pungency ranges from sweet to volcanic. All chilies contain capsaicin (cap-SAY-a-sin). Their heat is determined by the amount of capsaicin they contain, and is measured on a scale from 0 to 10 called the Official Chili Heat Scale. Chilies are used fresh or dried; whole, crushed, or ground; plain, pickled, or in adobo sauce. The most commonly available fresh chilies, listed from mild to hot, are the Anaheim (mild), poblano (mild), jalapeño (hot), serrano (very hot), habanero (painfully hot), and

Scotch bonnet, a Caribbean habanero, considered to be the hottest pepper in the world. Some commonly available dried peppers are the ancho (sweet earthy flavor), pasilla (mild), chipotle (hot smoky flavor), japones (hot), bird's eye (extremely hot), and dried habanero (why would you want to do this to yourself?). Ground chilies also run the gamut from mild to blistering. Cayenne and paprika, described on page 28, are the most common. Ground ancho, chipotle, pasilla, and the blend called chili powder — a blend of chiles, cumin, garlic, and other spices — are all delicious in southwestern offerings. The murderous Thai chilies are best suited to Asian cuisine.

Some chilies from other parts of the world are hardly known, but sublimely flavored. Syrian aleppo pepper is a gritty, dark red, oily pepper with a taste like a rich, robust paprika. Paula Wolfert mentions it frequently in her cookbooks. Although not readily available in markets, it can be obtained by mail order, and is definitely worth a search.

When working with the hotter chilies, please be careful. The hottest parts of chilies are the seeds and ribs. If you get a chili "burn" on your skin, rinse with a mild bleach solution, which makes the capsaicin water-soluble. Should you get some in your eyes, rinse with cool water. If you scorch your mouth, eat sour cream or yogurt, or drink cold milk or orange juice.

Chilies are used for flavor or revenge all around the world. The longer a chili is cooked, the hotter the flavor, so be especially careful with soups and stews. If you are burning to cook with these delicious demons, turn to Duck Picadillo Enchiladas, page 134, and Seafood Chili with Ancho and Pasilla Cream, page 110. Many chilies can be used interchangeably; try to use fresh or dried, as called for, and make an attempt to match hotness. Unfortunately, there is no substitute for the smoky uniqueness of the chipotle chile.

YOU WRITE CHILE, I WRITE CHILI . . .

It may be more difficult to spell *chile* than to cook with it. The original Spanish spelling is *chile*. All pods that come from the Americas are spelled *chile*, the plural being *chiles*. In Asia, pods are called *chili* or *chilies*. When referring to pods from both hemispheres, we use *chili* or *chilies*. To add to the confusion, the spicy southwestern bean or beef stew is known as *chili*, and the powder made of chiles and spices is called *chili powder*.

CHIPOTLE CHILES IN ADOBO SAUCE

When fresh jalapeño chiles are smoke-dried, the resulting withered chiles with a hot, smoky flavor are called chipotle chiles. These may be marinated and slow-cooked with spices and herbs to make an unbelievably rich, spicy Mexican adobo sauce. The most popular item in our mail-order catalog is this sauce. See Caesar Salad with Chipotle Chilem Dressing, page 176.

Chives

This medieval herb is the tiniest, most delicate member of the onion family. The chive's subtle taste is fragile; long cooking diminishes the flavor of chives, so add them at the end of cooking. They are delicious in omelets, with vegetables, and in herbed mayonnaise. Use the whole stems judiciously, poking out of salads, or allow them to float languidly on pale cold soups. Whole or cut, they are delicious in Jalepeño Clams in Fragrant Black Bean Sauce, page 101. In an emergency, scallions or shallots can fill in.

Cinnamon

Native to Sri Lanka, cinnamon was one of the first spices sought by the explorers of the 15th and 16th centuries. The Portuguese, the Dutch, and the English all fought bitterly over these diminutive brown scrolls of bark.

Cinnamon is available in two varieties. Cassia is the more readily available of the two, and generally referred to as just cinnamon in the United States. Ceylon cinnamon, harder to find than cassia, is lighter colored and has a milder, sweeter flavor. They are both produced from the barks of tropical evergreen trees. Cassia quills, or sticks, are larger and coarser than Ceylon cinnamon quills.

The Egyptians used cinnamon as an aromatic, and its fragrance still adds intrigue to potpourri and pomanders. Recorded in a Chinese herbal 5,000 years ago, and a frequent ingredient in medieval cookery, cinnamon has been used in savory and sweet dishes through the ages.

Ground cinnamon will enhance most meat stews, especially lamb. It adds character to pilafs and curries and is essential to baking.

No one has announced, "Aha, I suspect that this elaborate dish contains cassia, and not true cinnamon." So use what you can get, and use it with passion in Saffron Risotto, page 168.

CLOVES

The remarkable history of cloves contains all the ingredients of a screen spectacular: mystery, eroticism, intrigue, wicked villians, virtuous heroes, great sailing ships — and that's just part 1! Cloves' beginnings were peaceful enough when Chinese courtiers of the Imperial Court used them to sweeten their breaths. But during the Age of Exploration, events took a deadly turn, as the Portuguese and the Dutch battled for control of the spice trade — and thus the world — and an estimated 60,000 people were killed. The temporarily victorious Dutch restricted the growth of clove trees to one island. Their vigilance was for naught as Pierre Poivre (what a great name!) smuggled the spice out of the Moluccas and the hands of the Dutch.

Today, cloves are no longer the cause of wars; clove trees grow quietly by the sea in Tanzania and Madagascar. The buds are picked before they're ripe, and dried until they're brown as berries. Cloves have a warm and rich aroma; their bitingly sharp taste and their anesthetic properties simultaneously awaken and numb the tongue. Stud an onion with whole cloves and add to stews or lentil soup, but be wary of "overstudding," as cloves contribute a powerful flavor. Their pungency is especially welcome in ham and pork dishes. Cloves are used throughout India in various spice blends, and in South Africa they are an essential part of various lamb stews. A few cloves will add an interesting caramelized flavor to carrots, beets, and sweet potatoes. Along with cinnamon and ginger, cloves are one of the three most important spices in baking. Add them to simmering fruit. Push them into oranges and lemons to make pomander balls. James Beard reflected that this practice may result in "a domestic ailment known as clove pusher's thumb." Now that the spice wars are over, and the biggest controversy surrounds the issue of 1 clove or 2, use these little nails in Clove-Scented Onion Soup with Madeira and Paprika, page 80. Should you be cloveless, allspice works as a mild but acceptable substitute.

The European would have lived in former ages very comfortably without cloves. But by the 17th century that odoriferous pistil had been the cause of so many pitched battles and obstinate wars, of so much vituperating, negotiating, and intriguing, that the world's destiny seemed to have become almost dependent upon the growth of a particular gillyflower.

JOHN LOTHROP MOTHEY,
17TH-CENTURY HISTORIAN

CORIANDER

HISTORICAL RECIPE:
TO MAKE A BISKET CAKE

Take a pound of flower well dryd, a pound and a quart of fine sugar fine seavet, an ounce of Caraway, Coreander, sweet fenel seeds, 12 eggs and egght whites. Beat ym very well and then strew in your sugar and seeds and then your flower and 5 spoonfulls of rose water, beat ym very well together about half an hour; butter your tin, ym bake it.

*RECEIPT BOOK OF A LADY
OF THE REIGN OF QUEEN ANNE,
ELIZABETH WAINWRIGHT, 1711*

An ancient culinary herb, coriander possesses an aroma that has always stirred controversy. The Greeks named it after a bedbug, because of its astonishing scent. Mentioned in the Bible, coriander is one of the bitter herbs eaten at Passover. Coriander seeds were found in the tombs of the pharaohs and were a common ingredient in early Greek medicine. During the Middle Ages, coriander was highly regarded in Britain, where it was used in food, medicine, and love potions. Because it has a narcotic effect when eaten in large quantities, it has been called "dizzy corn." Spanish conquistadors introduced coriander to Mexico and Peru, where it has become an integral part of the cuisines.

Dry-roast coriander seeds lightly before using them to enhance their flavor, reminiscent of anise and orange peel. Use these ancient seeds in all forms of curry and in Indian spice blends. In Morocco, coriander is rubbed into lamb with other seasonings. In Europe, the seeds are part of an olive oil, lemon, and herb marinade. Ground coriander is found in sweet breads and cakes.

Fresh coriander leaf, commonly called Chinese parsley or cilantro, arouses passionate opinions. Those who love its pungent flavor say it tastes like anise; those who detest it liken its flavor to soap. Mexicans and Southeast Asians are clearly part of the first group, as fresh coriander is used lavishly in guacamole, salads, and seafood dishes. Since the leaf turns black when cooked in tomato-based sauces, add it at the last minute. For an even more intense cilantro flavor, use chopped coriander root in place of the leaves. Whether your cooking is inspired by the Pacific Rim, Mexico, or your own imagination, cook exuberantly with coriander in Endive with Shiitake Mushroom Relish, page 67, and Marinated Spice-Rubbed Spareribs, page 153.

Cumin

This ancient seed is a seasoned traveler, beginning its journey in the valley of the Nile 5,000 years ago. Cumin was heavily utilized by the Egyptians, both for medicinal and culinary purposes. To the Greeks, it symbolized miserliness, and Marcus Aurelius was secretly called "Cumin" because of his avaricious nature. Early Roman students drank a cumin infusion to appear pale and overworked

Today, cumin grows around the Mediterranean, and in the Middle East, India, and the United States. The seed has a piercing, lemony-hot bite. Used whole or ground, cumin is a vital flavor in Indian, Mexican, and North African cuisines. Black cumin seeds, available in Indian groceries and by mail, are smaller and have a more delicate flavor. Dry roast cumin before using in Curried Mahimahi in Bannana Leaves, page 90. Caraway is a passable substitute for cumin. Use one-half as much caraway as you would cumin.

Dill

In the world of fables and fairy tales, myths and legends, there is always a magic potion to induce sleep. Dill seeds contain a gentle sedative, and the name comes from the old Norse *dilla,* meaning *"to lull."*

In Scandinavia, where dill is the promise of spring, people sprinkle it on cured salmon and open-faced sandwiches. In the Middle East, dill weed appears in pastries and flavors Iranian salads. The flavor of dill is delicate, so add it as late as possible in the cooking process.

Dill seeds, the spice part of this duo, have a more pungent flavor; their taste is reminiscent of caraway seeds. Used frequently in the cuisines of Scandinavia, Germany, and Central and Eastern Europe, these little seeds are best known for their use in pickling liquids, breads, and potato dishes. Crush the seeds or dry-roast them lightly before using, to bring out their flavor. If dill weed is unavailable, parsley or fennel may be substituted, and caraway can fill in for dill seeds.

HISTORICAL REMEDY:

DIET DRINK

For to make one slender take Fennell and seeth it in water, a very good quantity, and wring out the juyce thereof when it is sod, and drinke it firste and laste . . .

THE GOOD HUSWIFE'S JEWELL,
THOMAS DAWSON, 1587

HISTORICAL RECIPE:

SPICED WINE

Take a gallon of Gascoign wine, of ginger, galingale, cinnamon, nutmegs and graines, annis seeds, fennell seeds, and carroway seeds, Of each a dram; of sage, mints, red roses, thyme, pellitory, rosemary, wild thyme, camomile, lavender, of each a handful, bray the spices small, and bruise the herbs, letting them macerate 12 hours, stirring it now & then, then distil by limbecke of pewter keeping the first cleare water that commeth, by it selfe, and so likewise the second. You shall draw much about a pinte of the better sort from everie gallon of wine.

DELIGHTS FOR LADIES,
SIR HUGH PLAT, 1602

Look, up on the hill — it's an herb, it's a spice, it's Super Spice! Disguised as a mild-mannered plant from Southern Europe and the Mediterranean, fennel has been physician and protector since antiquity. The Greeks called it *marathon,* named after the battlefield on which they were victorious, and fennel became their symbol of victory and success. Pliny recommended fennel as a treatment for 22 ailments, and since he believed fennel had restored sight to blind molting eagles, he was sure it would do the same for his weak-sighted fellowmen. Gerard also suggested fennel water to preserve eyesight, as did Culpeper. Eye remedies today still speak of the refreshing quality of fennel. Coles advised that fennel be added to broth "for those that are grown fat, to abate their unwieldiness and cause them to grow more gaunt and lank." During the Middle Ages, fennel was thought to be powerful against evil as well as disease. In the ancient Nine Herbs Charm, fennel is "great in power. It stands against pain, resists the venom, It has power against three and against thirty, Against a fiend's hand and against sudden trick, Against witchcraft of vile creatures."

Like coriander and dill, fennel is both a spice and an herb (and a vegetable, but we won't get into that). The leaves taste of anise and are used as a garnish on salads. The flavor of the seeds is stronger, and a little bitter. Called the fish herb, fennel is a traditional seasoning for seafood, and because of its digestive properties is commonly used with pork and other fatty meats. It contributes a sweet aniselike flavor to Mediterranean soups, sauces, and stews, and adds distinction to Southeast Asian curries.

Be an all-seeing superpower in your own kitchen. Add fennel, fresh or dry, whole or ground, to everything but the dishwater. Start with Lacquered Duck with Szechuan Fennel-Spiced Wine, page 133, and Garlic Fennel Prime Rib with Ginger Port Sauce, page 136.

Anise seeds, although stronger and sweeter, are an adequate substitute. Dill seeds, which are considerably milder, can be substituted if necessary.

Fenugreek

Fenugreek was once a star. The ancient Egyptians believed in its curative powers, and applied a fenugreek paste to reduce fevers. If that didn't work, fenugreek, used in embalming, was applied yet again after the patient expired. The Romans called it Greek hay and fed it to their cows. The emperor Charlemagne cultivated it for medicinal uses.

Like a forgotten film actress, fenugreek, with a flavor similar to celery, is now only a walk-on, never a star. It's been typecast as an ingredient in curries, and no one can see it in a different light. In fact, it is quite good with fish, in breads, and in cheese dishes. It appears without credit in gumbos, stews, and spice blends. Dry-roast the seeds before using them to develop their full aromatic flavor. Try them, whole or ground, in Spicy Mushrooms with Fenugreek and Lemon, page 159. There is no adequate substitute for fenugreek.

Galangal

This seasoning, whose name sounds like a medieval dance, was known to the ancient Egyptians, and became popular in Europe during the Middle Ages. Soon after, its use declined, and now it seldom appears anywhere other than Chinese or Southeast Asian cooking. We would like to change that.

If we could convince you to try one new seasoning, this would be the one. With an absolutely intoxicating aroma and flavor — like cardamom with a peppery bite — greater galangal deserves to be in everything. (Lesser galangal, with a more pungent eucalyptuslike flavor, is called *kentjur* and is not easy to find.) This rhizome, available fresh, frozen, or dried, can be obtained through mail-order sources. Make galangal your new secret ingredient. Use it in place of ginger or cardamom, or try it in Thai Shrimp Soup with Lime Leaves, Galangal, and Mushrooms, page 95. If galangal is not available, substitute a blend of 3 parts cardamom and 1 part ginger.

And, most dear actors,
eat no onions or garlic,
For we have to
utter sweet breath.

A MIDSUMMER NIGHT'S DREAM,
WILLIAM SHAKESPEARE

Dwellings were first redolent with garlic over 6,000 years ago in Sumer, Southwestern Asia. That aroma has provoked more controversy than any other seasoning. The Egyptians worshiped it as a god, yet because of its intense odor, it was considered laborers' food. The Greeks happily consumed great quantities of it. The Romans, like the Egyptians, considered it a plebeian flavoring, although Pliny credited it with 61 different uses. He noted that "garlic as well as onions gives an offensive smell to the breath, though when cooked it causes no smell" (uh, wrong). This love-hate relationship with garlic, like the aroma of the clove itself, has lingered in Europe for centuries. At different times during the Middle Ages it was thought to protect against vampires, the plague, and the evil eye. Until the 18th century, many Siberian villages paid taxes in garlic: 15 bulbs for a man, 10 for a woman, 5 for a child. (Personally, we'd pay more for the kid.)

Today, most cooks love "the stinking rose," and it is used liberally in almost every cuisine in the world. Nowhere is it more popular than in the Mediterranean, where it flavors stews, sauces, and vegetables. The French use it in Aioli, a garlic mayonnaise. They put 40 cloves of it in a chicken dish named, straightforwardly, Chicken with Forty Cloves of Garlic. In the Middle East, it complements yogurt and eggplant, and is used in pilafs. In Morocco, garlic is found in honey-flavored meat stews. In Ethiopia, it is essential to Wat, the spicy national stew. Garlic teams up with ginger in Chinese cooking. It show up in the Philippines in Chicken Adobo, and also in Malaysian curries. Garlic is a robust, pungent spice. You'll find it fresh and whole, peeled and crushed with oil in jars, and dry, as flakes or powders. Use it in food you love. If your warm-blooded passions get the best of you, pass out parsley, mint, or cardamom, all of which vaporize garlic odors as garlic (supposedly) vaporizes vampires. Find garlic recipes everywhere — our favorites are Scallops, Spinach, and Mushrooms, page 102, and Shrimp Fried Rice, page 173.

Ginger

Ginger, a gnarled and fibrous rhizome with a pungent, hot, sweet flavor, grows in almost every tropical region. The original ancient mariners, the Phoenicians, relied on it to calm their stomachs in rough seas. The Chinese, in the 2nd century, opened the arduous overland route known as the Silk Road, and traded ginger and silks to the Romans. It was ever-present in medieval Parisian dipping sauces, notably cameline sauce.

Ginger, processed into myriad forms, is versatile and popular. Its pungent flavor and crunchy texture permeate the cooking of China and flavor Malaysian lamb curry. It has a natural affinity with fish. On a rainy Saturday, children the world over probably make enough gingerbread people to encircle the earth. For 7,000 years, this ancient knobby hand has contributed to the flavor of food. It's time for you to try it in Soy Sauce Lamb Chops with Ginger Mint Pesto, page 148. There is no adequate substitute for the flavor of ginger.

Juniper

There must always be a protector of the meek and the small. The pinelike aroma of juniper is so powerful it was once believed to defeat the scent of hounds, and in folk tales, small hunted animals would retreat to the safety of its droopy branches. Juniper is protective of itself as well. The tiny pine needles are so prickly gatherers must wear gloves to retrieve the berries.

The bright blue berries are best known for flavoring gin, and are also classically used with sauerkraut. Used sparingly, they also add a cool eucalyptus flavor to pork, marinades, and stuffings. Try them in Chicken Liver Bruschetta with Pepper, Sage, and Juniper Berries, page 75, and Garlic Roast Duck with Blackberry Sauce, page 130. If you cannot locate juniper berries, use a small amount of gin in the recipe, and then make yourself a gin and tonic for being so smart.

HISTORICAL RECIPE:
CAMELINE SAUCE

Pound ginger, plenty of cinnamon, cloves, cardamom, mace, long pepper if you wish, then squeeze out bread soaked in vinegar and strain all together and salt it just right.

LE VIANDIER DE GUILLAUME TIREL (TAILLEVENT), 1375

JUNIPER LORE

During the Middle Ages, it was believed that if you hung a bunch of juniper over the doorway, the house would be protected against witches. The reasoning went that, upon seeing the juniper, a witch would be seized with an irrepressible desire to count all of the leaves, which are so tiny and numerous that the witch would be bound to make a mistake, and rather than start all over again, would flee, for fear of being seen.

THERAPEUTIC USE:

A PILLOW AGAINST HEADACHES

1   cup dried lemongrass
½   cup dried lavender
¼   cup dried marjoram
1   teaspoon crushed cloves

Combine all the ingredients, put into a small muslin bag, and slip between the pillow and the pillowcase.

LEMONGRASS

The flavor of lemongrass is so spectacular it deserves a rich history full of intrigue, romance, adventure, and mythology. Since we have been unable to uncover even the smallest piece of folklore, we have decided to make up a story worthy of this extraordinary grass.

Once upon a time, many centuries ago, a beautiful young woman fell in love with the prince of the realm. An Asian goddess, jealous of this alliance, cast down a spell upon the poor woman, and turned her into a beautifully plumed bird. The bird, in an attempt to attract the prince, threw down pieces of her only possession, her lemony nest. The dim-witted prince, annoyed at this bird who was circling the palace and throwing straw spears, had the bird killed. The straw spears stuck in the ground and became lemongrass.

This tall aromatic tropical grass, once Asia's best-kept secret, has become chefdom's *herbe du jour,* and for very good reason. The unique refreshing tartness of lemongrass adds a peppery lemon flavor to soups and other long-simmered dishes. It adds mouth-puckering mystery to stuffings and rubs. Buy fresh stalks, available in Asian markets and by mail. They will keep, refrigerated, for about 2 weeks. Fresh lemongrass can also be frozen, tightly wrapped, for several months. Even though lemongrass is available dried, powdered, and in brine, we still recommend that the fresh variety be used whenever a tart flavor is desired. Lemongrass works well with garlic, fresh coriander, coconut milk, and hot flavors. Crush the stalks before using, and soak them in oil or milk for 2-3 hours to soften them. We want lemongrass to become your *herbe du jour.* Use in traditional and nontraditional ways in Coconut Milk Chicken Soup with Rainbow Pepper and Lavender, page 84, and Hearty Lemon-Scented Beef Stew with Asian Aioli, page 138. A less-than-adequate substitute is lemon verbena with a pinch of freshly grated ginger.

Mace

Mace, the scarlet lacy cage clinging to nutmeg like white on rice, has always been nutmeg's forgotten twin. It should not be forgotten so quickly, however, for it is the most exquisite of spices. Cast in silver, it could be worn to a coronation.

The nutmeg tree is unique in that no other plant in the world offers up two separate spices — mace and nutmeg. Although similar, both the aroma and flavor of mace are much more potent than those of nutmeg. Mace is usually reserved for baked sweets, but it has a place in savory dishes as well. It enhances the flavor of vegetables, and is strong enough for bold soups, stews, and curries. A spice this beautiful and aromatic should not be relegated to the back of the spice closet. Bring it forward and use it in new ways in Chicken with 99 Spices, page 118. Nutmeg is a good substitute in recipes calling for mace.

Marjoram

Sweet marjoram and oregano are the joyful herbs of this collection. Marjoram plays the gentle, more refined spice to oregano's wild child. In spite of its delicate nature, sweet marjoram was used in Egyptian burial tombs. In Greece, bridal couples were crowned with marjoram, to ensure a long marriage.

This strongly perfumed, flowering herb has been cultivated in the Mediterranean since the dawn of time, and is now used in nearly every country in Europe. With a flavor similar to thyme but sweeter, marjoram is delicious in tomato dishes, or rubbed into lamb before roasting. Marjoram is well suited to salads, vegetables, and eggs. It is best to add marjoram at the end of cooking to preserve its fragile flavor. Try this kinder, gentler herb in New Orleans Beer-Braised Shrimp, page 105, or Paella Valencia, page 112. Substitute thyme if you're out of marjoram. A second choice is a smaller amount of the much-stronger oregano.

HOUSEHOLD USE:

AROMATIC SACHET POWDER

5 tablespoons dried marjoram
3 tablespoons dried thyme
3 tablespoons dried crushed basil
1 tablespoon dried caraway seeds
1 tablespoon dried lemon peel
1 tablespoon grated mace

Combine all the spices in a small cheesecloth bag and store among clothes to give them a sweet aroma.

HISTORICAL REMEDY:

TOOTHACHE

It [Marjoram] easeth the tooth ache being chewed in the mouth. The leaves dried and mingled with honey put away black and blew marks after stripes and bruses, being applied thereto.

THE HERBAL OR GENERAL HISTORY OF PLANTS,
JOHN GERARD, 1633

Mustard

MUSTARD LORE

During the night, ancient Hindus would light lamps and fill a deep vessel with water, into which they gently poured mustard seed oil. They would watch the oil as they pronounced the names of every woman in the village. If they saw the woman's shadow in the water as her name was called, there was no doubt that she was a witch.

Poor maligned mustard, always considered the "ho-hum" of spices: Here's a seed that's been around for thousands of years, flavoring everything from ancient hot dogs to fancy modern cream sauces, and no one accords it even a modicum of respect. Its most important role has been as the fat, round suspect in a mystery board game. How far this spice has fallen! Over 4,000 years ago in the great cities near the Indus River, mustard seeds were used in the earliest curry powders. The Greeks and Romans understood both their culinary and their medicinal uses: Mustard was commonly mixed into a plaster and spread on the chest to alleviate congestion. Pliny commented on its pungency and offered 40 remedies based on mustard. (He was also convinced that if lazy housewives were fed mustard, they would become industrious.) Apicius employed mustard in various recipes, and served it with boiled sausages. (Had he been really ahead of his time, he would have hawked them at chariot races.) In medieval Europe, mustard was inexpensive and therefore became a spice for the common folk. Until the discovery of chile peppers in the Americas, mustard was the hottest seasoning available.

Mustard seeds — always trying to please everyone — come in three colors: yellow, brown, and black. The yellow seeds are the most common; the brown and the black, usually used in India, are more pungent. To get the most flavor out of whole seeds, dry-roast before using. Ground mustard has no flavor or aroma until mixed with cool water; its flavor lasts only a short time, so add it late in recipes.

Prepared mustard, made from ground seeds, vinegar, salt, and spices, was served with food by the ancient Egyptians. Today it takes up more gourmet shelf space than any other item and is flavored with a variety of seasonings, including herbs, chilies, citrus, and honey. Dried mustard can be flavored with the same variety of herbs and seasonings as prepared mustard. It's time to start treating mustard with some respect. Begin with Fried Pork and Peanuts with Cumberland Sauce, page 152, and Caesar Salad with Chipotle Chile Dressing, page 176.

Nigella Seeds

Cooks would love nigella — if only they knew what it was. It is not a tiny black onion seed, even though it is sometimes called *kalonji,* which means "black onion seed." It is not black cumin, even though it is sometimes called *kala jeera,* which means "black cumin." It is not *love-in-a-mist,* even though its botanical name, *nigella,* is also the botanical name of the blue-flowered plant.

So what is it then? We thought you'd never ask. Nigella is a peppery seed with a mild oniony flavor. Add it to carrots and other sweet vegetables, or toss into a salad or pilaf. Become an adventurer; use nigella instead of pepper in Jerked Scallops with Asian Pear and Date Chutney, page 103.

It is difficult to decide where a spice ends and a shrub begins.

THE BOOK OF SPICES,
F. ROSENGARTEN JR., 1969

Nutmeg

Nutmeg, the Gemini of spices with its scarlet twin, mace, first appeared in Indonesia's Molucca Islands. Sheltered from the wind, it grew in tropical serenity by the sea. This comely seed with its elaborate covering was used by the Chinese for digestive disorders. In the Middle Ages, thought to possess magical powers, nutmeg was second only to pepper as the most popular spice. In the 16th century, the monopolistic Dutch banned nutmeg cultivation except on a few controlled islands. Pigeons ignored the colonial laws, eating nutmeg kernels and flying them to other islands. Soon the French and the English succeeded in smuggling out nutmeg as well, effectively breaking Holland's monopoly.

Nutmeg is an essential spice in Italian cooking, where it is used in many filled pastas and flavors a traditional white sauce. It has an astonishing affinity with spinach, and should be used whenever that good green is present. In Asia and Africa, it flavors curries and stews, and Scandinavia uses it liberally in baked goods. Try it in Pilaf-Stuffed Onions with Sumac and Nutmeg, page 161. If nutmeg is not available substitute mace.

HISTORICAL REMEDY:

DIZZINESS IN THE HEAD

A Very Good Powder for Dizziness in the Head and to prevent Apoplecktick Fitts. . . . Take the roots of a single Piony, of each a like quantity, dry and beat them severally into a fine powder, take the weight in Nutmeg, which you must beat and dry, and beat again: mix fine sifted sugar with this and take as much as will lie on a shilling every morning for a month constantly.

ENGLISH PHYSICIAN,
NICHOLAS CULPEPER, 1652

Cook and skim peas. Then put in a bunch of leeks and coriander. While cooking, grind pepper, lovage and oregano. Add a bouquet garni and mix. Blend with stock. Add olive oil. Cook over a slow fire and serve.

OF CULINARY MATTERS,
MARCUS GARVIUS APICIUS, 14 A.D.

OREGANO

Oregano is the quintessential Mediterranean herb. Fragrant and strongly flavored, it grows in such wild profusion on the mountainside that its Greek name means "joy of the mountain."

Oregano, also called wild marjoram, is essential to many dishes, flavoring English stews, Swedish soups, and Mediterranean meats. In Italy, the herb is used to complement the flavors of tomatoes, eggplant, cheese, beans, fish, and shellfish. In Latin American countries, oregano can be found in seviche, spicy soups, and chili powder blends. Put a little mountain joy in your kitchen. Use oregano in Chile–Black Bean Soup with Avocado Coriander Pesto, page 66. If oregano cannot be found, substitute a slightly greater quantity of the milder marjoram.

PAPRIKA

There's a beautiful folk tale of a young girl imprisoned in a harem who escaped to meet her lover. She took with her the seeds of a paprika plant, which he planted — and soon all of Hungary was awash in paprika vines.

Purists will demand that paprika be discussed in the chili pepper section where it rightfully belongs. Agreed: Like chili peppers, paprika comes from the capsicum family. But paprika is incredibly mild mannered compared to its fiery relatives. The finest paprikas come from Hungary; a very good strong paprika comes from Spain.

Whereas real chilies can be used for revenge, paprika doesn't have a mean bone in its body. Essential for goulash and chicken dishes, paprika is also at home in hearty soups and in seafood dishes. Find new and wonderful ways to use what may already be one of your favorite spices. Add its brilliance to Sautéed Asparagus with Black Peppered Pesto, page 156. If you're lacking in paprika, you may, if necessary, substitute a mild ground chile like a New Mexico.

PEPPER

This spice would make a *great* movie. We'll shoot in exotic locations and cover thousands of years. Big names, big budget, big bucks at the box office. Picture this: We could call it *The King of Spice,* kinda like *Raiders of the Lost Ark* meets *Gandhi.* Fade into a biblical scene. The Queen of Sheba — maybe we can get Julia Roberts for this — arrives at King Solomon's palace with her pepper-laden caravan. She tests him with hard questions. Think *Quiz Show* meets *The Ten Commandments.* Charlton could have a walk-on, sort of *Moses, The Later Years.* Cut to a Chinese herbalist mixing a black pepper potion. Cut again to Apicius (maybe a Sean Connery type) at a book signing in the 4th century as he recommends pepper for sweet dishes. Fade to the burning of Rome. Alaric, king of the Visigoths — perhaps Bobby De Niro here — demands 3,000 pounds of pepper be paid in tribute. Imagine, if you will, *Towering Inferno* meets *Lawrence of Arabia.* Cut to the Crusaders, who, under the guise of uniting the world in Christianity, are actually involved in trade wars to crush Byzantine control over pepper. *Monty Python and the Holy Grail* comes to mind. Fade out. Fade in to Vasco da Gama searching for a sea route to the East; we get images of *Mutiny on the Bounty* meets *Gypsy.* A lot of people get killed. Fade out. Slow fade in to a shot of a large pepper mill, slowly grinding. Fade out.

Black pepper, that tangy, pungent, crunchy taste sensation, is the star of the spice world. Cultivated in the hot and humid tropics of India, Indonesia, Ceylon, Madagascar, and Brazil, it accounts for one-quarter of the global spice trade, with the United States being the single largest importer. Black, white, and green peppercorns are all derived from the same berry. If one is picked when unripe, and then dried, it becomes the most pungent of the group, the black peppercorn. If instead of being dried, the unripe berry is freeze-dried or submerged in brine, it becomes the kinder, gentler green peppercorn, with its fruity, olivelike flavor. When the same berry is left to ripen on the

Pepper is the seed or fruit from a tree which grows on the south side of the Caucasus Mountains, in the hottest sunshine. The pepper forest is full of poisonous snakes that guard it. When the fruit is ripe, people come and set fire to the forest. The snakes flee, but the smoke and flames blacken the pepper fruits and make their taste sharper.

THE NATURE OF THINGS,
BARTHOLOMEUS, 14TH CENTURY

HISTORICAL RECIPE:
SAUCE FOR BOILED PIGEONS AND DOVES

In a mortar, crush celery seed, pepper, caraway, and parsley. Add country sauce, dates, honey, vinegar, wine, olive oil, and mustard.

OF CULINARY MATTERS,
MARCUS GARVIUS APICIUS, 14 A.D.

vine, and then is shorn of its outer skin, the mild white peppercorn is born. Following is the roster of pepper pretenders:

Pink Peppercorn A berry from a South American tree, the pink peppercorn adds mild pungency and stunning color to food.

Szechuan Pepper Long before the world initiated the food fights that surrounded pepper, the Chinese discovered their own version of that tasty spice. Also known as fagara and anise-pepper, this aromatic dried berry from the prickly ash tree grows from Pakistan to Japan, contributing a hot, woody flavor to Asian cuisine. It is one of the ingredients of Chinese Five-Spice Powder, page 52, and is commonly used in Asian fish dishes. Dry-roasting it before use heightens the flavor.

Cubeb Pepper Also known as tailed pepper, this romantic member of the group is one of the oldest known ingredients in love potions. It was extremely popular in the Middle Ages. A toll was collected for every pound of cubebs that passed over London Bridge. Native to Java, it lends its allspicelike flavor to Indonesian cuisine.

Grains of Paradise This exotic pepperlike spice, also known as melegueta pepper, makes its home on the coast and islands of West Africa. Discovered by Portugal in the 15th century, it became an inexpensive substitute for pepper. Most recently, brew masters have added it to their seasonal beers for a spicy kick.

Long Pepper Shaped like a tiny catkin, long pepper spread throughout Asia before black pepper, and was the first variety of pepper to reach the Mediterranean. It is used in pickles and preserves.

Rub cracked pepper on roasts, steaks, and poultry. Pepper enlivens the subtle flavors of seafood. Add it to mayonnaise and creamy dips. Pepper can also be ground into sweet custard and fruit salads to add a contrasting tang. Use these little balls interchangeably, separately, or all jumbled up like gumballs. Whole or ground, this rainbow coalition deserves your full attention. Use pepper everywhere, especially in Pink Peppercorn Pompano with Cream in Parchment, page 92, and Crispy Duck Breasts with Wild Mushroom and Green Peppercorn Sauce, page 132.

POMEGRANATE

Every storyteller from time immemorial has been drawn to the power of the pomegranate. Persephone, abducted by Pluto, god of the underworld, ate a few of the pomegranate seeds he offered her. She was forced to return to him for 4 months a year, leaving us winter in her absence. Some suggest that this "many-seeded apple" was the serpent's gift to Eve in the Garden of Eden. Anne of Austria, wife to Louis XIII, chose the pomegranate as her personal emblem.

Pomegranates are grown throughout the Tropics. Fresh pomegranate seeds add their rubylike appearance and their sweet-and-sour flavor to stuffed baked fish, green or fruit salads, and custards. They add a tartness to chutneys, curries, breads, and vegetables. Grenadine, a pomegranate-flavored syrup, is essential behind any truly suave bar.

Pomegranates are rich in symbolism and in taste. Create your own Garden of Eatin' and use them in Minted Pomegranate Eggplant, page 158.

POPPY SEEDS

If there were a single plant living in the Garden of Good and Evil, it would be the poppy. Its botanical name means "sleep inducer," and the poppy has remained the symbol of forgetfulness and sleep. (Remember the poppy field in *The Wizard of Oz*?) Opium was used for medicinal purposes by the ancient Egyptians, and by the Arabians and Asians in the 6th century. (It was not a heavily abused narcotic until the 19th century.) The poppy plant was the grail fought for during the Opium Wars in the 19th century.

Fortunately, those slate blue poppy seeds on your bagel are absolutely harmless — though since there are 800,000 of them to a pound, they can be a nightmare if you drop them on the floor. Roast blue poppy seeds, or the milder white seeds from India before using them to enhance their nutty flavor.

POMEGRANATE MOLASSES

An essential ingredient for cross-cultural cuisine, pomegranate molasses is used extensively in Eastern Mediterranean cooking. With its tart flavor and wonderful aroma, this thick sauce is delicious as a glaze on fish, poultry, or lamb, or when added to salads and pilafs. Buy the Cortas brand in Middle Eastern groceries or by mail. Refrigerated, it will keep indefinitely. Although there is no adequate substitute, a mixture of honey, lemon, and pomegranate or cranberry juice will suffice in a pinch.

[Poppies will] slake the peyne and distroye the mygreyn.

THE HERBAL OR GENERAL
HISTORY OF PLANTS,
JOHN GERARD, 1633

ROSEBUDS

Cut the white part from some scented rose petals. Let them dry thoroughly, then mix with a few drops of rose oil and ground cloves. Fill small bags to put in your drawers.

THE COMPLEAT CONFECTIONER,
MRS. HANNAH GLASSE, 1760

There is no more romantic flavoring than rosebuds. This traditional symbol of love has been known for centuries. It was once the custom to suspend a rose over a dinner table, as a sign that all that was spoken would be considered sacred and held in confidence.

Dried rose petals, usually made from pink damask roses, are used extensively in Tunisian cooking, and in the Moroccan blend Ras el Hanout, page 57. Use rose petals in pilafs or to garnish salads. Rose petal syrup or rosewater can be sprinkled on desserts. Rose petal jam from Greece is a sweet, indulgent confection. Store rose petals in a canister of sugar to give the sugar a delicate floral scent.

ROSEMARY

Boyle the [rosemary] leaves in white wine and washe thy face therewith and thy browes, and thou shalt have a faire face.

BANCKE'S HERBAL,
RYCHARDE BANCKE, 1525

Unruly Elizabethan rosemary grows in profusion in the Mediterranean. It is one of the most beautiful of herbs, and its very name, meaning "dew of the sea," inspires poetry in books and in the kitchen. Reminiscent of pine needles on a sultry hot day, rosemary is used abundantly in Italy, more discreetly elsewhere. It is incomparable in lamb dishes, and works well with shellfish, chicken, and vegetables. Its cool, minty flavor is welcome in cold beverages and fruity desserts.

Place a sprig in the cavity of a chicken before roasting, or in the stuffing with its complement, thyme. Drop a single fresh or dried sprig into soups, or add it to a bouquet garni and retrieve before serving. To release the flavor of dried leaves, crush them just before using them. Use dried ground rosemary in herbal rubs for chicken. Strip the needlelike leaves from rosemary stems and skewer mushroom caps and cherry tomatoes for broiling. Enthusiasm is usually a far-too-rare occurrence in the kitchen, but beware: Rosemary's crisp, woodsy fragrance can overwhelm a dish. Use a little restraint in Hot, Hotter, Hottest Jerk Chicken, page 121.

SAFFRON

Let's travel back to Mesopotamia, civilization's first light. The word *saffron* may have originated there. A Chinese medical book from 2600 B.C. contains the oldest known reference to saffron. The Phoenicians baked saffron into crescent-shaped cakes to honor their gods. Saffron is the "Karcom" of the Hebrews in Song of Solomon. In a painting from ancient Knossos in Crete, a trained monkey is seen gathering crocus flowers. In the Middle Ages in Europe, the penalty for selling adulterated saffron was death. Buddhist monks in Sri Lanka still wear saffron-tinted mantles as a mark of piety.

Three tiny threads, the stigmas, are removed from each of 70,000 purple crocuses to provide 1 pound of saffron, valued at about $800. Its flavor and aroma are subtle but sublime, like a delicate tea leaf that's been soaked in honey. Saffron is used in the world's most renowned dishes. It is added to Mediterranean bouillabaisse and classic Spanish paella. In Italy it flavors and colors risotto. In Morocco it is an intrinsic ingredient in couscous. In India it's required in creamy curries. It is used in Puerto Rican fish stews, and Colombian corn and avocado soup. In England it is used in saffron buns and cakes. It's important to use saffron threads, and not saffron powder, which is of lesser quality. Mexican saffron or azafran is not saffron, but safflower. Cooks love saffron, not only because it adds color and flavor to food, but also because it makes a statement about how important cooking is to them, and how far they are willing to go to provide an exceptional meal for their guests. We hope you'll use saffron too, in Fettuccine with Lobster and Avocado with Basil Vanilla Cream, page 167.

There is no adequate substitute for real saffron. You may leave it out of many-flavored, robust dishes. If you want to approximate the flavor and taste and look of saffron (we hope purists will forgive our heresy), use a pinch of turmeric for color; a pinch of excellent-quality black tea leaves and ¼ teaspoon of light floral honey for taste. But remember: This is no more the real thing than margarine is butter.

The moderate use thereof [of saffron] is good for the head, and maketh the senses more quick and lively, shaketh off heavy and drowsie sleep, and maketh a man merry. It is also such a speciall remedy for those that have consumption of the lungs, and are, as wee terme, at deaths doore, and almost past breathing, that it bringeth breath againe, and prolongeth life for certaine dayes.

THE HERBAL OR GENERAL
HISTORY OF PLANTS,
JOHN GERARD, 1633

I n medieval times, salt was placed in a monumental saltcellar just a little below the center of a lord's banquet table. Being seated "below the salt" was akin to being given a table "in Siberia" at Elaine's or some other chi-chi restaurant.

THE SALT MARCH OF MAHATMA GANDHI, APRIL 5, 1930

It was illegal to manufacture or sell salt except under license from the British. Seventy-eight ashramites left the Sarbamati Ashram outside Ahmedabad and marched some two hundred and forty miles to the beach at Dendi. There, the Mahatma, as he was known, ritually broke the law by picking up a handful of salt crystallised by the evaporation of sea water. By this symbolic march and simple act, Gandhi exhorted all fellow Indians to follow his example and break the law. The result was extraordinary.

IN SEARCH OF GANDHI,
RICHARD ATTENBOROUGH

SALT

A woman gathers seaweed, her source of salt, at the ocean's edge. As she stands she shields her eyes against the sun and looks across the ocean at the horizon. She wonders if, on the ocean's other shore, another woman is gathering seaweed. Salt has enjoyed greater importance and longer use than any other flavoring.

Before salt seasoned food, it was probably used to entice salt-deprived reindeer 10,000 years ago. This black, gray, or sometimes green substance contained a good deal of debris, seaweed, and sewage. Not only was it an essential flavoring, but salt was also a major preservative for meat and, especially, fish.

Sea, sun, and wind conspire to leave traces of salt on the shores. It is harvested from the sea, and other great bodies of water, as well as from places where the ocean used to be. Not technically a spice — there's no such thing as a salt bush or salt tree — salt enhances other flavors. Table salt is what we're used to. Kosher salt has a slightly mellower flavor. Sea salt comes from many oceans; salt from the Mediterranean may taste different from that from England, Japan, or New Zealand. Pickling salt is used solely for curing. Rock salt is crude and gray, more suitable for oyster beds than food, and is a common companion when making homemade ice cream. Indian black salt, colored from the presence of small quantities of trace minerals, smells like low tide, and is by far the most interesting. It can usually be purchased in Indian grocery stores and by mail. Use these salts interchangeably but judiciously.

SAVORY

I t must be awful to be the last herb anybody ever thinks of. Basil, oregano, marjoram, rosemary, tarragon, and thyme, and even sage are plucked off the shelf before anyone says, "Oh, what about savory?" Perhaps cooks are concerned that winter savory can only be used in cold weather, summer savory when the temperature rises; that the spice police will come to get them if they use savory out of season. And of course, most of us can't tell the difference between the two savories, even if one were wearing a bikini and the other snow shoes.

The point is, it doesn't matter. Summer savory is an annual from Southern Europe. Winter savory is a perennial from Southern Europe. Both have a strong, slightly peppery flavor resembling thyme and mint. Use either savory in bean and lentil dishes, with sausages, in stuffings, and in tomato sauces. Instead of calling it winter savory or summer savory, just call it savory savory and use it in Chicken and Sausage Filé Gumbo, page 82.

Sesame Seeds

 pen Sesame," and just like Ali Baba, find a treasure. Sesame seeds and the oil from them are ancient, never-weary world travelers and have provided light, food, and a soothing medicine. Originally from Africa, sesame found its way to India 6,000 years ago when civilizations flourished in the Indus Valley. Its medicinal properties were mentioned in the Ebers papyrus in 1550 B.C., and 2,000 years later it was used by the Persians for cooking. Finally it came to the New World in the 17th century.

Sesame seeds' creamy flavor is welcome throughout the world. In the Middle East, the brown seeds are ground to a thick paste called tahini, or used whole in za'atar, a spice blend. Black sesame seeds have a stronger flavor and are frequently the seed of choice in China and Japan. The white seed, the hulled version of the tan, is used to sprinkle on Japanese vegetables and fish. Dry-roast sesame seeds lightly before using them, and sprinkle them lavishly on rice, noodles, bread, cakes, cookies, and puddings. Sometime soon, stand at the kitchen door and proclaim, "Open Sesame." Let us know what happens. In the meantime, use sesame seeds in Stir-Fried Chicken Salad with Black Mushrooms, page 82.

SORREL

A nother ancient herb, sorrel's name means "sour." Sorrels were used in ancient Egypt, and also by the Romans to counteract their rich diet. It was extremely popular in England in the Middle Ages, and is currently loved by the French in sorrel soup and fish sauces.

Sorrel has a refreshing, somewhat bitter, sour flavor. Use the raw leaf chopped in salads and in chicken soups, or in herb mixtures for fish. Sorrel is available preserved in jars in European or Jewish markets labeled under the name *schav* or *chav*. Don't be sorry — use sour sorrel in super soups and savory salads.

Sorrel sharpens the appetite, assuages heat, cools the liver and strengthens the heart. . . . Sorrel imparts so grateful a quickness to the salad that it should never be left out.

A DISCORSE OF SALLETS,
JOHN EVELYN, 1698

STAR ANISE

C enturies ago, from a dusty corner of a Chinese apothecary, an exotic licorice aroma filled the air. An 8-pointed star, like a tiny brown pinwheel or mutant starfish, has been the secret ingredient in Chinese cuisine and medicine for hundreds of years. The Japanese acknowledged the beauty of star anise and planted the lovely tree in their temples. Sir Thomas Cavendish, mesmerized by its beauty and flavor, brought the spice to Europe in the beginning of the 17th century. Its first uses in the Western world were in jams and cordials.

If we were 16th-century explorers we would neglect pepper and covet this spice instead. Looking more like a tiny creature than a plant, star anise is the fruit of a small evergreen tree native to Southern China and Vietnam. It contributes its intense licoricelike flavor to Chinese Five-Spice Powder, page 52, and is a common ingredient in Chinese red sauces. The Malaysians use star anise in their curries, and the Vietnamese add it to beef soups. It adds a delicious flavor to seafood dishes, roast poultry, and puddings, and brings out the sweetness in beets, carrots, and yams. Add star anise to Poached Sea Bass with Vanilla and Tea, page 98. Substitute Five-Spice Powder or anise seeds if absolutely necessary.

HOUSEHOLD USE:
STAR ANISE

Make a spice necklace of star anise, allspice berries, cinnamon sticks, nutmegs, cardamom pods, and cloves for your favorite child.

Sumac

The leaves of Middle Eastern sumac, one of the most beautiful plants, turn an exquisite red in the fall, and the plant produces spikes of brilliant red berries. The fruity sourness of the dried berries enhanced ancient Roman dishes long before the arrival of lemon to Europe. So, given its beauty and interesting tartness, why has this spice been so neglected in this country? Perhaps people assume it shares the irritating characteristics of its American cousin, poison sumac, aka poison dogwood, when in fact they are related in name only.

Sumac is one of the Middle East's culinary secrets, where it is sprinkled on fish, added to salads, and mixed with chopped meats. It is also an ingredient in za'atar, a seasoning blend. Try it the next time a dish needs an explosive tart jolt, or in Beef Salad with Sumac and Lemongrass, page 181.

No man can be wise on an empty stomach.
GEORGE ELIOT

Tamarind

Shaped like a large, dark brown lima bean pod, the tamarind, also known as an Indian date, has been cultivated in East Africa and Southern Asia for centuries. The Spanish conquistadors introduced it to Mexico and the West Indies, where it is still a popular ingredient. In Tudor England a tamarind drink was a popular thirst quencher — kind of like Gatorade. Tamarind can be purchased in the pod, in dried bricks of pressed pulp and seeds, and in jars of seedless concentrate. It is available in Indian groceries and by mail.

The sour, fruity taste of the pulp is welcome whenever a tart flavor is needed. Use it in sauces for fish. Add it to all kinds of spicy relishes, chutneys, and curried dishes. Cook rice in tamarind-flavored water. A tamarind block or a jar of concentrate will keep indefinitely. Try some in Spicy Lamb Saté with Ancho Macadamia Sauce, page 76. Lemon juice is a less-than-adequate substitute.

Tarragon

I believe that if I ever had to practice cannibalism, I might manage if there was enough tarragon around.

JAMES BEARD

One herb deserves to be called classic. French tarragon is the Chanel of herbs. Timeless, always in vogue, it makes a clear, strong statement without ever being loud. It was believed by ancient Romans that if you carried a twig of this unassuming herb, it would protect against snakes and dragons, and so it was named "the little dragon." Tarragon, which may have originated in Russia, has been known in the Mediterranean for centuries.

Tarragon is one of the world's great culinary herbs. It is beloved by the French, who use it lavishly in their herbal blends, with chicken, and in sauces. Its sophisticated flavor enhances fish and shellfish dishes. Like basil, it perks up eggs and tomatoes. Use fresh tarragon if you can grow it or get it, wear your most chic apron, and reach new culinary heights when you make Vanilla-Infused Lobster Bisque with White Wine and Tarragon, page 86. If you cannot find tarragon, a less-than-adequate substitute is anise or fennel.

Thyme

THYME LORE

The Irish believed that mounds of thyme were loved by the fairies, who chose those aromatic herbal beds for hours of dancing.

This harmonious herb has grown wild on stony hillsides in Southern Europe for thousands of years. In ancient Greece, thyme's powerful aroma was used to perfume the body. During the Crusades ladies would embroider a bee and a sprig of thyme on the scarves worn by their knights. Medieval herbalists recommended it to fend off "wambling and gripings of the bellie."

There are over 100 species of thyme. Seldom the predominant herb, thyme is an essential ingredient in stews, soups, and braised dishes, where its strong flavor stands up to long simmerings. Its pungent flavor blends with the preferred flavors of the Mediterranean — tomatoes, olives, garlic, and wine. Thyme retains its strong aroma even when dried, so if you've got the thyme, we have the recipes, like Jambalaya, page 115.

Turmeric

If we were to create a myth about turmeric, it would be as follows: Once upon a time, an Indian troll kidnapped a beautiful princess, and took her into the underworld. The king, desperate for the return of his only daughter, sent a message to the troll asking for this. The troll responded, "I will return your golden-haired daughter on one condition. You are to catch the sun, grind it into a powder, and bring it to me, so that I may light up the netherworld." The king, who was quite creative, ground turmeric root and sent it to the troll, who, not being a troll genius, but rather a run-of-the-mill, double-digit-I.Q. troll, returned the princess unharmed.

Turmeric, the ground root of a tropical plant, has been cultivated for thousands of years in India, China, and the Middle East. It may have been one of the ancient Persian spices used in sun worship. While traveling in China, Marco Polo noted that the color of turmeric is reminiscent of saffron. Used for centuries as a medicine, dye, and flavoring, it was also worn around the neck by Pacific Islanders to ward off evil.

Turmeric's golden orange color is responsible for the hue of curry powders. A pinch of turmeric will make broccoli and other green vegetables a glow-in-the-dark green, will add an almost-radioactive red-orange tint to tomatoes, and will turn rice a golden copper color. Its musky flavor adds a subtle lemony edge to foods. In Southwestern Asia, it's rubbed on the skin of a pig before roasting, and added to curried coconut dishes. In Morocco, it appears frequently in couscous and soups. In India, it's used frequently in vegetarian dishes. Because of its intense color, it might be a good idea to serve turmeric-laden food on plastic placemats, not white tablecloths. Put yourself in the right mood, add a dab of turmeric to each cheek, like blusher, and prepare a visual feast with mysterious flavor: Steamed Seafood in Hobo Packs, page 104, and Spicy Smashed Potatoes with Garam Masala, page 163.

TURMERIC LORE

In an Indian marriage ceremony, the groom ties a sacred thread dipped in turmeric paste around the bride's neck for good fortune.

Vanilla

Many fairy tales require the successful completion of some arduous task. It may involve spinning straw into gold, searching for an object of great wealth, or slaying a dragon. The story surrounding vanilla is just such a tale: There are over 20,000 varieties of orchids on this earth. Of these, only one, growing in the tropical forests of Mexico, the West Indies, and Central America, is edible. Upon first glance, this particular plant is a rather plain climbing vine, exhibiting none of the heavily perfumed fragrance for which it is famous. That strong, unimaginably sweet smell and taste will develop only after a lengthy curing process. Only one insect, the *Melipona* bee, pollinates this orchid blossom, so it is often pollinated by hand. Since each flower blooms for only 1 day, pollination — natural or otherwise — must occur then. The task is to find the flower, which may grow several hundred feet above the ground, pollinate it, leave it to mature for 6 months, pluck the pod, cure it for several months more, and bring it back to be savored. If you succeed at this task, the aroma of the pod is a sweet reward.

Vanilla was first used by the Aztecs to sweeten their hot chocolate drink, and has been linked to chocolate ever since. When the Spaniards conquered Mexico in the 16th century, they took the prized vanilla bean, considered a powerful aphrodisiac, back to Europe.

All of the world's cuisines use vanilla to flavor their sweet desserts. It is available both as the vanilla bean (both the pod and the seeds impart their flavor) and as an extract. Store a cut-up vanilla bean in a canister of sugar, or add a small piece to coffee or tea before brewing. Of course, use it in pastries, flans, and cookies. What most cuisines have not yet ascertained is that vanilla is sublime in savory dishes as well. Be sure to try this fairy-tale spice in Vanilla Sweet Potato and Carrot Mousse with Cardamom Mint Cream, page 162. Synthetic vanilla is a poor substitute for real vanilla beans or extract.

Ah, you flavor everything; You are the vanilla of society.

LADY HOLLAND'S MEMOIR,
SIDNEY SMITH

HOUSEHOLD USE:

VANILLA

Use a vanilla bean to scent a bureau drawer.

BLENDS, RUBS, AND MARINADES OF THE WORLD

E very cuisine in the world has developed its own distinctive collection of spice mixtures to support and enhance its traditional dishes. They vary enormously in flavor, texture, and complexity. Following are authentic blends from different corners of the world. These blends have value outside of the traditional uses. We urge you to let the borders fade away and try these blends in nontraditional ways — whatever ways appeal to you and complement your style of cooking.

EUROPE

HISTORICAL EUROPEAN SPICE BLENDS

In the 14th century, apothecaries blended and sold several ready-to-use spice mixtures. Each shop had its own custom blends, but the general style and strength of each mixture was reflected in its name. Powdor Douce contained mild and sweet spices such as cinnamon and sugar. Powdor Fort almost always contained black pepper, ginger, cloves, cumin, or other strong spices.

POWDOR DOUCE

1 teaspoon ground coriander
½ teaspoon ground cinnamon
½ teaspoon brown sugar

HISTORICAL RECIPE:

POWDOR FORT

2 teaspoons ground cumin
¾ teaspoon freshly ground black pepper
¾ teaspoon ground ginger

MEDITERRANEAN EUROPE

In the Mediterranean, herbs are used far more than spices, with basil, bay, oregano, rosemary, sage, and thyme being the most popular.

ÉPICES FINES

Also called Spice Parisienne, this is a complex blend of herbs and spices usually used to enhance the flavor of pork.

6 bay leaves, crumbled
3 tablespoons freshly grated nutmeg
3 tablespoons white peppercorns
2 tablespoons cloves
2 tablespoons dried thyme, crumbled

2 tablespoons sweet paprika
1 tablespoon dried basil, crumbled
1 tablespoon ground cinnamon
1 tablespoon winter savory, crumbled

Grind finely in a spice grinder or food processor.

DRIED BOUQUET GARNI

4 dried bay leaves
1 tablespoon dried parsley

1 tablespoon dried thyme

Tie all ingredients into cheesecloth and remove at the end of cooking.

HERBES DE PROVENCE

A blend of summer herbs from the south of France.
Use in soups, stews, chicken dishes; with tomatoes and sauces;
or in anything that is even remotely Mediterranean.

2 teaspoons dried thyme	1 teaspoon dried savory
1 teaspoon dried basil	½ teaspoon ground fennel
1 teaspoon dried marjoram	½ teaspoon dried lavender
1 teaspoon dried rosemary	

Combine all ingredients.

QUATRE ÉPICES

A French spice mixture whose name means simply "four spices,"
Quatre Épices is frequently used in French charcuterie
and in slowly cooked meat and poultry dishes.

4 teaspoons freshly ground white peppercorns	3 teaspoons ground ginger
3½ teaspoons freshly grated nutmeg	1½ teaspoons freshly ground cloves

Combine all ingredients.

I feel sentimental about England now — English food, decent English waste! How much better than these thrifty French whose flower gardens are nothing but potential salad bowls. There's not a leaf in France that you can't "faire une infusion avec (make tea with)", not a blade that isn't "bon pour la cuisine (good for cooking)". By God, I'd like to buy a pound of the best butter, put it on the window sill and watch it melt to spite 'em.

THE COLLECTED LETTERS OF
KATHERINE MANSFIELD,
KATHERINE MANSFIELD,
1889

NORTHERN EUROPE

Historically subjected to far fewer invasions than southern parts of Europe, Northern Europe remained relatively insular, and its cuisines placed much greater emphasis on basic ingredients, with little reliance on added spices or flavorings.

Pickling Spice

Alter the ingredients according to the type of food being pickled. Cinnamon and cloves should predominate in fruit pickles, while mustard seeds, celery seeds, and turmeric should well be in evidence in savory pickling mixes.

1 tablespoon allspice berries
1 tablespoon dill seeds
1 tablespoon yellow mustard seeds
1 tablespoon freshly grated nutmeg
1 tablespoon black peppercorns

1 tablespoon hot red pepper flakes
1 cinnamon stick, broken into pieces
2 bay leaves, crumbled
2 teaspoons ground ginger
1 teaspoon cloves
1 teaspoon coriander seeds
1 teaspoon fennel seeds

Tie all the ingredients into a cheesecloth and remove after pickling.

Pudding Spice

An English blend of sweet spices.

1 tablespoon coriander seeds
1 cinnamon stick, broken into pieces
2 teaspoons allspice berries

2 teaspoons cloves
2 teaspoons ground mace
2 teaspoons freshly grated nutmeg

Grind finely in a spice grinder or food processor.

I have heard of a Cook that used six Pounds of Butter to fry twelve Eggs; when every Body knows, that understands Cooking, that Half a Pound is full enough, or more than need be used: But then it would not be French. *So much is the blind Folly of this Age, that they would rather be impos'd on by a* French *Booby, than give Encouragement to a good* English *Cook!*

THE ART OF COOKERY MADE PLAIN & EASY,
MRS. HANNAH GLASSE, 1747

The influence of invading empires — Turkish pastries, Austrian cakes, and Middle Eastern eggplants — have all been absorbed into the cuisines of Eastern Europe.

GEORGIAN BLEND

Paula Wolfert is the acknowledged expert on Moroccan and Eastern Mediterranean cooking. We have adapted the following Georgian Blend recipe from her book, The Cooking of the Eastern Mediterranean. *Use it in stews, in soups, and as a marinade for meat.*

1 tablespoon whole coriander seeds

2 teaspoons dried fenugreek leaves, crumbled, or ½ teaspoon ground fenugreek

1 teaspoon dried marigold petals, or ½ teaspoon saffron threads

1 teaspoon dried savory

¾ teaspoon dried basil

½ teaspoon dried mint, crumbled

½ teaspoon sweet paprika

½ teaspoon freshly ground black pepper

¼ teaspoon ground cinnamon

¼ teaspoon ground cloves

Grind in a spice grinder or food processor.

Middle East

In Greece and the land bridge called the Fertile Crescent, which includes Iran, Iraq, Jordan, Lebanon, Syria, and Turkey, the traditions surrounding food have remained essentially the same for centuries. Cooks blend simple Arabic dishes with complex, sweet Persian flavors, staples from North Africa, and Asian spices.

Kuwaiti Baharat

Baharat has as many permutations as curry powder. This usually sweet blend is similar in usage to the Indian garam masala. Add to meat loaf and meat pies, or use as a rub on grilled or roast chicken.

4 teaspoons ground Aleppo pepper or sweet paprika
4 teaspoons freshly ground black pepper
1 cinnamon stick, broken up
1 teaspoon cardamom seeds

1 teaspoon cloves
1 teaspoon coriander seeds
1 teaspoon cumin seeds
1 teaspoon ground ginger
1 teaspoon freshly grated nutmeg

Grind in a spice grinder or food processor.

Hawaj

This aromatic, earthy Yemenite blend is especially well suited for soups, broiled or barbecued meats, and cooked vegetables.

2 tablespoons black peppercorns
2 tablespoons caraway seeds
2 teaspoons green cardamom pods

2 teaspoons ground turmeric
1 teaspoon coriander seeds
1 teaspoon saffron threads

Grind in a spice grinder or food processor.

Saudi Arabian Kabsa Spice

Similar to harissa of North Africa, this very hot blend is tempered with the flavor of citrus.

1 tablespoon ground cayenne pepper
2 cinnamon sticks, broken up
1½ teaspoons cumin seeds
1 teaspoon ground cardamom
1 teaspoon cloves

1 teaspoon coriander seeds
1 teaspoon ground lime powder
1 teaspoon freshly grated nutmeg
1 teaspoon freshly ground black pepper

Grind in a spice grinder or food processor.

Syrian Za'atar

Za'atar refers to both an herb and a spice blend. Za'atar, the herb, is a hybrid of thyme, oregano, and marjoram. Za'atar, the blend, which varies from region to region, is used as a seasoning on breads, in dips, and with cheese.

¼ cup sesame seeds
3 tablespoons dried thyme, crumbled

2 tablespoons dried marjoram, crumbled
2 tablespoons ground sumac

Dry-roast the sesame seeds in a skillet over low heat for 2 minutes, or until aromatic. Cool, add the thyme, marjoram, and sumac, and mix well. Add 2 tablespoons ground pistachios to vary the recipe.

For cooking is the part of culture which remains closest to people and matters most; more than music and painting and clothing, more than language and sometimes even more than religion. For some generations of some peoples it may be all that is left, long after everything else has been lost; for it is that which makes people happy and comfortable.

COOKING IN ISRAEL:
A CHANGING MOSAIC,
CLAUDIA RODEN,
OXFORD FOOD SYMPOSIUM, 1981

India

Know that the knowledgeable use of spices is the principal base of prepared dishes, because it is the cement of cooking, and upon it cooking is built.

HISPANIC-MOORISH COOKERY TEXT,
13TH CENTURY

Profoundly influenced by the Muslim conquerors of India, food plays a major role in the religious and social rituals of the culture. Following are a few of the infinite varieties of aromatic blends.

Chaat Masala

Use this tart blend as counterpoint to the sweetness of fruits and vegetables.

1 teaspoon coriander seeds	½ teaspoon whole thyme
1 teaspoon black peppercorns	1 teaspoon ground sumac
½ teaspoon crushed dried mint leaves	½ teaspoon ground ginger
½ teaspoon pink peppercorns	¼ teaspoon asafetida
½ teaspoon black salt or coarse sea salt	¼ teaspoon ground cayenne pepper

Combine the coriander seeds, black peppercorns, mint leaves, pink peppercorns, salt, and thyme in a spice grinder or food processor and blend to a powder. Add the sumac, ginger, asafetida, and cayenne and blend to mix well.

BASIC CURRY POWDER

Add to chicken salad, lentil soups, carrots, and rice,
or mix with yogurt and serve as a dip.

6 dried red chili peppers,
  seeded
2 tablespoons coriander seeds
2 teaspoons cumin seeds
1 teaspoon fenugreek seeds
1 teaspoon black peppercorns
½ teaspoon cardamom seeds
½ teaspoon fennel seeds

½ teaspoon mustard seeds
One 1-inch piece cinnamon,
  broken up
10 fresh curry leaves
1 tablespoon ground turmeric
½ teaspoon ground cloves
½ teaspoon ground ginger

Combine the chilies, coriander seeds, cumin seeds, fenugreek
seeds, black peppercorns, cardamom seeds, fennel seeds, mustard
seeds, and cinnamon in a small saucepan over low heat. Dry-roast, stirring constantly, until the spices darken slightly. Add the curry leaves
and dry-roast for 3 minutes more. Allow to cool. Combine all ingredients in a spice grinder or food processor, and grind to a powder.

SRI LANKA CURRY POWDER

In Sri Lanka, spices are dry-roasted,
then blended into an intense, earthy curry powder.

10 fresh or dried curry leaves
1 cup coriander seeds
½ cup cumin seeds
1 tablespoon fennel seeds
1 teaspoon cardamom seeds

1 teaspoon cloves
1 teaspoon fenugreek seeds
1 cinnamon stick, broken up
1 teaspoon ground cayenne
  pepper

If using fresh curry leaves, preheat the oven to 200°F. Place them
in a single layer on a pie plate and roast for 10 minutes, or until dried.
Set aside. Combine all but the cayenne pepper in a skillet and dry-
roast until dark. Do not let this burn. Transfer to a food processor, add
the cayenne, and blend until finely powdered. Transfer to a jar. Crumble the curry leaves, add to the blend, and mix well.

Seated at his usual table, Keith ate pappadams and bombay duck while the staff fondly prepared his mutton vindaloo. "The napalm sauce, sir?" asked Rashid. Keith was resolved, in this as in all things. "Yeah. The napalm sauce." In the kitchen they were busy responding to Keith's imperial challenge: to make a curry so hot that he couldn't eat it. The meal arrived. Lively but silent faces stared through the serving-hatch. The first spoonful swiped a mustache of sweat on to Keith's upper lip, and drew excited murmurs from the kitchen. "Bit mild," said Keith when he could talk again. That day the Indian Mutiny had no other customers. Keith chewed steadily. His lion's hair looked silver in the shadows. Tears inched their way over his dry cheeks. "Bland, Rashid," said Keith, later, as he paid and undertipped. "What you looking at? It's five per cent. Bland. Dead bland."

LONDON FIELDS, MARTIN AMIS, 1989

Fragrant Garam Masala

Although garam masala can be a savory blend, it is usually milder and sweeter than curry and contains no turmeric. Use as a rub for poultry or fish, sprinkle on vegetables, or add to a curry blend to sweeten it.

¼	cup coriander seeds	1	teaspoon cloves
2	tablespoons cumin seeds	½	teaspoon dried rosebuds
1	tablespoon black peppercorns	1	teaspoon freshly grated nutmeg
2	teaspoons cardamom seeds	½	teaspoon saffron threads
	Four 3-inch cinnamon sticks, broken up		

Dry-roast the coriander seeds, cumin seeds, black peppercorns, cardamom seeds, cinnamon, and cloves in a small saucepan over low heat for 2–3 minutes, or until fragrant. Transfer to a spice grinder or food processor, add the rosebuds, and grind to a fine powder. Add the nutmeg and saffron and mix thoroughly.

Savory Garam Masala

Use this savory blend with vegetables and in bean casseroles.

¼	cup coriander seeds	2	teaspoons cloves
¼	cup cumin seeds	1	teaspoon cardamom seeds
¼	cup black peppercorns	1	teaspoon sesame seeds
4	small dried red chili peppers, seeded and broken up	½	teaspoon fennel seeds
		4	bay leaves
½	cinnamon stick, broken up	½	teaspoon ajowan
		½	teaspoon ground mace

Combine the coriander seeds, cumin seeds, black peppercorns, chili peppers, cinnamon stick, cloves, cardamom seeds, sesame seeds, fennel seeds, and bay leaves in a small skillet over moderate heat. Dry-roast for 3 minutes, or until fragrant. Allow to cool, and transfer to a spice grinder or food processor. Add the ajowan and mace and grind to a fine powder.

Panch Phora

*This five-spice mixture adds an interesting savory flavor
to vegetable dishes.*

Combine equal amounts of cumin seeds, fennel seeds, fenugreek
seeds, black mustard seeds, and nigella seeds. Mix well.

*Awake O north wind,
and come, thou south;
blow upon my garden, that the
spices thereof may flow out.*

SONG OF SOLOMON

Sambhar Powder

*Roasted beans add a nutty flavor to this fiery blend. Use it with braised
vegetables, or in lentil stews, spicy soups, and sauces.*

4 small dried red chili
   peppers, seeded
1 tablespoon coriander seeds
2 teaspoons cumin seeds
1 teaspoon mustard seeds
1 teaspoon black peppercorns
½ teaspoon fenugreek seeds

1 tablespoon ground turmeric
¼ teaspoon asafetida
1 tablespoon peanut oil
1 tablespoon white gram
   beans (urad dal)
1 tablespoon yellow split peas
   (channa dal)

Combine the chilies, coriander seeds, cumin seeds, mustard seeds,
black peppercorns, and fenugreek seeds in a small skillet over moderate
heat. Dry-roast for 3 minutes, or until aromatic. Add the turmeric and
asafetida, stir to mix, and set aside in a small bowl. Reduce the heat to
low and add the peanut oil to the skillet. Add the beans and peas and
sauté, stirring constantly, for 3 minutes, or until darkened. Add the
peas and beans to the spices and let cool. Grind to a powder.

Of the Many Uses of Spices Salts
(Sales Conditos ad Multa)

Spiced salts are good for the digestion, for promoting regularity, and for averting all sorts of sicknesses and plagues and chills. Moreover, they are more agreeable to the taste than you might expect. Take one pound of common ground salt, two pounds of ground Libyan salt, three ounces of white pepper, two ounces of ginger, one and one-half ounces of cumin, one and one-half ounces of thyme, one and one-half ounces of celery seed. If you do not want to take celery seed, take three ounces of parsley. Three ounces of oregano, one and one-half ounces of colewort seed, three ounces of black pepper, one ounce of saffron, two ounces of Cretan hyssop, two ounces of spikenard, two ounces of parsley, two ounces of aniseed.

OF CULINARY MATTERS,
MARCUS GARVIUS APICIUS, 14 A.D.

THE FAR EAST AND SOUTH PACIFIC

CHINA

In China, food is seen as an expression of inner harmony, and meals are an integral part of the ritual surrounding friendship. Food must gratify all the senses equally. The crunch and texture of water chestnuts are balanced by the visual brilliance of white rice and vibrant red peppers.

FIVE-SPICE POWDER

Easily the best-known Chinese blend, licorice-flavored Five-Spice Powder is used throughout China and Vietnam to flavor roast meats and poultry. Use as a rub or all-purpose sprinkle.

6 star anise pods	**2 teaspoons cloves**
1 tablespoon fennel seeds	**One 2-inch cinnamon stick,**
1 tablespoon Szechuan	**broken up**
peppercorns	

Combine all the ingredients in a spice grinder or food processor and grind to a powder.

SZECHUAN SALT

Use as a table salt.

3 tablespoons coarse salt	**1 teaspoon whole Szechuan**
	peppercorns

Combine in a small skillet, and dry-roast for 3 minutes, or until the Szechuan peppercorns darken slightly. Let cool, transfer to a spice grinder or salt mill, and grind to a coarse powder. Store in an airtight container for 4-6 months.

Japanese cooking is the most elegantly simple of the world's great cuisines. This simplicity carries into flavorings, and food is visually adorned but barely spiced.

SESAME SALT
(GOMASIO)

This Japanese table condiment is used as frequently as we use salt. Fill a salt shaker and keep it within easy reach to sprinkle on everything.

2 tablespoons black or white sesame seeds

1 tablespoon coarse sea salt

Dry-roast the sesame seeds in a small skillet over low heat for 2 minutes, stirring constantly. Cool, combine with the sea salt in a spice grinder, and grind finely.

SEVEN-SPICE SEASONING
(SHICHIMI TOGARASHI)

Use this popular blend liberally in soups, or with noodles, vegetables, and grilled meats.

1 tablespoon white sesame seeds

1 tablespoon Szechuan peppercorns

1 tablespoon minced tangerine zest

One 2-inch square Japanese seaweed (nori), finely chopped

1 teaspoon ground cayenne pepper

1 teaspoon white poppy seeds

1 teaspoon black sesame seeds

Combine all ingredients in a spice grinder or food processor and grind coarsely.

LEMONGRASS

In recipes where either fresh or dried lemongrass is not going to be processed in a food processor or slow-cooked as in a soup, it's best to pulverize it and soak it for 2 to 3 hours in milk or oil to soften it.

Embracing influences from China, India, and the South Pacific, Thailand has created a diverse and crisp cuisine, characterized by light, distinctly flavored dishes with a range of temperaments, from mild to incendiary, and from mouth-puckeringly sour to overpoweringly sweet.

Masaman Curry Paste

Curries are as important in Thailand as in India, but the Thais use ferociously hot pastes instead of powders. Cut the heat by reducing the amount of chilies, or by adding coconut milk.

2 fresh lemongrass stalks or 2 tablespoons dried chopped lemongrass	1 tablespoon cardamom seeds
12 small dried red chili peppers, seeded	2 teaspoons cumin seeds
One 1-inch piece fresh galangal, chopped, or 4 slices dried	½ cinnamon stick
2 red onions, chopped	1 teaspoon cloves
12 garlic cloves	1 teaspoon ground mace
2 tablespoons coriander seeds	1 teaspoon freshly grated nutmeg
	1 teaspoon whole black peppercorns
	1 teaspoon shrimp paste
	4 bay leaves

If using fresh lemongrass, remove and discard the outer leaves and upper half of the lemongrass stalks, and chop the bottom half into 1-inch pieces. Soak all the dried ingredients for 30 minutes, or until softened. Place all ingredients in a food processor and blend to a smooth paste. Add a little water if necessary to thin.

Panang Curry Paste

Unlike most Thai curries, panangs are almost dry.

2 lemongrass stalks, or ¼ cup dried chopped lemongrass	12 small dried red chili peppers, seeded

One 1-inch piece fresh
  galangal, chopped,
  or 4 slices dried
10 garlic cloves
 4 shallots, chopped
 1 tablespoon fresh Thai lime
  peel or lime peel, chopped
 2 coriander roots, chopped

2 teaspoons caraway seeds
2 teaspoons shrimp paste
1 teaspoon cardamom seeds
1 teaspoon ground mace
1 teaspoon Szechuan
  peppercorns
1 teaspoon salt

Follow the instructions for Masaman Curry Paste.

YELLOW CURRY PASTE

1 lemongrass stalk, or
  2 tablespoons dried
  chopped lemongrass
12 small dried red chili
  peppers, seeded
 2 shallots, chopped

2 coriander roots, chopped
1 tablespoon cumin seeds
1½ tablespoons ground
  turmeric
1 tablespoon peanut oil

Follow the instructions for Masaman Curry Paste.

◀ INDONESIA ▶

SAMBAL OELEK
This sambal is made from chilies, chilies, and more chilies.

1 cup fresh red chili peppers
1 teaspoon palm or brown sugar

1 teaspoon salt

Heat a heavy skillet until hot but not smoking. Add the chilies, and dry-roast for 5 minutes. Remove and discard the seeds for a milder (ha!) sambal. Let cool, and combine in a food processor with the palm sugar and salt. Store in an airtight container in the refrigerator for about a week.

There is an abundant quantity of game of all kinds, such as roebucks, stags, fallow deer, hares, and rabbits, together with partridge, pheasants, francolins, quails, common fowls, capons, and such number of ducks and geese as can scarcely be expressed; for so easily are they bred and reared on the lake, that for the value of a Venetian silver groat, you may purchase a couple of geese and a couple of ducks.

THE TRAVELS OF MARCO POLO,
MANUEL KOMROFF, TRANS., 1953

AFRICA

The food of Africa is surprising and complex. Nowhere else on earth have the influences of the Phoenicians, Carthaginians, Arabs, Turks, and Europeans combined with the indigenous cuisine to create such splendid results.

SAVORY BAHARAT

*Use this palate-buster from
the Gulf States judiciously on grilled meat and vegetables.*

¼ cup sweet paprika
2 tablespoons cloves
2 tablespoons coriander seeds
2 tablespoons cumin seeds
2 tablespoons black
   peppercorns

2 teaspoons freshly grated
   nutmeg
2 teaspoons cardamom seeds
1 cinnamon stick, broken up
1 teaspoon ground cayenne
   pepper

Combine all ingredients in a spice grinder or food processor and blend to a fine powder.

HARISSA

Harissa is found all over Tunisia, Algeria, and Morocco.
Use it whenever a blistering hot sauce is in demand.

4 large dried guajillo or other
chili peppers, quartered,
seeded, and stemmed
1 teaspoon crushed dried
mint leaves

1 tablespoon olive oil
1 tablespoon coriander seeds
1 tablespoon caraway seeds
8 garlic cloves
1 teaspoon cumin seeds

Soak the chilies and the mint leaves in ⅓ cup of hot water for 30 minutes, or until softened. With a slotted spoon, transfer the chilies and mint to a food processor and add the remaining ingredients. Blend to a smooth paste.

RAS EL HANOUT

The most renowned Moroccan blend, Ras el Hanout, translates literally
"head of the shop." Although these blends are as varied as the cooks who
create them, most are a complicated mix of warm, sweet spices.

4 whole nutmegs
10 dried rosebuds
6 cinnamon sticks
12 mace blades
2 quarter-size slices fresh
or dried galangal
1 small dried chili pepper
4 teaspoons green cardamom
pods
1 tablespoon cubeb pepper
or black peppercorns

2 teaspoons allspice berries
1 teaspoon anise seeds
1 teaspoon brown cardamom
pods
1 teaspoon cloves
1 teaspoon coriander seeds
1 teaspoon cumin seeds
1 teaspoon sesame seeds
½ teaspoon dried lavender
flowers
2 teaspoons turmeric

Combine all ingredients in a spice grinder or food processor and blend to a fine powder.

AJOWAN

With no written history to speak of, no glorious or romantic quotes dedicated to it, ajowan is the poor little step-sister of the more storied spices and herbs. It is, nevertheless, quietly essential in Indian savory dishes and snacks, and in *chat masala* — an Indian spice blend used in fruit and vegetable salads. Native to southern India, this herb determinedly grows in Afganistan, Pakistan, Iran, and Egypt as well. Also called bishop's weed, ajowan is related to caraway and cumin, looks like celery seed, and tastes like thyme. It flavors flat breads like *paratha*, enhances spicy lentil dishes, and is especially good with fish. Although it lacks the subtely of thyme, it can easily be replaced by that herb in recipes. However, if you are replacing thyme with ajowan, use half the quantity to compensate for its stronger flavor.

Tunisian Quatre Épices

This very popular Tunisian blend is quite different from the French blend of the same name.

2 garlic cloves
2 tablespoons coriander seeds
1 teaspoon dried mint
1 teaspoon black peppercorns
1 teaspoon dried rose buds

Combine all ingredients in a food processor and blend to a paste. Stored in an airtight container in the refrigerator for up to 1 week.

Berbere

Berbere is the blend that flavors wat, a traditional Ethiopian stew. Add it to soups, or use it as a very hot rub for roast chicken or lamb.

1 tablespoon ajowan
1 tablespoon cardamom seeds
1 tablespoon black cumin seeds or cumin seeds
1 tablespoon fenugreek seeds
½ cinnamon stick, broken up
1 teaspoon cloves
1½ cups New Mexican chile powder
3 tablespoons onion flakes
2 tablespoons garlic flakes
2 tablespoons ground ginger
1 tablespoon coarse sea salt

Combine the ajowan, cardamom, cumin, fenugreek, cinnamon, and cloves in a skillet over low heat and dry-roast, stirring constantly, for 5 minutes, or until aromatic. Stir in the chile powder and dry-roast for 1 minute more. Let cool, and transfer to a food processor. Add the onion flakes, garlic flakes, ginger, and salt and blend to a fine powder.

North America

Every wooden-spoon-wielding immigrant grandmother who ever landed on these shores brought traditional ways to cook with her. Over time, traditional ethnic tables have softened as chefs and foodies have begun to borrow from these diverse cuisines, cooking what they love rather than what is traditional.

Barbecue Rub

Rub it over other spices, rub it into chicken, rub it on steak.

- 2 tablespoons freshly cracked black pepper
- ½ cup ground aleppo pepper or sweet paprika
- 2 tablespoons chili powder
- 2 tablespoons ground cumin
- 2 tablespoons brown sugar
- 1 tablespoon ground cayenne pepper
- 1 tablespoon garlic powder
- 1 tablespoon salt
- 1 teaspoon Five-Spice Powder (page 52)

Combine all ingredients and mix well.

Crab Boil

- 1 teaspoon allspice berries
- 1 teaspoon cloves
- 1 teaspoon coriander seeds
- 1 teaspoon dill seeds
- 1 teaspoon mustard seeds
- 1 teaspoon black peppercorns
- 1 teaspoon crushed red pepper
- 1 teaspoon salt
- 1 teaspoon dried thyme
- 3 bay leaves
- ½ teaspoon celery seeds

Tie all the ingredients into cheesecloth. Add to water for boiling seafood. Remove and discard at the end of cooking.

The ordinary mode of living is abundant, but not delicate. They consume an extraordinary quantity of bacon. Ham and beef-steaks appear morning, noon, and night. In eating, they mix things together with the strangest incongruity imaginable.

DOMESTIC MANNERS OF THE AMERICANS,
FRANCES TROLLOPE, 1832

Cajun Seasoning

Cajun blends evoke memories of New Orleans — café au lait, beignets, the Jazz Festival — one of the world's truly fascinating cities. It's impossible not to like this blend; use it on everything.

2 shallots, chopped
1 garlic clove, peeled
1 teaspoon dried oregano, crumbled
1 teaspoon sweet paprika
1 teaspoon freshly cracked black pepper
1 teaspoon salt

1 teaspoon dried thyme, crumbled
½ teaspoon ground cayenne pepper
½ teaspoon celery seeds
½ teaspoon cumin seeds
½ teaspoon mustard seeds
½ teaspoon dried sage, crumbled

Combine all the ingredients in a food processor and blend well.

Chili Powder

Chile powder (with an "e") is usually one kind of chile that has been ground. Chili powder (with an "i") is a blend of several chiles and other spices. Use it in anything even remotely southwestern, in meat loaf, or mixed into red sauces.

¼ cup ground New Mexican chiles
1 tablespoon ancho chile powder
1 tablespoon garlic powder
1 tablespoon pasilla chile powder

2 teaspoons ground cumin
2 teaspoons ground oregano
1 teaspoon ground cayenne pepper
1 teaspoon chipotle chile powder

Combine all ingredients and mix well.

I was watching everyone else and didn't see the waitress standing quietly by. Her voice was deep and soft like water moving in a cavern. I ordered the $4.50 special. In a few minutes, she wheeled up a cart and began off-loading dinner: ham and eggs, fried catfish, fried perch fingerlings, fried shrimp, chunks of barbecued beef, fried chicken, French fries, hush puppies, a broad bowl of cole slaw, another of lemon, a quart of ice tea, a quart of ice, and an entire loaf of pastry-wrapped white bread. The table was covered. "Call me if y'all want any more." She wasn't joking.

BLUE HIGHWAYS,
WILLIAM LEAST HEAT MOON, 1983

CARIBBEAN

A hot, colorful cuisine with names that never stop dancing — Coconut Run Down, Solomon Gundy, Stamp and Go, Jamaican Jerk — Caribbean cooking celebrates the flavors of Africa, Spain, and Portugal. Even though each island has its own regional specialties, they share affection for the abundant fruits and fish of the New World, along with its most jolting gift — the chile pepper.

CARIBBEAN CURRY POWDER

Migrant workers from India and Sri Lanka brought the idea of curry powder with them in the 1800s. Different islands of the Caribbean each add their own particular sweet spin.

2 **tablespoons cumin seeds**	1 **teaspoon poppy seeds**
1 **tablespoon allspice berries**	2 **tablespoons ground**
1 **tablespoon coriander seeds**	**turmeric**
1 **teaspoon anise seeds**	1 **tablespoon ground ginger**
1 **teaspoon cloves**	1 **teaspoon ground fenugreek**
1 **teaspoon mustard seeds**	½ **teaspoon ground cinnamon**

Combine the cumin seeds, allspice, coriander, anise, cloves, mustard, and poppy seeds in a small skillet over low heat. Dry-roast for 2 minutes, or until the mustard seeds start jumping. Let cool, transfer to a spice grinder or processor, and blend to a fine powder. Add the turmeric, ginger, fenugreek, and cinnamon, and blend to mix well.

POUDRE DE COLOMBO

*In Martinique and Guadeloupe,
this curry powder is usually fried in oil before use.*

1	teaspoon ground coriander	3 garlic cloves, crushed
1	teaspoon ground mustard	2 fresh hot red chile peppers,
½	teaspoon ground turmeric	seeded and chopped

Combine all ingredients in a food processor and blend to a paste.

JAMAICAN JERK

*This volatile paste is contributed by Cinnabar Specialty Foods, Inc.,
suppliers of, among other things, a dynamite, dry Jamaican Jerk blend.
Use this paste for all your grilling — it will enliven shrimp,
fish, chicken, meats, and vegetables.*

6 scallions, minced
3 garlic cloves, minced
2 tablespoons minced red bell pepper
2 tablespoons minced green bell pepper
1 fresh Scotch bonnet or habanero chile pepper, seeded and minced
2 tablespoons ground allspice

1 tablespoon crushed red chile pepper
¾ tablespoon coarsely ground black pepper
¾ teaspoon freshly grated nutmeg
½ teaspoon salt
¼ cup fresh lemon juice
2 tablespoons malt vinegar
2 tablespoons canola oil

Combine all the ingredients. Use to marinate meat for 8–12 hours prior to grilling; marinate chicken, fish, and vegetables for substantially less time.

Mexico and South America

The cuisines of ancient Aztec and Mayan civilizations, with their cornerstones of chiles, chocolate, and corn, were the perfect base for the sweet marinades, sauces, and faraway foods — citrus fruits, pork, and rice — brought by the Spanish conquerors.

Annatto Paste

Rub this flavorful paste on chicken or pork before roasting or grilling.

1	tablespoon vegetable oil	1	teaspoon allspice berries
½	cup crushed annatto seeds	1	teaspoon cumin seeds
1	cup fresh orange juice	2	garlic cloves, unpeeled
¼	cup fresh lemon juice	½	teaspoon ground cayenne
1½	teaspoons dried oregano, preferably Mexican		pepper
		½	teaspoon salt

Heat the oil in a small skillet over medium heat until hot but not smoking. Add the annatto and sauté, stirring constantly, for 5 minutes. Transfer to a small bowl and add the orange and lemon juices. Let soak for 3 hours, or until softened. Combine the oregano, allspice, and cumin in a small skillet over low heat and dry-roast for 2 minutes, or until aromatic. Transfer the spices to a bowl. Place the garlic in the skillet, increase the heat to high, and dry-roast, turning frequently, for 5 minutes, or until darkened on all sides. Allow to cool; peel. Drain the annatto and transfer to a food processor. Add the roasted spices, garlic, cayenne pepper, and salt and blend to a paste.

Tortillas, which are the common food of the people, and which are merely maize cakes mixed with a little lime, and of the form and size of what we call scones, I find rather good when very hot and fresh-baked, but insipid by themselves. They have been in use all through this country since the earliest ages of its history, without any change in the manner of baking them, excepting that, for the noble Mexicans in former days, they used to be kneaded with various medicinal plants, supposed to render them more wholesome. They are considered particularly palatable with chile, to endure which, in the quantities in which it is eaten here, it seems to me necessary to have a throat lined with tin.

LIFE IN MEXICO,
MME CALDERON DE LA BARCA, 1843

Adobo Seasoning

Use this traditional chile marinade on pork chops, ribs, or fish.

8 garlic cloves, unpeeled
4 ancho chile peppers, stemmed, seeded, and torn into pieces
6 guajillo chile peppers, stemmed, seeded, and torn into pieces
½ teaspoon ground cinnamon
½ teaspoon dried oregano
½ teaspoon freshly ground black pepper
½ teaspoon dried thyme
¼ teaspoon ground cloves
¼ teaspoon ground cumin
2 bay leaves
1 teaspoon salt
¼ cup cider vinegar

In a small skillet over low heat, dry-roast the garlic, turning frequently, for 10 minutes, or until darkened all over and very soft. Remove the garlic and let cool. Place the chiles in the skillet, press down with a metal spatula, and dry-roast, turning frequently, for 1 minute, or until blistered and dark all over. Remove the chiles and soak in hot water to cover for 30 minutes. Peel the garlic. Transfer the chiles to a food processor. Add the peeled garlic and the remaining ingredients and blend to a paste, using a little of the chile water if necessary.

Chimichurri

Throughout Argentina this deliciously spiced parsley sauce is traditionally used on grilled meats, but is also wonderful on vegetables and in soups.

½ cup olive oil
6 tablespoons red wine vinegar
½ cup finely chopped onion
½ cup finely chopped fresh Italian parsley
6 large garlic cloves, minced
1 tablespoon dried oregano
1 teaspoon freshly ground black pepper
½ teaspoon hot red pepper flakes
Salt, to taste

Combine the oil and vinegar in a bowl, and mix well. Stir in the onions, parsley, garlic, oregano, pepper flakes, black pepper, and salt. Let stand for 3 hours before serving.

RECIPES

Join us on our culinary adventure, from small-plate appetizers to start your spice-laden meal, to comforting or searingly hot soups, bold main courses and pastas, unusual and refreshing salads, all the way through to mouthwatering desserts and beverages.

Small Plates

When you find that you cannot get dinner ready at the time appointed, put the clock back . . .

JONATHAN SWIFT, AROUND 1731

HOT SAUCES

These potato chips are the perfect opportunity to serve one or more bottled hot sauces. Inner Beauty sauces are very tasty, as is River Run. If you're seeking revenge, put Melinda's XXXXtra Hot Reserva on the table. All are available in gourmet specialty shops or by mail.

Potato Chips
WITH CAJUN SEASONING, HOT SAUCE, AND BLUE CHEESE
It's actually better to serve these as a snack than as an appetizer, because they will surely ruin everyone's appetite for dinner.

4 SERVINGS

2 sweet potatoes, peeled and sliced ⅛ inch thick	¼ cup Cajun Seasoning (page 60)
2 Idaho potatoes, peeled and sliced ⅛ inch thick	½ cup blue cheese, crumbled
Peanut oil, for frying	Hot sauce, preferably Melinda's, Inner Beauty, or Tabasco, to taste

1. Soak the sweet potatoes and Idaho potatoes in separate bowls of ice water in the refrigerator for 4 hours.

2. Preheat the oven to 250°F. Heat oil in a deep fryer to 370°F. Drain the potatoes and pat dry with paper towels. Fry the potatoes in small batches until nicely browned. Bring the oil back to temperature before frying the next batch. Drain the chips on brown paper bags or paper towels and sprinkle with the Cajun Seasoning. As you finish each batch, place chips in a single layer on a baking sheet in the oven to keep warm and crisp.

3. When all of the chips are fried, crumble the blue cheese on top and heat in the oven for 5 minutes, or until the cheese is soft. Serve with the hot sauce on the side.

Endive

WITH SHIITAKE MUSHROOM RELISH

Jeff Loshinsky, one of the most versatile and imaginative chefs we know, turns out an unbelievable array of traditional and cross-cultural dishes for the catering arm of Adriana's Caravan. This mushroom relish is as versatile as the chef. Add it to egg salads, spread it on sandwiches, or serve it on the side with grilled vegetables.

4 SERVINGS

SHIITAKE MUSHROOMS

Similar to the Chinese black mushroom, the Japanese shiitake is cultivated on oak logs. This delicately flavored mushroom is available fresh and dried in Asian markets, in gourmet shops, and by mail.

INDIAN MANGO PICKLE

Traditional fruit or vegetable condiments, similar to relishes or sambals, are served with Indian curries. The sweeter relishes are called chutneys, the saltier and hotter ones pickles. Both are available in a variety of flavors in Indian groceries, in gourmet shops, and by mail.

4 ounces dried shiitake
   mushrooms, stemmed
6 scallions, trimmed and
   sliced into thin rounds
1 red bell pepper, cored,
   seeded, and diced
½ cup imported Indian mango
   pickle

¼ cup dark brown sugar
1 tablespoon whole coriander
   seeds
½ cup extra-virgin olive oil
Freshly ground black pepper,
   to taste
1 endive, separated into leaves
   and rinsed

1. Soak the mushrooms in boiling water to cover for 10 minutes, or until soft. Drain the mushrooms and rinse carefully to remove any residual grit. Squeeze out all excess water and cut into ½-inch pieces.

2. Combine the mushrooms, scallions, and bell pepper in a bowl. In a food processor, combine the mango pickle, brown sugar, and coriander and process until smooth. Gradually add the olive oil in a steady stream until incorporated into the mixture. Remove from the processor and add to the mushroom mixture, blending well. Season with black pepper.

3. Put 1 tablespoon of the shiitake relish in each endive leaf, arrange around a plate, and serve.

Stuffed Mushrooms

with Spinach, Cream, Anchovies, and Nutmeg

*The richness of this appetizer is offset slightly by the tingle of cayenne
pepper in the back of your throat. To make a bigger splash,
you may want to substitute 12 gargantuan portobello mushrooms.*

8–12 SERVINGS

3 pounds fresh spinach, rinsed and stemmed	½ teaspoon ground nutmeg
24 large white mushrooms	½ teaspoon sweet paprika, plus 1 tablespoon for garnish
¼ cup (½ stick) butter	
One 2-ounce can anchovies	¼ teaspoon cayenne pepper
3 garlic cloves, minced	Freshly grated Parmesan cheese, for garnish
1 cup heavy cream	

1. Bring a large pot of water to a boil, add the spinach, and boil for 5 minutes, or until completely wilted. Drain, allow to cool, and squeeze out all of the water. Mince the spinach and set aside.

2. Preheat the oven to 350°F. Remove the mushroom stems, chop them finely, and set aside. Melt the butter over low heat. Place the mushroom caps, round-side up, on a baking sheet, and brush with melted butter. Bake for 10 minutes, or until tops are hot and dry but still firm.

3. Drain the anchovies, pouring the anchovy oil into a medium saucepan. Mince half or all of the anchovies, depending on your love of anchovies. Save the remainder for another use. Heat the anchovy oil over medium heat and add the minced anchovies and garlic. Sauté for 1 minute.

4. Add the spinach to the anchovies and garlic and mix well. Add the cream, nutmeg, paprika, and cayenne pepper and stir to blend. Reduce the heat to low and cook for 5 minutes; do not allow the cream to boil.

5. Stuff each mushroom cap with about 1 tablespoon of the spinach mixture and sprinkle with the paprika and Parmesan. Bake, stuffed-side up, for 10–15 minutes, or until heated through.

Among those foods which are eaten thoughtlessly, I would justly place mushrooms. Although their flavor is excellent, mushrooms have fallen into disgrace by a shocking instance of murder: They were the means by which the Emperor Tiberius Claudius was poisoned by his wife Agrippina; and by doing this she gave to the world and to herself another poison, one worse than all the others: her own son, Nero.

NATURAL HISTORY,
PLINY THE ELDER, 77 A.D.

Marinated Shrimp and Onions

in Rémoulade Sauce

*These shrimp are best if allowed to marinate
in the rémoulade sauce for 2–3 days.*

4–6 SERVINGS

1 cup homemade or
   commercial mayonnaise
¼ cup freshly squeezed lemon
   juice
1 tablespoon prepared
   horseradish
2 tablespoons ketchup
1 garlic clove, crushed
¼ teaspoon hot sauce,
   preferably Melinda's
   or Tabasco (optional)

Salt and freshly cracked black
   pepper, to taste
1 large onion, thinly sliced
¼ cup chopped fresh parsley
1 bay leaf or ½ teaspoon
   ground bay leaf
1 pound large shrimp,
   unpeeled

*Shrimps and prawns are
found in the summer season on
the Southern coasts. They are
similar in form to a lobster, but
very small. They should be
cooked in boiling salted water
from five to eight minutes.
Remove the shells and head; the
part that is eaten resembles in
shape the tail of a lobster. They
are used in fish sauces, and are
very effective as a garnish.*

MRS. LINCOLN'S BOSTON COOK BOOK,
MRS. D. A. LINCOLN, 1884

1. Combine the mayonnaise, lemon juice, horseradish, ketchup,
garlic, and hot sauce in a food processor and blend until well mixed.
Pour into a large glass jar or bowl with a tight-fitting lid. Season with
salt and pepper, add the onion, parsley, and bay leaf, and stir to mix.

2. Bring a large pot of water to a boil, drop in the shrimp, and boil
for 3–4 minutes, or until the shrimp are firm and opaque. Do not
overcook. Remove from heat and drain. Shell and devein the shrimp.
Add the shrimp to the rémoulade sauce and refrigerate for 2–3 days, or
at least overnight, stirring once or twice a day. Serve cold.

VIETNAMESE RICE PAPER

Vietnamese rice paper is one of the world's great secret ingredients. These thin, brittle rice paper crêpes require no cooking, although some recipes call for them to be deep-fried. Just soak for a minute and wrap around shrimp, noodles, vegetables, salads of any kind, and even fruit. Rice paper rounds are available in Asian markets or by mail, and will keep indefinitely without refrigeration. If you absolutely cannot get rice paper rounds, use red leaf lettuce instead.

RICE VINEGAR

Made from fermented rice, Asian rice vinegar is mild in flavor and strength. It is available in most specialty and Asian food stores. Cider or white wine vinegars may be substituted, although both have a slightly more intense flavor.

HERBED SHRIMP ROLLS
WITH MINTED GINGER AND CHILI SAUCE

Beautifully translucent and simple to make, these refreshing rice-wrapped rolls are great for summer picnics or as appetizers in the dead of winter. Any leftover sauce will keep for up to 3 days in the refrigerator; use it as a cocktail sauce with simple boiled shrimp, or as a spicy dressing tossed with your favorite greens.

8 SERVINGS

1 **pound medium shrimp, unpeeled**	2 **ounces rice vermicelli**
1 **small onion, thinly sliced**	1 **cup fresh bean sprouts**
1 **garlic clove, minced**	2 **tablespoons chopped macadamia nuts or peanuts**
1 **tablespoon rice vinegar**	
1 **tablespoon fresh lime juice**	
1 **teaspoon fish sauce (nuoc mam or nam pla) or anchovy paste**	3 **tablespoons chopped fresh mint**
Eight 8-inch round rice paper wrappers	3 **tablespoons chopped fresh coriander**
	Minted Ginger and Chili Sauce (recipe follows)

1. Bring a large pot of water to a boil, drop in the shrimp, and boil for 3–4 minutes, or until the shrimp are firm and opaque. Refresh the shrimp under cold water to stop the cooking, and drain. Shell, devein, and cut in half lengthwise.

2. Combine the shrimp, onion, garlic, vinegar, lime juice, and fish sauce in a medium bowl. Stir to mix well. Marinate in the refrigerator for 1–2 hours.

3. Soak the rice vermicelli in very hot water to cover for 15 minutes and drain well in a colander. They should be soft and pliable. Cut the vermicelli into 4-inch lengths.

4. Immerse one rice paper round in warm water, remove quickly, and set on a plate or paper towel until softened, about 1 minute. Place ⅓ cup of the shrimp mixture (about 8 shrimp halves) about 2 inches from the bottom of a rice paper round. Cover with a shrimp-size bunch of rice vermicelli. Add 1 tablespoon of the bean sprouts and sprinkle with a scant teaspoon of the nuts. Add 1 teaspoon of mint and 1 teaspoon of coriander. Fold the bottom of the rice paper up over the shrimp mixture and fold in both sides. Roll into a compact cylinder. Repeat the process with the remaining shrimp mixture and rice paper wrappers. Pour the Minted Ginger and Chili Sauce into a mustard dispenser and drizzle artfully on a serving platter or 8 small plates. Arrange the shrimp rolls on top and serve, passing the additional sauce.

MINTED GINGER AND CHILI SAUCE

2 CUPS

- 1 cup fresh mint leaves, stemmed
- ⅔ cup sour cream
- 2 tablespoons chopped fresh chives
- 2 tablespoons minced fresh ginger

- 2 tablespoons rice vinegar or white vinegar
- 1 tablespoon honey
- 1 teaspoon fresh lemon juice
- 1 small fresh Thai or jalapeño chili pepper

Blend all ingredients in a food processor until smooth.

FISH SAUCE

Fish sauce is a strongly flavored pungent seasoning sauce used much the same way as soy sauce. Called *nam pla* in Thailand, *nuoc mam* in Vietnam, and *patis* in the Philippines, fish sauces are similar to the ancient Roman anchovy sauce called *laser*. If you'd rather not know the messy details of how fish sauce is made, stop reading now. Okay, you've been warned: Dead fish are allowed to "age" in a barrel for 6 months. Fine fish sauce may be aged for as long as 2 years. The resulting "sauce" at the top of the barrel is refined and bottled. Available in Asian markets and by mail, fish sauce is an absolutely essential ingredient in Southeast Asian cooking.

GARNISH

For a decorative touch, place cookie cutters, carrot rounds, small leaves, or other shaped objects on top of the shrimp and, with a sieve, lightly dust with cinnamon.

The first course comes with a flourish of trumpets, with many bright banners hanging from them; the noise of drums and the fine pipes make wild warbles that delight the eye and cheer the heart. Dainty dishes of exotic foods are served; abundant, fresh, so many and various that it is difficult to find a place before the guests to set the silver platters. Everyone helps himself without stint. Each two guests share twelve dishes between them and good beer and bright wine. There is no lack of anything that could be wished. A new fanfare signals the start of eating.

FABULOUS FEASTS,
MADELEINE PELNER COSMAN, 1976

SHRIMP AND MUSHROOMS
WITH CINNAMON AND SAFFRON IN ALMOND SAUCE

The use of cinnamon in savory dishes is well documented in ancient Roman recipes, and is welcomed in this sublimely sauced dish. Requires overnight marinating.

4 SERVINGS

½ cup dry Spanish sherry
4 slices onion
2 small carrots, sliced
2 garlic cloves, crushed
1 bay leaf
½ teaspoon ground cinnamon
½ teaspoon saffron threads
½ teaspoon dried tarragon
Salt and freshly ground black pepper, to taste

1 pound jumbo shrimp, shelled and deveined
Flour, for dusting
3 tablespoons olive oil
12 cherry tomatoes, halved
1 cup fish broth or clam juice
4 large white mushrooms, quartered
3 tablespoons ground blanched almonds

1. Combine the sherry, onion, carrots, garlic, bay leaf, cinnamon, saffron, tarragon, salt, and pepper in a bowl. Add the shrimp and stir to mix. Cover and refrigerate for 6–8 hours or overnight, stirring occasionally if you're awake.

2. Strain, reserving both the liquid and the contents of the strainer. Discard the bay leaf. Pick out the shrimp, pat dry with paper towels, and dust with the flour.

3. Heat the olive oil in a skillet over medium heat and sauté the shrimp for 1 minute, turning once. Remove to a medium bowl. Add the reserved onion, carrots, and garlic to the skillet and sauté for 2–3 minutes, or until the onion is wilted. Add the tomatoes and cook for 1 minute more, then add the reserved marinade and the fish broth. Simmer, uncovered, for 10 minutes. Strain the sauce and return it to the skillet. Stir in the mushrooms, almonds, and shrimp. Cover and cook for 3 minutes, or until the shrimp are firm and opaque. Serve.

Garlicky Clams in Parsley Sauce

*This Argentinian-inspired dish comes together in a snap and works
equally well with shrimp or scallops. We could eat this and still adhere
to any diet, as long as it included garlic and clams.*

4 SERVINGS

3 tablespoons olive oil
¼ cup finely chopped onion
6 garlic cloves, minced
2 tablespoons all-purpose
   flour
½ cup dry white wine
1 cup fish broth or clam juice

¼ cup milk
¾ cup minced fresh parsley
Salt and freshly ground black
   pepper, to taste
2 dozen Manila or other small
   clams, soaked and
   scrubbed

Heat the oil in a medium saucepan or flameproof casserole over
medium heat. Add the onion and sauté for 2–3 minutes, or until
wilted. Stir in the garlic. Add the flour, stir again, and cook for 1
minute. Gradually add the wine, broth, and milk, then the parsley,
salt, and pepper. Cook, stirring constantly, for about 5 minutes, or
until thickened and smooth. Add the clams, reduce the heat to
medium-low, and cover. Cook for 6–10 minutes. Discard any
unopened clams. Serve.

PARSLEY

Parsley has long been renowned
and beloved throughout the world
for its curative and culinary powers.
If ever there was an herb pageant,
parsley would win the Ms. Congeniality Award, because this univer-
sal herb gets along with everything.
Cooks add small quantities of
chopped parsley to food as instinc-
tively as they add salt and pepper. It
brightens soups, stews, and marinades. It's an enhancement to meat,
fish, vegetables, and stuffings. In
general, all cooking is unthinkable
without parsley.

CHINESE BEAN SAUCE

Strongly flavored and salty, Chinese bean sauce is made from dried soybeans that are salted, dried, or mixed with brine. Essential to Szechuan and Hunan cuisines, bean sauces are derived from some of the world's oldest flavorings.

HOISIN SAUCE

Made from fermented soybean paste, sugar, garlic, Five-Spice Powder, and chili, hoisin sauce is a sweet, thick, reddish brown sauce. Annatto seeds give it its red color. Available in Asian markets and by mail, it can be used to glaze roast pork or poultry.

MIRIN

Mirin is a sweetened golden wine used solely as a cooking ingredient in Asian foods and not as a beverage.

CARDAMOM AND GINGER CHICKEN WINGS

IN SILVER WRAPS

Our passion for wrapped food surfaces again (the first wrap occurs in Herbed Shrimp Rolls, page 70) in these Asian-inspired silver surprises.

12 SERVINGS

24 chicken wings (about 4 pounds)	2 tablespoons sesame oil
½ cup brown sugar	4 teaspoons minced fresh ginger
6 tablespoons dark soy sauce	3 garlic cloves, minced
¼ cup Chinese bean sauce	1 teaspoon ground cardamom
¼ cup hoisin sauce	1 teaspoon salt
4 scallions, thinly sliced	½ teaspoon Five-Spice Powder (page 52)
¼ cup chopped fresh coriander	Twelve 9-inch foil squares
2 tablespoons mirin (Japanese rice wine) or dry sherry	Vegetable oil, for deep-frying

1. Cut each chicken wing into 3 pieces: main bone, second joint, and wing tip. Discard the tips. Set aside.

2. Combine the sugar, soy sauce, bean sauce, hoisin, scallions, coriander, mirin, sesame oil, ginger, garlic, cardamom, salt, and Five-Spice Powder in a large glass bowl. Stir to mix well. Add the chicken and stir until well coated. Cover and refrigerate for 8 hours or overnight, stirring once or twice if you're awake.

3. Place a foil square on a work surface, with one corner pointing at you. Place 4 chicken pieces in the center and drizzle about 1 tablespoon of the marinade on them. Fold the bottom corner up and over the wings. Fold in the sides. Roll up securely. Repeat with the remaining chicken.

4. In a deep-fryer or cast-iron skillet, heat the oil to 350°F. Carefully deep-fry the chicken, 1 or 2 packages at a time (since the oil will bubble furiously), for 6–8 minutes, or until the chicken is cooked through. (Remember, it's better to peek than to serve raw chicken.) Drain the packages on paper towels and serve hot and unopened.

Chicken Liver Bruschetta
WITH PEPPER, SAGE, AND JUNIPER BERRIES

Bruschetta, the garlicky Italian toast,
is a perfect foil for the smooth texture of chicken livers.

6 SERVINGS

BRUSCHETTA
- 1 loaf crusty Italian bread
- 1 garlic clove, halved
- ¼ cup extra-virgin olive oil

CHICKEN LIVERS
- 3 tablespoons extra-virgin olive oil
- 1 medium onion, thinly sliced
- 3 garlic cloves, thinly sliced
- 1 pound chicken livers, washed, trimmed, halved, and dried

- 1 tablespoon balsamic vinegar
- 6 fresh sage leaves, minced, or ¾ teaspoon dried sage, crumbled, plus additional sage leaves for garnish (optional)
- 8 juniper berries, smashed
- ¾ teaspoon freshly ground black pepper
- ½ teaspoon fine sea salt or salt
- ½ teaspoon cinnamon
- Pomegranate seeds, for garnish (optional)

1. To make the bruschetta, cut twelve ¾-inch-thick slices of bread. Reserve the rest for another use. Grill or broil slices for about 1 minute on each side, or until golden brown and crisp on the outside but still soft on the inside. Rub one side of the toasts with garlic, and drizzle olive oil on that same side. Set aside.

2. Heat the olive oil in a large skillet over medium heat until hot but not smoking. Add the onion and sauté, stirring, until golden. With a slotted spoon, remove the onion to a paper towel to drain.

3. Add the garlic to the skillet and cook over medium heat until golden. Add the chicken livers and sauté until browned, about 2 minutes on each side. Stir in the vinegar, sage, juniper berries, pepper, salt, and cinnamon and cook for 1 more minute. Remove the chicken liver mixture to a flat surface and chop coarsely. Mound 2 teaspoons of the mixture on the oiled side of each bruschetta. Garnish with the onion and sage leaves, dot with pomegranate seeds, and serve.

BALSAMIC VINEGAR

Crafted for almost a millennium in north-central Italy, balsamic vinegar is produced from grape juice that is simmered and then slowly fermented for several years. The vinegar then ages for decades or even centuries, transferred to sequentially smaller oak barrels as it condenses and reduces. Very fine balsamic vinegar has been aged a minimum of 12 years.

HISTORICAL RECIPE:
CHICKENS' LIVERS WITH MADEIRA SAUCE

Clean and separate livers, sprinkle with salt and pepper, dredge with flour, and sauté in butter. Brown two tablespoons butter, add two and one-half tablespoons flour, and when well browned add gradually one cup Brown Stock; then add two tablespoons Madeira wine, and reheat livers in sauce.

THE ORIGINAL BOSTON COOKING SCHOOL COOK BOOK,
FANNIE MERRITT FARMER, 1896

I gape open-mouth at the way you compensate for the sharpness of one herb with the sweetness of another. It takes no small skill to match the pungency and the bite of one leaf with the savor, neither pungent nor biting, of a different one until the whole is a mixture so tasty that it would satisfy satiety itself.

PIETRO ARETINO, 1537

SOY SAUCE

First used in China over 3,000 years ago, this salty condiment is made now as it always was, from fermented soybeans mixed with a toasted grain. Yeast is added to begin fermentation. The mixture is left in vats for many months, and then filtered. Dark or thick soy sauces usually contain caramel or molasses. Mushroom soy is made with straw mushrooms. *Tamari,* a Japanese soy sauce, is smoother and has a more refined flavor. All are available in Asian markets and by mail.

Spicy Lamb Saté
WITH ANCHO MACADAMIA SAUCE

Texas meets Thailand in this cross-cultural saté. Interestingly, both places share a passion for fresh coriander. Requires marinating for 2 hours.

4 SERVINGS

1 small onion, minced
2 garlic cloves, minced
2 tablespoons shredded dried coconut, moistened with 1 tablespoon hot water
1 tablespoon dark soy sauce
1 teaspoon dried rosemary
1 teaspoon Sambal Oelek (page 55) or chili sauce
1 teaspoon tamarind concentrate or 1½ teaspoons tamarind pulp

½ teaspoon shrimp or anchovy paste
½ teaspoon salt
1 pound boneless lamb from the leg, cut into 1-inch cubes
12 bamboo skewers, soaked in warm water for 15 minutes
Ancho Macadamia Sauce (recipe follows)

1. Combine the onion, garlic, coconut, soy sauce, rosemary, sambal oelek, tamarind, shrimp paste, and salt in a large glass bowl. Add the lamb and stir to mix well. Cover and let stand at room temperature for 2 hours.

2. Thread the lamb onto bamboo skewers and grill or broil, turning frequently, for 3–5 minutes, until cooked through, taking care that the coconut does not burn. Place 3 skewers on each of 4 plates, drizzle with Ancho Macadamia Sauce, and serve.

ANCHO MACADAMIA SAUCE
ABOUT 1½ CUPS

1 cup unsweetened coconut milk

¾ cup macadamia nuts, finely ground

1 tablespoon dark soy sauce

1 teaspoon fresh lime juice

1 teaspoon palm sugar or brown sugar

1 teaspoon ground ancho chile

1 teaspoon hot red pepper flakes

Minced fresh coriander, for garnish

Combine the coconut milk, nuts, soy sauce, lime juice, palm sugar, ground chile, and red pepper flakes in a small pan over medium heat. Bring to a simmer and cook, stirring occasionally, for about 10 minutes, or until thickened. Transfer to a small bowl and allow to cool. Garnish with the coriander and serve.

SAMBAL OELEK

Indonesian and Malaysian relishlike side dishes are known as *sambals*. Most sambals are hot, with some form of chili as their main ingredient. Sambal oelek is one of the simplest, made from red chilies, salt, and vinegar. Use sambal oelek wherever a hot jolt is desired. Stir it into soups (carefully), use it as a dip, or add it to curries and sauces.

SOUPS

CHILE–BLACK BEAN SOUP
WITH AVOCADO-CORIANDER PESTO

*Please don't be deterred by the required overnight bean soak. We know, we
know, your creative spontaneity might be compromised by the wait. If you
must, compromise the beans instead and use good-quality canned beans.*

4 SERVINGS

3 tablespoons olive oil
1 Spanish onion, finely
   chopped
3 garlic cloves, minced
3 small carrots, sliced
2 celery stalks with leafy tops,
   coarsely chopped
1–2 fresh hot chile peppers
   (jalapeño or serrano),
   seeded and sliced
One 2-inch piece of ginger,
   peeled
2 bay leaves
2 tablespoons fresh coriander,
   chopped
1 teaspoon anise seeds

1½ teaspoons dried crumbled
   oregano, preferably
   Mexican
1 teaspoon ground cumin
6 cups chicken stock
1 pound dried black beans,
   soaked overnight in water
   to cover and drained, or
   one 15-ounce can black
   beans, rinsed and drained
2 chipotle chile peppers
Salt and freshly ground black
   pepper, to taste
½ teaspoon dried epazote
Avocado Coriander Pesto
   (recipe follows)

78

1. Heat the olive oil in a soup pot over medium heat until hot but not smoking. Add the onion and garlic and cook, stirring occasionally, for about 5 minutes, or until the onion is wilted and golden.

2. Add the carrots, celery, fresh chiles, ginger, bay leaves, coriander, anise seeds, oregano, and cumin. Reduce the heat to low and cook, uncovered, for 15 minutes, stirring occasionally.

3. Add the stock, beans, chipotle chiles, salt, and pepper and bring to a boil. Reduce the heat to low and simmer, partly covered, for 1–2 hours, until the beans are tender. (If using canned black beans, simmer for 30 minutes.)

4. Remove from heat and let cool slightly. Remove the bay leaves and chipotle chiles. Transfer the soup to a food processor in 2 or more batches, if necessary, and puree. Return to the saucepan and reheat to the boiling point. Ladle into 6 soup bowls, spoon a dollop of Avocado Coriander Pesto in each, and serve. Pass additional pesto at the table.

AVOCADO CORIANDER PESTO

2 CUPS

¼ cup pine nuts
3 garlic cloves, minced
2 cups fresh coriander, chopped
1 cup fresh Italian parsley, chopped
½ cup avocado, pitted and peeled

½ cup extra-virgin olive oil
¼ cup fresh lemon juice
Salt and freshly ground black pepper, to taste
½ cup freshly grated Parmesan cheese

Combine all the ingredients in a food processor and process until smooth.

EPAZOTE

We cannot pretend we use *epazote* with wild enthusiastic abandon in the kitchen. Epazote is like brussels sprouts: Nobody really likes it. It could use some marketing genius to exclaim its virtues. How about a catchy slogan — the little leaf that tames bellicose bellies.

Epazote, aka goosefoot, Mexican tea, pigweed, and wormseed, could do with a name change. We'll call it Le Paz-oo-tè, and cash in on French chic. Varieties of this pungent herb grow wild all over the United States, Mexico, and Central America. Its piney flavor, like minted hay, and its carminative (gas-reducing) effect are especially welcome in the cooking of the Yucatán peninsula. The Mayans used epazote to flavor their food centuries ago. Use fresh or dried epazote sparingly in black bean soup and in south-of-the-border sauces.

Clove-Scented Onion Soup

WITH MADEIRA AND PAPRIKA

*There's a world of flavor in this soup, reminiscent of Portugal,
the Mediterranean, and the Middle East.*

4 SERVINGS

*If a lump of soot falls into the
soup, and you cannot
conveniently get it out, scum it
well, and it will give the soup a
high French taste . . .*

JONATHAN SWIFT, AROUND 1731

¼ cup unsalted butter
2 tablespoons extra-virgin
   olive oil
3 pounds Spanish onions,
   peeled and thinly sliced
6 cups beef broth
3 tablespoons golden seedless
   raisins

1½ teaspoons sweet paprika
½ teaspoon ground mace
8 whole cloves
Salt and freshly ground black
   pepper, to taste
4 large egg yolks, lightly
   beaten
¼ cup dry Madeira wine

1. Heat the butter and olive oil in a soup pot over medium heat.
Add the onions and cook, stirring occasionally, for about 20 minutes,
or until the onions are wilted and golden. Add the broth, raisins,
paprika, mace, and cloves. Raise the heat to high and bring to a boil.
Lower the heat, partially cover, and simmer for 30 minutes.

2. Season with salt and pepper. Stir ¼ cup of the soup into the egg
yolks. Add the yolk mixture to the pot and cook, stirring, for about
4 minutes, or until slightly thickened. Add the Madeira, stir once
more, and serve.

Peanut and Sweet Potato Soup
with Sweet Potato–Allspice Cream
African, Caribbean, and Mexican influences
all contribute to this spicy curried soup.

6 SERVINGS

1 large sweet potato
2 tablespoons peanut oil
1 onion, diced
3 celery stalks, diced
2 leeks, diced
4 garlic cloves, minced
2 teaspoons curry powder
1 teaspoon ground cumin
1 teaspoon ground coriander
½ teaspoon cayenne pepper
½ teaspoon ground cinnamon
3 tomatoes, seeded and roughly chopped
2 cups salted roasted peanuts, plus 2 tablespoons, chopped, for garnish
4 cups vegetable broth
½ cup chilled heavy cream
¼ teaspoon allspice

Of soup and love, the first is best.

SPANISH PROVERB

1. Wrap the sweet potato in a paper towel and microwave on high for 8 minutes. Allow to cool, still wrapped in the paper towel.

2. Heat the oil in a soup pot over medium heat until hot but not smoking. Add the onion, celery, leeks, and garlic and cook, stirring occasionally, for about 15 minutes, until the vegetables wilt.

3. Add the curry powder, cumin, coriander, cayenne pepper, and cinnamon and cook for 5 minutes more. Stir in the tomatoes and the peanuts and cook for 5 minutes more. Add the broth, bring to a boil, reduce the heat, and simmer, covered, for 20 minutes.

4. Scoop out the sweet potato from its skin and place in a food processor. Process until smooth and creamy. Reserve 2 tablespoons of the sweet potato puree. Add the rest to the soup, stir, and cook for 5 minutes more. Add 1 tablespoon of the heavy cream, bring to just short of boiling, and remove from the heat.

5. In a bowl with an electric mixer, beat the remaining cream until stiff. Fold in the reserved sweet potato puree and allspice. Ladle the soup into 6 soup bowls, spoon a dollop of Sweet Potato–Allspice Cream in each, and sprinkle with the chopped peanuts.

COOK'S NOTES:

ROUX

A passable prepared roux can be found in New Orleans gourmet shops or purchased by mail from Adriana's Caravan.

FILÉ POWDER

Coming from the deep heart of Louisiana bayou country, filé powder is the ground dried leaves of the sassafras tree (listen: the name sounds like drops of fat in a skillet — or the feet of a spunky dancer in the streets of New Orleans: sass-a-frasss). It's both a seasoning and a thickener, with a woodsy flavor that is essential to Creole gumbos. It should be added at the end of cooking, as it becomes stringy if boiled.

Chicken and Sausage Filé Gumbo

There's no American city we love more than New Orleans — the music, the romantic architecture, and the food! And there's nothing that epitomizes New Orleans cooking like gumbo, the thick, spicy Creole stew with hundreds of variations. We like it with andouille sausage, chicken, and ham.

8 SERVINGS

One 3–4 pound chicken, cut into serving pieces
2 tablespoons Cajun Seasoning (page 60)
1½ pounds andouille or other smoked pork sausage, sliced ½ inch thick
⅓ cup vegetable oil
½ cup all-purpose flour
½ pound lean baked ham, cut into ½-inch cubes
2 cups chopped onions
½ cup chopped green bell pepper
½ cup chopped celery
8 scallions (white and 2 inches of green), thinly sliced

2 tablespoons finely minced fresh parsley
3 garlic cloves, finely minced
8 cups chicken stock or water
2 teaspoons salt
1 teaspoon freshly ground black pepper
1 teaspoon dried savory
¼ teaspoon ground cayenne pepper
2 whole bay leaves, crushed, or 1 teaspoon ground bay leaf
2½ tablespoons filé powder
6 cups cooked jasmine or long-grain white rice

1. Preheat the oven to 175°F. Rub the chicken with the Cajun Seasoning and set aside. In a heavy casserole, sauté the sausages for 5–10 minutes, or until they give up some of the fat. Drain on paper towels and set aside. Discard the fat.

2. Add the oil to the casserole and heat over medium heat until hot but not smoking. Carefully add the chicken pieces and cook, turning occasionally, for about 15 minutes, or until browned. Drain on paper towels and put in the oven to keep warm.

3. Make a roux by gradually adding the flour to the oil left in the casserole, stirring constantly. Reduce the heat to low, and cook, always stirring, for about 15 minutes, or until the roux is a medium brown, the color of nutmeg. Add the sausage, ham, onions, bell pepper, celery, scallions, parsley, and garlic. (If there is a delay in adding the ingredients, turn off the heat until you're ready. If you burn the roux, you'll have to start over or go out to dinner.)

4. Continue cooking for 10 minutes, stirring constantly. Add ¼ cup of the stock, the chicken, salt, pepper, savory, cayenne pepper, and bay leaves; stir well to mix. Gradually stir in the rest of the stock. Raise the heat to high and bring the gumbo to a boil. Reduce the heat and simmer, stirring frequently, for 1 hour, or until the chicken pieces are tender. Remove the pot from the heat and let stand for 5 minutes. Add the filé powder and stir. Let stand for an additional 5 minutes and serve with the rice.

HISTORICAL RECIPE:

GOMBO

Cut up and season the chicken, meat or other material to make the soup; fry to a light brown in a pot, and add boiling water in proportion to your meat. Two pounds of meat or chicken, with ½ pound of ham, or less of breakfast bacon, will flavor a gallon of soup, which, when boiled down, will make gombo for 6 people. When the boiling water is added to the meat, let it simmer for at least 2 hours. Take the large bones from the pot, and add okra or a preparation of dried and pounded sassafras leaves called filée. This makes the difference in gombo. For gombo for 6 people use 1 quart sliced okra; if filée be used, put in a coffee-cupful. Either gives the smoothness so desirable in this soup. Oyster, crabs and shrimp may be added when in season, as all improve the gombo. Never strain gombo. Add green corn, tomatoes, etc., if desired. Serve gombo with plain boiled rice.

LA CUISINE CREOLE,
LAFCADIO HEARN, 1885

UNSWEETENED COCONUT MILK

Coconut is the "hard to get, pick, husk, break, and grate" fruit. Use the store-bought variety when your schedule does not leave time for climbing palm trees. Unsweetened coconut milk is available in canned or powdered forms from Asian supermarkets and by mail. Use it in seafood curries, soups, rice, and desserts.

LAVENDER

There is no shortage of odes to lavender. This Mediterranean herb has been praised by every minor poet and his mother. It perfumes and protects every garment in an English chest of drawers. In spite of all that praise, no one ever uses it. It's time to let lavender out of the closet. Dried lavender is an essential ingredient in the Moroccan blend Ras el Hanout, and the French blend Herbes de Provence. The lemon-peppermint flavor enhances marinades for venison and lamb, and lavender honey is a marvel. Use the flowers lavishly as a garnish but add sparingly to foods.

Coconut Milk Chicken Soup
WITH RAINBOW PEPPER AND LAVENDER

Coconut milk adds smoothness, flakes of pepper enliven the flavor, and lavender flowers impart a subtle perfume.

4 SERVINGS

2½ cups unsweetened coconut milk

6 cups chicken broth

One 3-inch piece fresh galangal, peeled and thinly sliced, or 12 dried slices

8 fresh or dried Thai lime leaves or 1 teaspoon grated lime zest

3 fresh lemongrass stalks, cut into 2-inch pieces, or 2 teaspoons chopped dried lemongrass

3 pounds skinless boneless chicken breasts, trimmed and cut into 1-inch cubes

¾ cup fresh lime juice

3 tablespoons Asian fish sauce (nuoc mam or nam pla)

2 small fresh Thai or other hot chili peppers, seeded and thinly sliced

1 teaspoon dried lavender flowers

1 teaspoon Tellicherry peppercorns, cracked

1 teaspoon pink peppercorns, cracked

½ teaspoon green peppercorns, cracked

Mint leaves, for garnish

1. Pour the coconut milk into a food processor and blend until very smooth. Pour into a saucepan and add the broth, galangal, lime leaves, and lemongrass.

2. Simmer, partially covered, for 30 minutes. Stir in the chicken, lime juice, fish sauce, chilies, lavender flowers, and peppercorns and simmer for 5 minutes, or until the chicken is cooked through. Remove the lemongrass. Garnish with the mint leaves and serve.

Thai Shrimp Soup

with Lime Leaves, Galangal, and Mushrooms

This soup is easy to prepare, spicy, and low in fat — like most Thai food.

4 SERVINGS

1 pound medium shrimp, preferably with heads on

2 fresh lemongrass stalks, or 3 tablespoons chopped dried lemongrass

6 cups chicken stock

6 fresh or dried Thai lime leaves,

4 quarter-size pieces fresh or dried galangal

1 garlic clove, minced

3 tablespoons fresh lime juice

1 tablespoon Thai fish sauce (nam pla) or ½ teaspoon anchovy paste in 1 tablespoon water

1 teaspoon roasted or unroasted chili paste

One 15-ounce can straw mushrooms, drained, or 12 medium mushrooms, thinly sliced

1 fresh hot green chili pepper, seeded and julienned

6 thin lime slices and 3 tablespoons coarsely chopped fresh coriander, for garnish

THAI LIME LEAVES

The clear floral aroma of Thai limes wafts from Southeast Asian kitchens on a daily basis. Grown in Florida, and so now readily available, these shiny double leaves can be obtained fresh or dry from Asian markets and by mail. Use them incessantly in any even remotely Asian-inspired dishes, with coconut sauces, and whenever a lime flavor is desired.

1. Peel and devein the shrimp, reserving the heads and shells. Refrigerate the shrimp, covered. If using fresh lemongrass, remove and discard the outer leaves and upper half of the lemongrass stalks. Cut the bottom half into 2-inch lengths, and bruise the pieces by rolling with a rolling pin or bottle.

2. Combine the shrimp heads and shells, the lemongrass, stock, lime leaves, galangal, and garlic in a medium saucepan. Bring to a boil, reduce the heat, and simmer for 15 minutes. Strain, discarding the solids, and add the lime juice, fish sauce, and chili paste and stir.

3. Add the mushrooms and bring just to a boil. For a hotter soup, add the chili pepper now. Add the shrimp and cook for about 2 minutes, or until the shrimp are firm and opaque. Add the chili pepper if you haven't already, garnish with the lime and coriander, and serve.

VANILLA-INFUSED LOBSTER BISQUE
WITH WHITE WINE AND TARRAGON

The most elegant ingredients in the world — lobster, vanilla bean, saffron,
and white wine — are combined in this fabulously rich soup.

6 SERVINGS

1½ gallons water	¼ vanilla bean, sliced in half lengthwise
6 cups fish stock or clam juice	1 teaspoon dried tarragon
4½ cups dry white wine	½ teaspoon saffron threads
2 onions, quartered	½ teaspoon dried thyme
4 celery stalks	¼ teaspoon ground cayenne pepper
4 garlic cloves, 2 whole, 2 minced	3 tablespoons unbleached all-purpose flour
4 bay leaves	2½ cups milk
2 live lobsters (1¼–1½ pounds each)	¾ cup heavy cream
½ cup (1 stick) unsalted butter	Salt and freshly ground black pepper, to taste
½ cup cognac	2 large egg yolks
¾ cup chopped shallots	
3 tablespoons tomato paste	

1. Bring the water, stock, and 2 cups of the wine to a boil in a large stockpot. Add the onions, celery, whole garlic, and 2 of the bay leaves. Carefully place the lobsters into the stockpot and boil, covered, for 15 minutes. Remove the lobsters from the pot and reserve 4 cups of the lobster broth. Allow the lobsters to cool.

2. When the lobsters are cool, crack the shells and remove all of the lobster meat. Reserve the shells. Chop the meat finely and reserve.

3. Melt ¼ cup of the butter in a skillet over medium heat. Add the lobster shells and cognac, reduce the heat to low, and cook just until the cognac is warmed. Carefully light the cognac with a long kitchen match, shaking the pan until the flames subside. Add the minced garlic, 2 remaining bay leaves, shallots, tomato paste, vanilla bean, tarragon, saffron, thyme, cayenne pepper, remaining 2½ cups of wine, and 2½ cups of the reserved broth. Simmer, uncovered, for 30 minutes. Remove from the heat and strain through a fine-mesh strainer.

4. Melt the remaining ¼ cup of butter in a saucepan over medium heat. Gradually add the flour and cook, whisking constantly, for 1 minute. Slowly pour the lobster broth into the pot and whisk until well blended. Add the milk and cream and continue cooking and whisking until hot. Season with salt and pepper.

5. In a small bowl, beat the egg yolks. Whisk in ½ cup of the hot soup, then add the egg mixture to the saucepan and whisk until thoroughly blended. Add the reserved lobster meat, heat thoroughly but do not let simmer, and serve.

Soup does its loyal best, no matter what undignified conditions are imposed upon it. . . . Soup is sensitive. You don't catch steak hanging around when you're poor and sick, do you?

JUDITH MARTIN, AKA MISS MANNERS

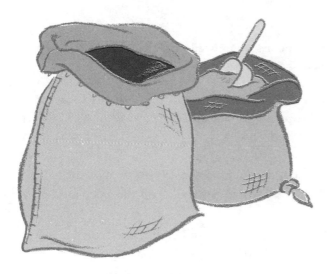

Fish

Want some seafood mama!

FATS WALLER

HISTORICAL RECIPE:
AN EXCELLENT WAY TO DRESS FISH

Dredge the fish well with flour, sprinkle salt and pepper on them, and fry them a nice brown; set them by to get cold; put a quarter of a pound of butter in a frying pan; when it boils, fry tomatoes with the skins taken off, parsley nicely picked, and a very little chopped onion; when done, add as much water as will make a sauce for the fish — season it with pepper, salt, and pounded cloves; add some wine and mushroom catsup, put the fish in, and when thoroughly heated, serve it up.

THE VIRGINIA HOUSEWIFE OR, METHODICAL COOK,
MARY RANDOLPH, 1824

LEMON PEPPER BLUEFISH
WITH CHIPOTLE CHILE CREAM

Going fishing for "blues" with my father is one of my best childhood memories. The intense oily flavor of bluefish stands up beautifully to bold seasoning.

4 SERVINGS

2 tablespoons cumin seeds	1 teaspoon salt
2 tablespoons lemon-pepper blend	Four 8-ounce bluefish fillets, 1 inch thick, skin on
2 tablespoons dried oregano	¼ cup olive oil
2 tablespoons ground annatto or sweet paprika	Chipotle Chile Cream (recipe follows)

1. Combine the cumin seeds, lemon-pepper, oregano, annatto, and salt in a small bowl and mix well. Rub the spice mixture all over the bluefish.

2. Heat the olive oil in a skillet over medium heat until hot but not smoking. Add the fillets, skin-side up, and cook, turning once, for 5–6 minutes, or until completely opaque. Serve with the Chipotle Chile Cream.

CHIPOTLE CHILE CREAM

2 CUPS

1 or 2 canned chipotle chiles
   in adobo sauce, or dried
   chipotles
2 tablespoons olive oil
1 teaspoon coriander seeds
1 teaspoon anise seeds

½ teaspoon ground cinnamon
¼ cup minced onion
2 tablespoons golden raisins,
   chopped
2½ cups heavy cream

1. Drain the chiles, coarsely chop, and set aside. (If using dried chiles, soak in hot water for 30 minutes and coarsely chop.) Heat the oil in a large saucepan over medium heat until hot but not smoking. Add the coriander, anise, and cinnamon and cook, stirring, for 1 minute, or until the anise begin to darken.

2. Add the chiles and the onion and continue to cook and stir for about 10 minutes, or until the onion is wilted. Add the raisins and cook for 1 minute more. Add the cream and bring the mixture to a boil, still stirring. Boil the mixture, stirring occasionally, until it has reduced to about 2 cups.

In Japan, chefs offer the flesh of the puffer fish, or fugu, which is highly poisonous unless prepared with exquisite care. The most distinguished chefs leave just enough of the poison in the flesh to make the diner's lips tingle, so that they know how close they are coming to their mortality. Sometimes, of course, a diner comes too close, and each year a certain number of fugu-lovers die in midmeal.

DIANE ACKERMAN

BANANA LEAVES

Banana leaves are a remarkable culinary contraption. Used either as a garnish or a wrapping, they impart an exotic elegance to dishes. Available in Asian and Latin markets and by mail, they may be kept for months in the freezer.

Curried Mahimahi in Banana Leaves
with Coriander Chutney

Our parcel fetish surfaces again, but for good reason. Moisture is preserved and flavor is enhanced when fish are wrapped up tightly with other ingredients.

4 SERVINGS

1 large lemon, thoroughly peeled, seeded and chopped
4 shallots, chopped
2 garlic cloves, peeled
2 fresh hot green chili peppers, seeded and chopped
½ cup chopped fresh coriander leaves
1 teaspoon finely chopped fresh ginger
1 teaspoon ground cumin
½ teaspoon ground fenugreek

½ cup shredded dried unsweetened coconut
2 tablespoons olive oil
1 onion, finely chopped
1 teaspoon Garam Masala (page 50)
½ teaspoon ground turmeric
½ teaspoon salt
Four 8-ounce mahimahi or kingfish fillets
4 banana leaves or 9-inch foil squares
Coriander Chutney (recipe follows)

1. Combine the lemon, shallots, garlic, chilies, coriander, ginger, cumin, and fenugreek in a food processor. Blend until thoroughly pureed, add the coconut, and blend for 20 seconds more.

2. Heat the olive oil in a large skillet until hot but not smoking. Add the onion and sauté for 4–5 minutes, or until wilted and translucent. Add the blended mixture and cook, stirring, for 5 minutes. Remove from the heat and add the Garam Masala, turmeric, and salt and mix thoroughly.

3. Place a fish fillet on a banana leaf or piece of foil and pour one-fourth of the sauce on top. Turn the fish over once so that it is completely covered in sauce. Fold the bottom of the leaf or foil up over the fish, fold the top down over the fish, and fold in both sides, making

sure the fish is securely wrapped. Repeat with the remaining fish and banana leaves or foil.

4. Place the parcels in a steamer over simmering water and steam for 30 minutes, turning the parcels occasionally. Peek to make sure the fish is completely opaque. Serve in the packets, with Coriander Chutney on the side.

CORIANDER CHUTNEY

ABOUT 1 CUP

1 cup packed fresh coriander
  leaves
¼ cup packed fresh mint leaves
6 scallions, quartered
1 fresh hot green chili pepper,
  halved and seeded
1 garlic clove, halved

½ cup lemon juice
2 tablespoons water
1 teaspoon chopped fresh
  ginger
1 teaspoon sugar
1 teaspoon Garam Masala
  (page 50)
½ teaspoon salt

Put all of the ingredients in a food processor and blend until finely pureed.

A widowed bonito, a really fine beast, I passed through just enough oil and then swaddled it in fig leaves, sprinkled it with oregano and hid it like a firebrand in a heap of hot ashes.

LOCKED-UP WOMEN,
SOTADES, 350 B.C.

Pink Peppercorn Pompano

with Cream in Parchment

*If pompano is unavailable, make this dramatic dish with
red snapper. Although brown paper bags or aluminum foil don't
have the panache of parchment, they will work as well.*

4 SERVINGS

Four 12-inch squares
  parchment or foil, or 4
  medium brown paper bags
10 tablespoons unsalted butter
8 scallions, finely chopped
¼ cup all-purpose flour
1 tablespoon minced fresh
  chervil
½ cup fish stock or clam juice
½ cup dry white wine
¼ cup heavy cream
½ teaspoon lemon juice

1 teaspoon freshly ground
  pink peppercorns
½ teaspoon salt
¼ teaspoon cayenne pepper
1 pound shrimp, peeled,
  deveined, and minced
½ cup lump crabmeat, picked
  over
Four 8-ounce pompano fillets,
  skinned

1. Butter the parchment, foil, or the insides of the paper bags with 4 tablespoons butter. Oil a shallow baking dish. Preheat the oven to 425°F.

2. In a saucepan over low heat, melt the remaining 6 tablespoons of butter and sauté the scallions for about 10 minutes, or until softened. Gradually add the flour and cook, stirring constantly, for 2 minutes. Add the chervil and cook, stirring frequently, for 5 more minutes.

3. Add the fish stock, wine, cream, lemon juice, peppercorns, salt, and cayenne pepper and mix thoroughly. Add the shrimp and crabmeat. Cook, stirring frequently, for 3 minutes. Remove from the heat.

4. Place 1 pompano fillet on each piece of parchment and top with one-fourth of the shrimp-and-crabmeat sauce. Fold the bottom of the parchment up over the fish. Put the sealed packets in the prepared baking dish and bake for 18–20 minutes, or until the parchment begins to brown and the fish is cooked through. Serve.

CHERVIL

This mild-mannered member of the parsley family has a subtle, fresh taste, with a hint of anise. Also called sweet cicely, chervil is one of the *fines herbes,* and is essential to French cooking. Although dried chervil is readily available, it doesn't have the delicate flavor of fresh.

Halibut Puttanesca

*Pungent puttanesca sauce, usually served with pasta,
surrounds halibut with earthy flavors.*

6 SERVINGS

**Six 8-ounce halibut or
swordfish steaks**
**1 teaspoon dried ground
thyme**
¼ cup extra-virgin olive oil
**2 Spanish onions, thinly
sliced**
**One 28-ounce can tomatoes,
drained and coarsely
chopped**
5 garlic cloves, minced
**1 teaspoon freshly cracked
black pepper**

1 teaspoon dried oregano
**1 bay leaf, crushed, or ¾
teaspoon ground bay leaf**
**½ teaspoon hot red pepper
flakes**
**1½ cups niçoise olives, pitted
and coarsely chopped**
3 tablespoons drained capers
**1 tablespoon anchovy fillets,
chopped**
**½ cup chopped fresh Italian
parsley**

1. Preheat the oven to 350°F. Rub the fish lightly with the thyme
and arrange in a single layer in an oiled baking dish. Set aside.

2. Heat the olive oil in a heavy skillet over medium heat until hot
but not smoking. Add the onions and sauté for 4–5 minutes, or until
wilted and translucent. Add the tomatoes, garlic, black pepper,
oregano, bay leaf, and red pepper flakes. Cover and simmer for 10
minutes. Stir in the olives, capers, and anchovies. Pour the sauce over
the fish in the baking dish and bake for 30 minutes, or until the fish is
opaque. Garnish with the parsley and serve.

*Fish, on account of its
abundance, cheapness, and
wholesomeness, is invaluable as
an article of food. It is less
nutritious and less stimulating
than meat, as it contains less
solid matter and more water.
An exaggerated idea of the value
of fish as brain food has
prevailed; the latest authorities,
however, state that there is no
evidence to prove that fish is any
richer than meat in phosphorus.
But as it contains little fat,
the white varieties particularly,
it is easily digested, and as it
has a large proportion of
nitrogenous material, it is
especially adapted to all those
upon whom there are great
demands for nervous energy.*

MRS. LINCOLN'S BOSTON COOK BOOK,
MRS. D. A. LINCOLN, 1884

STEAMED RED SNAPPER
WITH FRESH AND CRYSTALLIZED GINGER SAUCE

This dish is an absolute delight, quick and easy to make, and leftovers can be rolled up in rice paper wrappers for lunch the following day. If you are deterred by the idea of a whole fish with its big, guilt-provoking eyes staring at you, by all means use fish fillets.

4 SERVINGS

2 fresh lemongrass stalks, or 1 tablespoon dried chopped lemongrass, or 1 tablespoon finely grated lemon zest

One 1-inch cube fresh galangal or 6 slices dried

6 fresh or dried Thai lime leaves

One 2-pound whole red snapper, cleaned, or four 8-ounce snapper fillets

One 1-inch piece fresh ginger, julienned

1 fresh hot green chili pepper, seeded and julienned

3 scallions (white and 2 inches of green), thinly sliced

½ cup minced fresh coriander

4 teaspoons fish sauce (nam pla or nuoc mam)

½ cup each finely diced yellow, orange, red, green, and purple bell peppers (optional)

Fresh and Crystallized Ginger Sauce (recipe follows)

1. Remove and discard the outer leaves and upper half of the lemongrass stalks and bruise the bottom half by rolling with a rolling pin or bottle. Coarsely chop. (If using dried lemongrass, soak in ¼ cup of hot water for 30 minutes.) Julienne the fresh galangal. (If using dried galangal, soak in the hot water with the lemongrass.) Julienne the fresh lime leaves. (If using dried lime leaves, soak in the hot water with the lemongrass.)

2. If using a whole fish, cut 4 deep diagonal slits on both sides of the body. If using dried lemongrass, galangal, and/or lime leaves, remove from the water, drain, and finely chop. Reserve the water.

3. On a plate large enough to hold the fish and fit inside a steamer or wok, put half of the lemongrass, galangal, ginger, chili, scallions, and coriander. Place the fish on top of the seasonings and add the rest of the same seasonings. Combine the fish sauce, reserved soaking water or ¼ cup of water, and Thai lime leaves and pour over the fish.

4. Put 1 inch of water in a steamer or wok and heat to boiling. Place the plate with the fish on a rack in the steamer or wok and steam for 5–8 minutes for fish fillets, 10–15 minutes for a whole fish, or until the fish is opaque and flakes with a fork. Garnish with the diced peppers (carefully placed in a geometric design if you have time, or carelessly flung about if you don't) and serve with Fresh and Crystallized Ginger Sauce.

FRESH AND CRYSTALLIZED GINGER SAUCE
ABOUT 1 CUP

8 dried shiitake or Chinese black mushrooms
1 cup hot water
6 tablespoons rice vinegar
2 tablespoons packed brown sugar
2 tablespoons soy sauce
2 tablespoons finely chopped scallions (white and 2 inches of green)

1 tablespoon cornstarch dissolved in 1 tablespoon water
2 tablespoons fresh ginger, peeled and thinly sliced
¼ cup crystallized ginger, diced

1. Soak the mushrooms in the water for 30 minutes. Drain, reserving the liquid. Discard the tough mushroom stalks and slice the caps thinly.

2. Combine the mushroom-soaking liquid, mushrooms, vinegar, sugar, and soy sauce in a saucepan over medium-high heat. Bring to a boil and cook for 5 minutes. Add the scallions and stir to combine. Stir the cornstarch mixture once or twice and stir into the sauce. Cook, stirring, about 5 minutes, or until clear and thickened. Stir in the fresh and crystallized ginger and serve.

Helen — Isabel and Ron were here last night and everything about my dinner went wrong. I had beautiful red snappers and did them in foil with butter, tarragon and onion, and they were just god-awful — part of them cooked to perfection and part horribly. I can't understand it. And my rice got too much herb in it because I was called to the phone . . . but sometimes nothing goes right in the kitchen.

LOVE & KISSES & A HALO OF TRUFFLES: LETTERS TO HELEN EVANS BROWN
JAMES BEARD, 1994

Spice-Rubbed Sea Bass

with Stuffed Dates and Fiery Cucumber Salsa

Throughout North Africa and Southeast Asia, sweet and scorchingly hot flavors are often paired to great effect, as evidenced in this Moroccan- and Thai-inspired wonder. Long-grain jasmine rice adds a seductive perfumed element to this dish. Have a needle and thread handy to sew up the fish.

6 SERVINGS

¼ cup unsweetened coconut milk
¼ cup water
¼ cup jasmine rice
1 tablespoon coriander seeds
1 tablespoon cumin seeds
1 tablespoon sweet paprika
1 tablespoon black peppercorns
1 teaspoon ground cayenne pepper
1 teaspoon whole allspice
6 green cardamom pods
¼ cup macadamia nuts

1 tablespoon packed brown sugar
½ teaspoon ground ginger
¼ teaspoon ground white pepper
6 tablespoons unsalted butter
2 cups pitted dates, preferably Medjool
One 4-pound whole sea bass or shad, cleaned, but not split end to end
½ cup white wine or water
1 teaspoon nutmeg
Fiery Cucumber Salsa (recipe follows)

1. Combine the coconut milk and water in a small saucepan over medium-high heat and bring to a boil. Add the rice and return to a boil. Reduce heat to low, cover, and simmer for 12–15 minutes, or until the liquid is absorbed and the rice is soft. Set aside.

2. Heat the coriander seeds and cumin seeds in a small skillet over medium heat for 1 minute, or until their aroma is quite apparent; do not allow to brown. Combine the coriander seeds, cumin seeds, paprika, black peppercorns, cayenne pepper, allspice, and cardamom pods, in a spice grinder or food processor and blend until well ground. Set aside.

3. Grind the macadamia nuts in a spice grinder or with a mortar and pestle. In a small bowl, combine the rice, nuts, sugar, ginger, white

The fishery is a great nursery for seamen, and brings more ships to Yarmouth than assembled at Troy to fetch back Helen.

MEDIEVAL ENGLISH

pepper, and 1 tablespoon of the butter, mashing the rice grains and blending well. Slit the dates and stuff with the rice mixture.

4. Preheat the oven to 450°F. Oil a large, shallow ovenproof dish. Fill the fish with as many stuffed dates as possible and, with a needle and thread, sew up the cavity. Rub the fish all over with the reserved spice blend and place in the prepared dish. Pour the wine around the fish, place any remaining stuffed fruit in the dish, and dab the fish with the remaining 5 tablespoons of butter. Bake for 45 minutes, basting frequently.

5. Remove the fish from the oven and raise the oven temperature to 500°F. Cut and remove the thread. Remove all the dates from the cavity and place around the fish. Sprinkle the fish and the fruit with the nutmeg, return to the oven, and bake for 15 minutes, or until browned. Serve with Fiery Cucumber Salsa.

FIERY CUCUMBER SALSA
ABOUT 4 CUPS

2 large cucumbers, peeled, seeded, and chopped	3 tablespoons fresh lime juice
16 scallions (white and 2 inches of green), chopped	2 tablespoons packed brown sugar
1 small red bell pepper, chopped	3 garlic cloves, minced
¼ cup chopped fresh mint	1 small fresh hot chili pepper, seeded and minced
3 tablespoons minced fresh ginger	2 teaspoons roasted sesame oil
	½ teaspoon ground cayenne pepper

Combine all the ingredients in a bowl and stir to mix well. Cover and refrigerate for 1 hour. Serve cold or at room temperature.

POACHED SEA BASS

WITH VANILLA AND TEA

Carefully brewed tea complements the sweet flavors of vanilla and tamarind.

4 SERVINGS

2 teaspoons jasmine or other fine black tea leaves

5 cups boiling water

2 small white onions, coarsely chopped

One 3-inch piece fresh ginger, peeled and sliced

¼ cup fresh mint, coarsely chopped

¼ teaspoon ground cayenne pepper (optional)

1 cup white wine

2 tablespoons tamarind pulp or concentrate, or 1 tablespoon lime juice

2 teaspoons dark brown sugar

1 teaspoon salt

Four 8-ounce skinless sea bass fillets

6 Thai lime leaves

½ vanilla bean, split

½ teaspoon saffron threads

1 star anise pod

2 scallions (white and 2 inches of green), thinly sliced

1 starfruit, thinly sliced, for garnish (optional)

1. Steep the tea in the boiling water for 5 minutes. Discard the tea leaves. Combine the onion, ginger, mint, cayenne pepper, and 3 tablespoons of the tea in a food processor and process until pureed.

2. Combine the white wine and remaining tea in a large skillet over medium heat. Add the onion mixture, tamarind pulp, sugar, and salt. Bring to a simmer and simmer for 5 minutes. Cut each sea bass fillet in half lengthwise and carefully place in the poaching liquid. Add the lime leaves, vanilla bean, saffron, and star anise and cook for 1 minute. Turn the fish over and cook, basting frequently, for another 6–8 minutes, or until the fish is thoroughly opaque. Add the scallions and cook for 1 minute more. Divide the fish onto 4 plates, garnish with the starfruit, and serve.

HISTORICAL RECIPE:

SAUCE FOR POACHED FISH

(IUS IN PISCE ELIXO)

[Combine] pepper, lovage, parsley, oregano, dried onion, honey, vinegar, fish stock, wine and a little olive oil. When [the sauce] has been brought to the boil, thicken it with starch and serve [the poached fish] on a platter.

OF CULINARY MATTERS,
MARCUS GARVIUS APICIUS, 14 A.D.

Herb- and Pepper-Encrusted Tuna
with Lemon Thyme Oil

The use of Herbes de Provence softens the bite of the peppers.
Feel free to substitute another firm-fleshed fish.

4 SERVINGS

2 cups all-purpose flour
2 tablespoons Herbes de Provence (page 43)
1 tablespoon freshly ground black pepper
½ teaspoon ground cayenne pepper

Four 8-ounce tuna steaks
1 egg, lightly beaten
3 tablespoons extra-virgin olive oil
3 tablespoons unsalted butter
Lemon Thyme Oil (recipe follows)

Put 1 cup of flour in each of 2 shallow bowls. Add the Herbes de Provence, pepper, and cayenne pepper to 1 of the bowls of flour. Dredge the tuna steaks in the unseasoned flour, then in the egg, then in the seasoned flour. In a large skillet over medium heat, heat the olive oil until hot but not smoking. Add the butter and heat for 1 minute more. Cook the tuna steaks, turning once, for 6–8 minutes, or until opaque and evenly browned. Remove the steaks to 4 plates, drizzle with 1 tablespoon of Lemon Thyme Oil, and serve.

LEMON THYME OIL
1 CUP

1 lemon
4 fresh thyme sprigs

1 cup extra-virgin olive oil

Peel the yellow zest from the lemon, leaving the white pith on the fruit. (Reserve the lemon for another use.) Wash the thyme and bruise by rolling with a rolling pin. In a medium saucepan over low heat, combine the lemon zest, thyme, and olive oil and heat for 5 minutes. Pour into a sterilized, heatproof jar, cool, cover, and let steep in the refrigerator for 1–2 days, if there's time. Drain the oil and discard the solids before using.

They fried the fish with bacon and were astonished; for no fish had ever seemed so delicious before. They did not know that the quicker a freshwater fish is on the fire after he is caught the better he is, and they reflected little upon what a sauce open air sleeping, open air exercise, bathing, and a large ingredient of hunger makes, too.

MARK TWAIN

GARNISH

Play up the pomegranate connection: Garnish with very thinly sliced starfruit or lemon, studded with fresh pomegranate seeds.

One of the most delicate fishes in the world is caught in the Volga, where it abounds. It is called Sterled, and unites the flavour of the sea and fresh water fishes, without, however, resembling any that I have eaten elsewhere. This fish is large, its flesh light and fine; its head pointed and full of cartilages, is considered delicate; the monster is seasoned very skillfully, but without many spices: the sauce that is served with it unites the flavour of wine, strong meat broth, and lemon-juice.

THE EMPIRE OF THE CZAR,
MARQUIS DE CUSTINE, 1843

GRILLED SALMON
GLAZED WITH POMEGRANATE MOLASSES

Old World Mediterranean pomegranates and the hot flavors of the New World are held together by pungent Asian influences.

4 SERVINGS

¼ cup orange juice
¼ cup pomegranate molasses*
1½ teaspoons thinly sliced scallion (mostly white)
1 teaspoon Cajun Seasoning (page 60) or other hot seasoning blend

1 garlic clove, minced
Four 8-ounce salmon fillets
2 tablespoons roasted sesame oil
Salt and cracked black pepper, to taste

1. In a medium saucepan over medium heat, combine the orange juice, pomegranate molasses, scallion, Cajun Seasoning, and garlic and cook for 3 minutes, or until all the ingredients are mixed thoroughly. Set aside.

2. Prepare a medium fire for grilling or preheat the broiler. Rub the salmon lightly with the roasted sesame oil and sprinkle with salt and pepper. Grill or broil the salmon for 6–7 minutes, or until each piece is well seared on one side. Remove from the heat and brush the pomegranate molasses mixture on the seared side. Return to the heat, seared side to the fire, and grill or broil for about 30 seconds, being careful to caramelize but not burn the glaze. Flip the fillets over and grill or broil the uncooked side for 6–7 minutes, or until the salmon is thoroughly opaque. Brush the newly cooked side with the pomegranate molasses mixture and grill or broil, newly cooked side to the heat, for 30 seconds, to caramelize the glaze. Serve.

* If you absolutely can't find pomegranate molasses, substitute 3 tablespoons pomegranate or cranberry juice mixed with 1 tablespoon honey and 1 teaspoon lemon juice.

Shellfish

Jalapeño Clams
IN FRAGRANT BLACK BEAN SAUCE

*This multi-culti, stir-fried clam dish is delicious alone
or ladled over pasta.*

4 SERVINGS

¼ cup roasted sesame oil
4 garlic cloves, minced
One 2-inch piece fresh ginger,
    peeled and sliced
3 scallions, thinly sliced
1 jalapeño chile pepper,
    seeded and minced
2 tablespoons fermented black
    beans, coarsely chopped
3 dozen very small littleneck
    or cherrystone clams,
    soaked and scrubbed

¼ cup dry white wine
2 tablespoons soy sauce
1 teaspoon sugar
1 cup water
1 tablespoon cornstarch
    dissolved in 2 tablespoons
    water and 1 tablespoon
    roasted sesame oil
1 tablespoon chopped chives
¼ cup diced red bell pepper,
    for garnish

1. Heat the roasted sesame oil in a wok or skillet over medium-high
heat until hot but not smoking. Add the garlic, ginger, scallions,
jalapeño, and black beans and stir to mix. Add the clams and stir for 1
minute. Add the wine, soy sauce, and sugar. Stir again to mix and add
the water. Cover and steam for 5 minutes. Discard any unopened clams.

2. Stir the cornstarch mixture once or twice and add to the wok.
Cook, stirring, for 2–3 minutes, or until thick and smooth. Stir in the
chives, garnish with red bell pepper, and serve.

FERMENTED
BLACK BEANS

There is nothing to equal the
almost-garlicky flavor of fermented
black beans, which are soybeans that
have been preserved in salt. They are
especially good with chicken, vegetables, pasta, and seafood. They will
keep almost indefinitely tightly
wrapped or in a jar. Available in
Asian markets and by mail.

A CLAM BAKE
*An impromptu clam bake may be
had at any time at low tide along
the coast where clams are found.
If you wish to have genuine fun,
and to know what an appetite
one can have for the bivalves,
make up a pleasant party and
dig for the clams yourself. A
short thick dress, shade hat,
rubber boots — or, better still, no
boots at all, if you can bring your
mind to the comfort of bare feet,
— a small garden trowel, a fork,
and a basket, and you are ready.*

MRS. LINCOLN'S BOSTON COOK BOOK,
MRS. D. A. LINCOLN, 1884

Scallops, Spinach, and Mushrooms
with Fennel Saffron Cream
4 SERVINGS

*Why sometimes I dream
of the shell-fish of Marseilles,
and wake up crying.*

THE WIND IN THE WILLOWS,
KENNETH GRAHAME, 1908

½ teaspoon saffron threads
¼ cup dry white wine
1 pound spinach leaves, rinsed
  and stemmed
2 tablespoons unsalted butter
½ cup white mushrooms,
  thinly sliced
6 cherry tomatoes, quartered
1 pound sea scallops

1 teaspoon fennel seeds,
  lightly dry-roasted
Salt and freshly ground black
  pepper, to taste
1 tablespoon olive oil
2 large shallots, minced
1 large garlic clove, minced
⅔ cup heavy cream
2 tablespoons fish stock
2 teaspoons fresh lemon juice

*A well made sauce will
make even an elephant or a
grandfather palatable.*

GRIMOD DE LA REYNIÈRE,
19TH CENTURY

1. Bruise the saffron threads and combine with the wine in a small bowl. Set aside. Bring a large pot of water to a boil, add the spinach, and boil for 5 minutes, or until completely wilted. Drain the spinach, chop coarsely, and set aside.

2. Melt the butter in a large skillet over medium heat. Add the mushrooms and tomatoes and sauté for 5 minutes, or until softened. With a slotted spoon, remove the mushrooms and tomatoes and set aside. Add the scallops, fennel seeds, salt, and pepper to the skillet. Cook, stirring, for 3 minutes, or until the scallops are thoroughly opaque. Transfer the scallops and any liquid to a medium bowl and set aside.

3. Heat the olive oil in the skillet until hot but not smoking. Add the shallots and sauté for 5 minutes, or until softened. Add the garlic and cook for 1 minute more. Add the wine and saffron, increase the heat to high, and boil until the wine is reduced by half.

4. Reduce the heat to medium, stir in the cream and fish stock, and bring to a simmer. Add the spinach, mushrooms, and tomatoes and simmer for 1 minute, or until heated through. Add the scallops and their liquid and cook for about 2 minutes more, or until thoroughly hot. Stir in the lemon juice and serve.

JERKED SCALLOPS
WITH ASIAN PEAR AND DATE CHUTNEY

*Spice blends and rubs were designed for those of us who subscribe
to the "Blink School of Cooking." Blink — it's done, and delicious.
Jamaican jerk is the ketchup of Jamaica, flavoring anything
that walks, flies, or swims with a blistering heat.*

4 SERVINGS

2 pounds sea scallops
¼ cup Jamaican Jerk
    Seasoning (page 62)
3 tablespoons unsalted butter

3 tablespoons olive oil
¼ cup dry white wine
Asian Pear and Date Chutney
    (recipe follows)

Rub the scallops all over with the jerk seasoning. Heat the butter
and oil in a large skillet over medium heat until hot but not smoking.
Add the scallops and sauté for 4 minutes, or until opaque. Add the
wine and simmer for about 1 minute, or until thoroughly hot. Serve
plain or over rice, with Asian Pear and Date Chutney on the side.

ASIAN PEAR AND DATE CHUTNEY
ABOUT 4 CUPS

2 Asian pears, or Bosc or
    Bartlett pears, cored and
    diced small
1 cup Medjool dates, pitted
    and coarsely chopped
½ cup rice or white vinegar
½ cup golden raisins
2 tablespoons brown sugar

1 tablespoon minced fresh
    ginger
1 teaspoon nigella seeds
½ teaspoon ground cayenne
    pepper (optional)
Salt and freshly ground black
    pepper, to taste

Combine all of the ingredients in a saucepan over medium heat.
Cook for 10 minutes, stirring frequently, to blend the flavors. Remove
from the heat, cool, and serve.

JERK SEASONING

Any good-quality, high-powered
blend will work with these scallops.
Either make your own or buy one
off the shelf. When buying, make
sure that salt, if mentioned at all, is
low on the list of ingredients.

ASIAN PEARS

Asian pears have the crunchiness
of a good apple and the succulence
of the juiciest pear that's ever
dripped down your chin. Originally
from Asia, they are now grown
domestically. Look for this apple-
shaped fruit with tan skin the next
time you're surrounded by exotic
produce.

Steamed Seafood in Hobo Packs

with Lime Leaves and Tamarind

Sweet, tart, and hot flavors are never more pungent than when packaged in your choice of wraps. Macadamia nuts add crunch to these seafood treasures.

4 SERVINGS

- 8 macadamia nuts
- 1 onion, thinly sliced
- 4 garlic cloves
- ¼ cup water
- 2 teaspoons tamarind pulp or concentrate
- 1 teaspoon brown sugar
- ½ teaspoon ground turmeric
- ½ teaspoon salt
- ½ teaspoon ground cayenne pepper
- 16 small clams, soaked and scrubbed
- 16 mussels (about 1 pound), soaked, scrubbed, and debearded
- 16 medium shrimp (about ½ pound), shelled and deveined
- 16 sea scallops (about ½ pound)
- 8 fresh or dried Thai lime leaves
- Eight 9-inch squares wrapping (banana, Romaine lettuce, cabbage leaves, or foil)

1. In a food processor, combine the nuts, onion, garlic, water, tamarind, brown sugar, turmeric, salt, and cayenne pepper and process until smooth. Set aside.

2. Bring 1 cup of water to a boil in a large pot and add the clams and mussels. Cover and steam for 5 minutes. Discard any clams or mussels that do not open. Remove the clams and mussels from their shells and discard the shells.

3. Preheat the oven to 350°F. Combine the clams, mussels, shrimp, and scallops in a large bowl. Add the nut-onion paste, stir well to mix, and allow to stand for 15 minutes. If using dried lime leaves, soak in warm water to cover for 15 minutes and drain.

4. Divide the seafood mixture among the leaves or foil and add a lime leaf to each. For each packet, fold up the bottom edge, securely fold in the sides, and fold down the top edge. Place the packets on a cookie sheet and bake, turning once, for 15 minutes, or until the seafood is cooked through. (Peek into the packets to make sure.) Serve.

SAUCE FOR LOBSTER AND CRAYFISH

(IUS IN LOCUSTA ET CAMMARI)

Brown chopped pallacanian onions. . . . Add pepper, lovage, caraway, cumin, a date, honey, vinegar, wine, fish stock, oil, and boiled new wine. Add mustard to the sauce while it is still boiling.

OF CULINARY MATTERS,
MARCUS GARVIUS APICIUS, 14 A.D.

ΠEW ORLEAΠS BEER-BRAÍSED SHRÍMP

These glorious messy shrimp taste better if cooked in their shells and eaten with your fingers. Make them only for people who love you; it is probably a wise idea to serve something neater to visiting dignitaries.

4 SERVINGS

2 dozen jumbo shrimp (about 2 pounds), preferably with heads and shells on
1 teaspoon ground cayenne pepper
1 teaspoon freshly ground black pepper
¾ teaspoon dried thyme
½ teaspoon dried basil
½ teaspoon dried marjoram

½ teaspoon dried rosemary, crushed
½ teaspoon dried savory
½ teaspoon salt
10 tablespoons unsalted butter
4 garlic cloves, minced
1 teaspoon oyster sauce
½ cup shrimp stock, fish stock, or clam juice
¼ cup beer at room temperature

OYSTER SAUCE

Living near the Pearl River in Nam Shui, China, Mr. Kum Sheung Lee invented the first oyster sauce in 1888. It revolutionized Chinese cooking. A thick, dark brown seasoning sauce, oyster sauce is flavored with oyster extract. Its smoky, meaty flavor is good for dipping, marinating, and stir-frying, or as a gravy base or table seasoning. Refrigerated, it will keep indefinitely.

1. Rinse the shrimp and drain well. Trim and discard each head from the eyes forward, leaving a point. Set aside.

2. Combine the cayenne pepper, black pepper, thyme, basil, marjoram, rosemary, savory, and salt in a small bowl and mix thoroughly. In a large skillet over high heat, combine the spice-and-herb mix with 6 tablespoons of the butter, the garlic, and the oyster sauce and cook, stirring, for 2 minutes, or until the butter is melted. Add the shrimp and cook, stirring, for 2 minutes more. Add the remaining 4 tablespoons of butter and the stock and cook until the butter is melted. Add the beer and cook until thoroughly heated. Serve with crusty bread.

To lick greasy fingers or to wipe them on your coat is impolite; it is better to use the tablecloth or the serviette.

THE FIFTY COURTESIES
OF THE TABLE, 1480

Fragrant Shrimp

WITH ETHIOPIAN SPICED BUTTER

This is a mild curry, especially if you leave out the chili pepper.
Serve it with rice and a chutney of your choice.

4 SERVINGS

3 cups fish stock, clam juice, or water
2 pounds large shrimp
½ cup Ethiopian Spiced Butter (recipe follows)
3 onions, finely chopped
½ cup plain yogurt
1 fresh hot green chili pepper, seeded and minced (optional)
¼ teaspoon asafetida
¼ cup heavy cream

1. Bring the fish stock to a boil in a large saucepan, add the shrimp, and boil for 4 minutes, or until firm and opaque. Drain, reserving the fish stock. Let the shrimp cool. Shell, devein, and rinse the shrimp and set aside.

2. Heat the Ethiopian Spiced Butter in a large skillet over medium heat until hot. Add the onions and cook, stirring constantly, for 15 minutes, or until golden brown. Add 1½ cups of the reserved fish stock, bring to a boil, and cook for 10 minutes. Add the remaining fish stock and continue to cook, stirring frequently, for 20 minutes, or until the sauce is slightly thickened.

3. Stir in the yogurt, chili, and asafetida, and cook for 2 minutes, stirring. Reduce the heat to low and add the cream and reserved shrimp, cooking just long enough to warm thoroughly. Serve.

Shrimps are found largely in our Southern waters, the largest and best coming from Lake Pontchartrain. They are about two inches long, covered with a thin shell, and are boiled and sent to market with heads removed. Their grayish color is changed to pink by boiling. Shrimps are in season from May first to October first, and are generally used for salads. Canned shrimps are much used and favorably known.

THE ORIGINAL
BOSTON COOKING SCHOOL COOK BOOK,
FANNIE MERRITT FARMER, 1896

ETHIOPIAN SPICED BUTTER

*Normally, butter spoils easily without proper refrigeration.
It also burns quickly when heated. If butter is clarified (the milk solids
removed), it will keep well without refrigeration, and can be heated to a
much higher temperature without burning. Here is an adaptation of
Ethiopian Niter Kebbeh, a highly seasoned clarified butter.*

ABOUT 1 CUP

2 cups (4 sticks) butter
½ onion, chopped
3 garlic cloves, sliced
1 tablespoon dried basil
One 1-inch piece fresh ginger,
    peeled and sliced

1 cinnamon stick
¾ teaspoon ground turmeric
½ teaspoon cardamom seeds
½ teaspoon cloves
½ teaspoon coriander seeds
½ teaspoon ground mace

Place the butter in a small saucepan over low heat and heat until
foamy. Add the onion, garlic, basil, ginger, cinnamon, turmeric, cardamom, cloves, coriander, and mace and cook for 45 minutes, or until
the butter sauce is transparent and the milk solids have drifted to the
bottom. Strain the sauce through several layers of cheesecloth into a
heat-resistant container. Discard the spices and milk solids. Stored in
an airtight container, Ethiopian Spiced Butter will remain fresh for 2
months.

*Never eat more
than you can lift.*

MISS PIGGY

HERBED SHRIMP IN PEPPER SAUCE
WITH AVOCADOS AND MUSHROOMS

Another entry from the Blink School of Cooking (see Jerked Scallops, page 103). Ground aleppo pepper, similar to paprika, adds an earthy, sweet, and hot flavor to this shrimp-and-vegetable mélange. Serve these beauties in shells for friends, shelled for company.

4 SERVINGS

2 avocados (preferably Haas), pitted, peeled, and sliced
2 jumbo portobello mushrooms or 8 large white mushrooms, stemmed and sliced
4 tablespoon fresh lemon juice
2 pounds medium shrimp
2 garlic cloves, quartered
1 tablespoon freshly cracked black pepper

2 teaspoons oyster sauce
1 teaspoon dried basil, crumbled
1 teapoon dried oregano, crumbled
1 teaspoon ground aleppo pepper or sweet paprika
½ teaspoon ground cayenne pepper
½ cup unsalted butter
4 scallions (white and 2 inches of green), thinly sliced

1. Preheat the oven to 450°F. Combine the avocados and mushrooms in a medium bowl. Drizzle with 2 tablespoons of the lemon juice, coating them thoroughly. Set aside. If you're going to shell and devein the shrimp, do it now.

2. In a food processor, combine the remaining 2 tablespoons of lemon juice, the garlic, black pepper, oyster sauce, basil, oregano, aleppo pepper, and cayenne pepper and blend until well mixed. Add the butter and blend thoroughly.

3. Place the mushrooms and avocados in 1 layer in a shallow baking dish. Drop dollops of the butter mixture over them, sprinkle with the scallions, and bake for 5 minutes. Add the shrimp in 1 layer and bake, stirring once or twice, for 5 minutes more, or until the shrimp are firm and opaque. Serve.

LOBSTER FRA DIAVOLO

Wear short sleeves and a big bib.

4 SERVINGS

6 tablespoons olive oil
1 Spanish onion, chopped fine
5 garlic cloves, minced
1 teaspoon dried basil
1 teaspoon dried oregano
1 teaspoon freshly ground black pepper
1 teaspoon crushed red pepper flakes
1 teaspoon dried thyme
One 28-ounce can tomatoes, coarsely chopped, with their juice

1 cup fish stock or clam juice
½ cup dry white wine
3 tablespoons tomato paste
1 bay leaf
2 live lobsters, 1½–1¾ pounds each, killed, cut lengthwise and into serving pieces
1 dozen littleneck clams, soaked and scrubbed
1 pound vermicelli or linguine
¼ cup chopped Italian parsley, for garnish

1. Heat 3 tablespoons of the olive oil in a saucepan over medium heat until hot but not smoking. Add the onion and garlic and sauté 6–8 minutes, or until wilted and just barely browned. Stir in the basil, oregano, black pepper, red pepper flakes, and thyme and mix well. Add the tomatoes and their juice, the stock, wine, tomato paste, and bay leaf. Bring to a simmer and cook, stirring frequently, for 30 minutes.

2. Heat the remaining olive oil in a large skillet over medium heat until hot but not smoking. Add the lobster pieces and sear, turning once or twice, for 5 minutes, or until their shells are bright red.

3. Pour the sauce over the lobster, bring to a simmer, and cook, stirring frequently, for 10 minutes. Add the clams, cover, and cook for 5 minutes more. Discard any unopened clams.

4. In a large pot of salted boiling water, cook the pasta until al dente, 3–4 minutes or according to manufacturer's directions.

5. Put the pasta on a large serving platter, place the lobster pieces and clams around, and pour the Diavolo Sauce over all. Garnish with parsley and serve.

OF LOBSTERS

In winter lobsters seek out sunny coasts, but in summer they withdraw into the shade of the sea. All members of this class are afflicted by winter but become fat in the autumn and spring, and even more so at the full moon since by night the moon makes them mellow by the warmth of its gleams.

NATURAL HISTORY
PLINY, THE ELDER, 77 A.D.

WHERE'S IT FROM?

The controversy surrounding the origins of Lobster Fra Diavolo are heated enough to provoke another spice war. Italian restaurateurs say it's from Italy, but some critics claim its origins are in Westchester. Whether it's from Sicily or Scarsdale has hardly ever mattered to us. This luscious sloppy dish has been our favorite special meal for years.

SEAFOOD CHILI
WITH ANCHO AND PASILLA CREAM

Chipotle chiles in adobo sauce will add body and smoky, potent flavor to the chili sauce. The Ancho and Pasilla Cream, made with crème fraîche, is a respite from the heat.

6 SERVINGS

2 tablespoons extra-virgin olive oil

1 small onion, minced

3 garlic cloves, minced

2 canned chipotle chiles in adobo sauce, coarsely chopped, plus 2 tablespoons of the adobo sauce

1 red bell pepper, cut into medium dice

1 orange or yellow bell pepper, cut into medium dice

One 28-ounce can tomatoes

4 husked fresh tomatillos or 4 canned tomatillos, cut into medium dice

1½ cups dry white wine

2 tablespoons tomato paste

1 tablespoon minced fresh coriander

2 teaspoons chili powder

1 teaspoon dried basil, crumbled

1 teaspoon dried oregano, crumbled

1 teaspoon salt

1 teaspoon freshly ground black pepper

½ dozen oysters, scrubbed

1 dozen small clams, soaked and scrubbed

¾ pound mussels, soaked, scrubbed, and debearded

¾ pound large shrimp, shelled and deveined

¾ pound halibut fillets, cut into 1½-inch cubes

½ pound sea scallops

Ancho and Pasilla Cream (recipe follows)

1. Heat the olive oil in a large skillet over medium heat. Add the onion and garlic and sauté for 2 minutes, or until wilted. Stir in the chipotle chiles, adobo sauce, and red and orange bell peppers and cook, stirring, for 3 minutes.

2. Drain and chop the tomatoes, reserving the juice. Add the tomatoes, tomatillos, wine, tomato paste, coriander, chili powder, basil, oregano, salt, and pepper to the skillet. Simmer for 10 minutes, or until the ingredients are softened and well blended. If the sauce is too thick, add some of the reserved tomato juice.

3. Add the oysters and simmer for 1 minute. Add the clams, cover, and simmer for 1 minute. Add the mussels, cover, and simmer for 1 minute. Add the shrimp, cover, and simmer for 1 minute. Remove any oysters, clams, and mussels that have opened to a plate. Add the halibut and scallops, cover, and simmer for 1 minute. Return the opened oysters, clams, and mussels to the skillet, stir, simmer for 1 more minute, and remove from the heat. Remove and discard any clams and mussels that have not opened. Ladle the chili into soup bowls. Pour the Ancho and Pasilla Cream into a mustard dispenser and use to decorate the chili.

ANCHO AND PASILLA CREAM

ABOUT ½ CUP

1 **ancho chile pepper, stemmed and seeded**	1 **pasilla chile pepper, stemmed and seeded**
	6 **tablespoons crème fraîche**

Pour boiling water over the ancho and pasilla chiles to cover and soak for 10 minutes, or until softened. Drain, coarsely chop, and put into a food processor. Add the crème fraîche and process until smooth.

HISTORICAL RECIPE:
SCALLOPED OYSTERS

oysters
coarse bread or cracker crumbs
butter

Wash them thoroughly clean in their own liquor and put them into your scallop shells; strew over them a few crumbs of bread. Lay a slice of butter on the first you put in, then more oysters and bread and butter successively till the shell is full. Put them into an oven to brown, and serve them up hot in the shells.

THE YOUNG WOMAN'S COMPANION, 1813

When invading in the 8th century, the Moors gave the gift of paella to Spain — and the rest of the world — by introducing rice and saffron. Valencians will argue that the only true paella comes from Valencia, on the coast of Spain. But versions of this famous seafood stew are found in other countries as well, sometimes called by different names, but always enhanced by the culture in which they reside.

Tomatoes and oregano make it Italian. Wine and tarragon make it French. Sour cream makes it Russian. Lemon and cinnamon make it Greek. Soy sauce makes it Chinese. Garlic makes it good.

ALICE MAY BROCK

PAELLA VALENCIA

This is the respected original and deserves the very best ingredients. Use authentic balsamic vinegar and don't skimp on the saffron.

6 SERVINGS

2 garlic cloves, minced, plus 1 unpeeled head garlic
About ¼ cup extra-virgin olive oil
1 tablespoon balsamic vinegar
¾ teaspoon dried marjoram, crumbled
¾ teaspoon dried thyme, crumbled
½ teaspoon freshly ground black pepper
¼ teaspoon salt
1 chicken (about 2½ pounds), cut into serving pieces
1 pound medium shrimp, unpeeled
1 live lobster (about 2 pounds), killed, cut lengthwise and into serving pieces
½ pound sea scallops
2 chorizos or hot Italian sausages

1 onion, diced small
½ cup drained, chopped canned tomatoes
2 tablespoons capers, rinsed
1 teaspoon saffron threads, crumbled
1 teaspoon sweet paprika
3½ cups chicken broth
½ cup dry white wine
2½ cups Spanish paella rice or short-grain Italian rice
Salt and freshly ground black pepper, to taste
1 pound mussels, scrubbed and debearded
1½ dozen small clams, scrubbed
½ cup water
½ cup freshly cooked or frozen peas
One 4-ounce jar pimentos, drained

1. In a small bowl, combine the minced garlic with 1 tablespoon of the olive oil, the vinegar, marjoram, thyme, pepper, and salt. Mix well. Rub the chicken with this mixture and allow to stand for 30 minutes.

2. Heat 1 tablespoon of olive oil in a paella pan or large skillet over medium heat until hot but not smoking. Add the shrimp and sauté for 2 minutes, or until just firm and opaque. Do not overcook. Remove and reserve. Add 1 tablespoon of olive oil, if necessary, and sauté the lobster for 5 minutes, or until opaque. Remove and reserve. Add 1 tablespoon of oil, if necessary, and sauté the scallops for 3 minutes, or until opaque. Remove and reserve. Add the chorizos and sauté for 15 minutes, or until cooked through. Remove from the pan, slice, and reserve. If desired, peel and devein the shrimp.

3. Sauté the chicken pieces in the oil left in the pan, turning frequently, for about 8 minutes, or until browned all over. Add the onion, tomatoes, capers, saffron, and paprika and stir to mix. Stir in the broth, wine, rice, salt, and pepper. Wedge the garlic head in the center of the pan. Bring to a simmer, reduce the heat to low, and simmer, covered, for 15 minutes, or until most of the liquid is absorbed and the rice is tender.

4. Meanwhile, in a medium saucepan, bring the water to a boil and add the mussels and clams. Cover and steam for 5 minutes. Discard any that do not open and reserve the water.

5. When the rice is done, discard the garlic head and raise the heat to medium. Add the shrimp, lobster, scallops, and peas and cook, stirring, for 5 minutes. Add some of the shellfish-steaming water if all of the liquid has been absorbed; the rice should be moist but not sloppy. Stir in the chorizos, mussels, and clams and heat for 1 minute. Garnish artfully with the pimentos and serve.

The husband, who can ask a friend to partake of his dinner in full confidence of finding his wife unruffled by the petty vexations attendant on the neglect of household duties — who can usher his guest into the dining-room assured of seeing that methodical nicety which is the essence of true elegance — will feel pride and exultation in the possession of a companion, who gives to his home charms that gratify every wish of his soul, and render the haunts of dissipation hateful to him.

THE VIRGINIA HOUSEWIFE
OR, METHODICAL COOK,
MARY RANDOLPH, 1824

CURRIED PAELLA

This flavorful dish from the Indian Ocean shares Spain's love of saffron and seafood but adds its own distinctive bite.

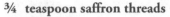

4 SERVINGS

¾ teaspoon saffron threads
¼ cup warm water
3 tablespoons olive oil
1 onion, diced
1½ cups basmati or long-grain rice
2 cups low-sodium chicken broth
1 cup clam juice
1½ cups coarsely chopped fresh or drained canned tomatoes
1 fresh hot red chili pepper, seeded and minced
2 tablespoons curry powder

1 teaspoon nigella seeds
1 cinnamon stick
1 teaspoon preserved lemon or grated lemon zest
½ teaspoon ground cardamom
½ teaspoon ground cloves
¼ teaspoon asafetida or garlic powder
1 dozen small clams, soaked and scrubbed
1 pound mussels, soaked, scrubbed, and debearded
8 jumbo shrimp, shelled and deveined
Fresh coriander, for garnish

1. Combine the saffron and the water in a small bowl and set aside. Heat the oil in a large skillet over medium heat until hot but not smoking. Add the onion and sauté for 5 minutes, or until wilted and translucent. Add the rice and stir to coat well with the oil. Add the stock, clam juice, tomatoes, chili pepper, curry powder, nigella seeds, saffron, and saffron water and cook for 5 minutes, stirring frequently. Add the cinnamon, preserved lemon, cardamom, cloves, and asafetida and stir to mix well. Reduce the heat to low.

2. Add the clams and mussels to the skillet, cover, and cook for 5 minutes. Add the shrimp and cook for 3 minutes more, or until the shrimp are firm and opaque, the rice is tender, and most of the liquid is absorbed. If the seafood is done, but the rice requires a few more minutes, remove the seafood to a plate, finish cooking the rice, and return the seafood to the skillet. Discard any clams or mussels that do not open. Garnish with coriander and serve.

BASMATI RICE

Basmati rice is prized throughout the world for its supreme flavor. This fine, long, perfumed rice grows in India and on the foothills of the Himalayas, with the best grains coming from India.

JAMBALAYA

New Orleans, the City that Care Forgot, tenders its spicy entry.
We find it helpful to pre-assemble all the ingredients in individual
zippered bags so they can be added quickly, on cue.

8 SERVINGS

¾ pound andouille sausage, chorizo, or hot Italian sausage, sliced
2 onions, finely chopped
3 celery stalks, finely chopped
2 red bell peppers, seeded and finely chopped
½ green bell pepper, seeded and finely chopped
4 large garlic cloves, minced
One 28-ounce can tomatoes, chopped
½ pound cooked ham, cut into ¾-inch cubes
½ cup minced fresh parsley
2 bay leaves

1 teaspoon dried thyme, crumbled
1 teaspoon hot sauce, or to taste, plus more for serving
Salt and freshly ground black pepper, to taste
1 cup fish broth or clam juice, plus more if necessary
1 cup water
1 pint shucked oysters, drained, liquor reserved
1½ cups long-grain rice
2½ pounds medium shrimp, shelled and deveined
1 pound sea scallops

1. Sauté the sausage in a paella pan or large skillet over medium heat, stirring occasionally, for 10 minutes. Add the onions and cook for 5 minutes, or until wilted. Add the celery, red and green peppers, and garlic and cook, stirring occasionally, for 2 minutes.

2. Stir in the tomatoes, ham, parsley, bay leaves, thyme, hot sauce, salt, and pepper. Add the broth, water, and oyster liquor. Cook, stirring frequently, for 10 minutes.

3. Add the rice and stir to mix. Reduce the heat to low, cover, and cook for 15 minutes, or until the rice is tender and has absorbed all the liquid. Stir once or twice to prevent the rice from sticking. Add more broth if necessary. When the rice is done, add the oysters, shrimp, and scallops, and cook for 2 minutes more, or until the seafood is firm and opaque. Serve with a bottle of hot sauce on the side.

HISTORICAL RECIPE:

JIMBALAYA

Cut up and stew a fowl (with an onion and 1–2 stalks celery in 1–1½ quarts water); when half done, add 1 cup of raw rice, 1 slice of ham minced, and pepper and salt; let all cook together (covered) until the rice swells and absorbs all the gravy of the stewed chicken, but it must not be allowed to get hard or dry. (Now add the powdered sassafras or filée powder.) Serve in a deep dish. Southern children are very fond of this; it is said to be an Indian dish, and very wholesome as well as palatable; it can be made of many things.

LA CUISINE CREOLE,
LAFCADIO HEARN, 1885

BLACK RICE

WITH MANILA CLAMS, SHRIMP, AND SCALLOPS

I've saved the best for last. Romy Dorotan,
chef of Cendrillon in Manhattan, offers this Philippine version of paella.

6 SERVINGS

PANDAN LEAVES

This aromatic screw pine is used for both color and fragrance in many Southeast Asian cuisines. Sold frozen, dried, or as an intensely strong extract, in Asian markets and by mail, pandan leaves have no acceptable substitutes. If you cannot find them, just omit them from recipes.

2 cups black rice
6 tablespoons extra-virgin olive oil
1 small yellow onion, diced
1 carrot, diced
4 cups water
2 pandan leaves (optional)
Salt, to taste
¾ cup Thai Green Curry Paste (recipe follows) or prepared Thai green curry paste
2 leeks, sliced and washed well
½ pound fresh shiitake mushrooms or other wild mushrooms, stemmed and sliced

2 plum tomatoes, diced
1 pound large shrimp with heads, unpeeled
3 blue crabs, cleaned and cut in half
1½ dozen Manila clams or small clams, soaked and scrubbed
2 pounds sea scallops
1 cup unsweetened coconut milk
2 tablespoons Thai fish sauce (nam pla), preferably Tiparos
1 tablespoon fresh lemon juice

1. Rinse the black rice in cold water. Heat 3 tablespoons of the olive oil in a small skillet over medium heat until hot but not smoking. Add the onion and carrot and sauté for 8 minutes, or until the onion is slightly brown. Add the rice and sauté, stirring frequently, for 3 minutes. Add the water and bring to a boil. Add the pandan leaves and salt, reduce the heat to low, and cover. Simmer for about 20 minutes, or until the water has been absorbed and the rice is almost cooked. Transfer the rice to a deep, flameproof casserole and keep warm.

2. Heat the remaining 3 tablespoons of olive oil in a wok over medium heat until hot but not smoking. Add the Green Curry Paste

and cook, stirring, for 2 minutes. Add the leeks, mushrooms, and tomatoes and cook, stirring frequently, for 2 minutes.

3. Add the shrimp, crabs, clams, scallops, and coconut milk and stir well to mix. Add the fish sauce and lemon juice and stir again.

4. Add the seafood to the rice in the casserole and place over medium heat. Bring to a simmer and cook for 3 minutes. Remove the shrimp with a slotted spoon and keep warm. Cook the remaining seafood for 2 minutes more. Remove the scallops and any opened clams. Cook for 2–5 minutes more, until the rice is tender. Return the seafood to the casserole, discard any unopened clams, and serve.

BLACK RICE

Grown in the Philippines and Indonesia, these long black grains of rice resemble wild rice. Black rice can be used interchangeably with white rice, but the cooking time is slightly longer.

GREEN CURRY PASTE

ABOUT ¾ CUP

1 lemongrass stalk
One 1-inch cube fresh ginger, peeled
3 garlic cloves
3 shallots

1 bunch fresh coriander, stemmed
2 small fresh green Thai chili peppers or other hot chili peppers

Remove and discard the outer leaves and upper half of the lemongrass stalks and cut the bottom half into 1-inch pieces. Combine all the ingredients in a food processor and blend until smooth.

POULTRY

Chicken with 99 Spices

*Well now, there are not really 99 spices in this dish, but Jeff Loshinsky,
chef extraordinaire, has managed to create 99 levels of flavor.*

4 SERVINGS

2 large skinless bone-in chicken breasts with wings attached, preferably Bell and Evans, split
2 tablespoons 99 Spice Blend (recipe follows)

1 tablespoon olive oil
Juice of 2 lemons
½ cup minced fresh parsley
Flour, for dredging
Peanut oil, for frying
Lemon wedges, for garnish

*Woe to the cook whose
sauce has no sting.*

GEOFFREY CHAUCER

1. Cut off the first joint of the chicken wings and discard. Combine the 99 Spice Blend with the olive oil and half of the lemon juice to make a paste. Rub the paste all over the chicken and place in a glass roasting pan. Drizzle with the remaining lemon juice and sprinkle with the parsley. Cover and refrigerate for 6–8 hours or overnight, turning once or twice if you're awake.

2. Bring chicken to room temperature. Dredge each piece liberally in flour, shaking off excess. Heat ½ inch of peanut oil in a heavy skillet over medium heat to 350°F, or until a pinch of flour sizzles when dropped in the oil. Place the chicken breasts in the oil, being careful

not to crowd them. (Fry in 2 batches if necessary.) Fry the chicken, turning once, for 8–10 minutes, until the juices run clear when the thickest part of the chicken is pierced with a sharp knife. Transfer the chicken to brown paper and drain. Garnish with lemon and serve.

99 SPICE BLEND
ABOUT 1 CUP

6 large bay leaves
3 tablespoons Spanish paprika
3 tablespoons light brown sugar
2 ancho chile peppers, stemmed, seeded, and broken into pieces
2 tablespoons black mustard seeds
2 tablespoons sea salt
1 tablespoon allspice berries

1 tablespoon cumin seeds
1 tablespoon dried lemon peel
1 tablespoon mace blades or ground mace
1 tablespoon black peppercorns
1 tablespoon dried rosemary leaves
1 tablespoon dried thyme leaves

Recipe for Boiled Owl. Take feathers off. Clean owl and place in cooking pot with lots of water. Add salt to taste.

THE ESKIMO COOKBOOK, 1952

Combine all ingredients in a bowl and blend well. Transfer to a spice grinder or food processor and process until finely ground.

TO BOILE A CAPON WITH ORENGES AND LEMONS

Take Orenges or Lemmons pilled, and cutte them into your best broth of Mutton or Capon with prunes or currants and three or fowre date, and when these have been well sodden put whole pepper, great mace, a good piece of sugar, some rose water, and either white or claret Wine, and let all these seeth together a while, and so serve it upon coppers with your capon.

THE GOOD HUSWIFE'S JEWELL,
THOMAS DAWSON, 1587

CHICKEN AND SWEET POTATO STEW
WITH AROMATIC SPICES AND FRUIT

*Every cuisine in the world has a chicken stew of some sort.
This dish is inspired by North Africa and the Mediterranean. It conjures
up romantic images of deserts and heat, and a palm tree oasis.*

6 SERVINGS

1 cup blanched almonds
3 medium sweet potatoes
1 onion, finely chopped
2 teaspoons vegetable oil
1 teaspoon ground cinnamon
½ teaspoon freshly grated nutmeg
½ teaspoon anise seeds
1 chicken (about 3 pounds), cut into serving pieces
2 tablespoons unsalted butter
¼ cup dried apricots, chopped
¼ cup dried dates, pitted and chopped
¼ cup dried figs, chopped
¼ cup chicken broth
1 tablespoon pomegranate molasses
½ teaspoon freshly ground black pepper
½ teaspoon saffron threads, crumbled
½ teaspoon orange flower water (optional)

1. Dry-roast the almonds in a small skillet over medium heat, turning frequently, for 3 minutes, or until lightly browned. Remove from the heat, chop coarsely, and set aside. In a large pot of boiling water, cook the sweet potatoes for 10 minutes. Drain and allow to cool. Peel, slice, and set aside.

2. Combine the onion, vegetable oil, cinnamon, nutmeg, and anise seeds in a small bowl and stir to mix well. Add the chicken pieces and stir to coat thoroughly. Let stand for 15 minutes.

3. Melt the butter in a large skillet over medium heat. Add the chicken and the marinade and sauté, turning frequently, for 10 minutes, or until the chicken is evenly browned.

4. Stir in the sweet potatoes, almonds, apricots, dates, figs, broth, pomegranate molasses, pepper, saffron, and orange flower water. Bring to a boil, reduce the heat to low, and simmer, partially covered, for 1 hour, or until the chicken is tender and the sauce is thickened.

HOT, HOTTER, HOTTEST JERK CHICKEN

*Dig a hole 4 feet deep in your back yard — only kidding,
this version of this devilishly hot dish can be put together in the kitchen.
Use a milder chile pepper, like jalapeño, if you can't take the heat, or serve
with grilled bananas and a sweet chutney to counteract it.*

4 SERVINGS

6 garlic cloves, minced
1 tablespoon ground allspice
1 tablespoon dried thyme, crumbled
1 tablespoon brown sugar
2 teaspoons freshly ground black pepper
1½ teaspoons ground sage
1 teaspoon dried rosemary leaves, crushed
1 teaspoon ground cayenne pepper
1 teaspoon ground cinnamon
1 teaspoon grated nutmeg
1 teaspoon salt

¾ cup white vinegar
½ cup fresh lemon juice
¼ cup olive oil
¼ cup soy sauce
3 tablespoons fresh lime juice
1 fresh Scotch bonnet chile pepper, or other fresh hot red chile pepper, seeded and finely chopped
2 onions, chopped
4 scallions (white and 2 inches of green), finely chopped
2 bone-in chicken breasts (about ¾ pound each), split

1. Combine the garlic, allspice, thyme, sugar, black pepper, sage, rosemary, cayenne pepper, cinnamon, nutmeg, and salt in a medium bowl and mix well. Gradually add the vinegar, lemon juice, olive oil, soy sauce, and lime juice and stir until thoroughly mixed. Add the chile pepper, onions, and scallions and mix well. Add the chicken and stir to coat. Cover, refrigerate, and let marinate for 1–2 hours.

2. Prepare a medium fire for grilling or preheat the broiler. Remove the chicken breasts from the marinade and grill or broil, turning once, for 12–15 minutes, or until cooked through. Baste the chicken with some of the marinade until 4 minutes before the end of grilling. Heat the remaining marinade in a small saucepan until just simmering. Serve the chicken, passing the remaining marinade at the table.

Cooking ought not to take too much of one's time. One hour and a half to two hours for lunch, and two and a half for dinner is sufficient, providing that the servant knows how to make up the fire in order to get the stove ready for use.

A HANDBOOK
OF COOKERY FOR A SMALL HOUSE,
JESSIE CONRAD, 1923

Wipe your spoon before dipping it into a fresh dish, for there are people so fastidiously constituted that they object to eating what you have disarranged with a spoon which you have just taken out of your mouth.

ANTOINE DE COURTIN

GARNISH

Instead of sprinkling cinnamon and sugar willy-nilly over the tops of the pies, place a cookie cutter or a shaped object on the top of the pie and sprinkle on the sugar and cinnamon through a sieve.

PHYLLO

The thin pastry called phyllo is wonderful for wrapping both sweet and savory fillings. It is available in most supermarkets in the freezer section. A 1-pound package contains about 24 sheets of pastry. Defrost the unopened package at room temperature. Phyllo dries out quickly, so keep unused sheets of phyllo between 2 sheets of waxed paper covered by a damp kitchen towel. Well wrapped in plastic wrap, it will keep in the freezer for 6 months, or for about a week in the refrigerator.

Moroccan Chicken and Almond Pies

When I owned the gourmet food and spice shop Adriana's Bazaar, the most intriguing and popular item I sold was the Moroccan bisteeya — *a chicken pie made with phyllo dough. Weeks after you serve these mysterious layered pies your guests will daydream about their haunting flavor.* — R.Z.

6 SERVINGS

¼ cup (½ stick) unsalted butter, plus ¾ cup (1½ sticks) butter, melted, for phyllo dough
1 cup blanched whole almonds
¼ cup confectioners' sugar, plus ¼ cup for garnish
1½ teaspoons ground cinnamon, plus 2 tablespoons for garnish
1 medium onion, finely chopped
3 garlic cloves, minced
½ cup finely chopped fresh parsley
½ cup finely chopped fresh coriander

2 teaspoons Ras el Hanout (page 57)
½ teaspoon coarse sea salt
½ teaspoon freshly ground black pepper
½ teaspoon saffron threads, crumbled
3 pounds chicken breasts and thighs
3 cups chicken broth
3 cinnamon sticks, preferably Ceylon cinnamon
¼ cup fresh lemon juice
5 large eggs, well beaten
1 pound phyllo dough (about 24 sheets), thawed according to package directions

1. Melt 2 tablespoons of the butter in a small skillet over medium heat. Add the almonds and sauté for 5 minutes, or until lightly browned. Remove the almonds, drain on paper towels, and chop coarsely. In a small bowl, combine the almonds with the sugar and ground cinnamon. Set aside.

2. Melt 2 tablespoons of the butter in a skillet over medium heat. Add the onion and garlic and sauté for 5 minutes, or until wilted and translucent. Remove to a medium bowl and stir in the parsley,

coriander, Ras el Hanout, salt, pepper, and saffron. Add the chicken and mix well to coat thoroughly. Cover and refrigerate for 30 minutes.

3. In a large saucepan over medium-high heat, combine the chicken mixture, broth, and cinnamon sticks. Bring to a boil, reduce the heat to low, and simmer for 1 hour. Remove the chicken pieces from the broth and shred, discarding the skin and bones. Set the chicken aside. Simmer the broth over medium heat for 10 minutes, or until reduced to 2 cups. Remove and discard the cinnamon sticks. Add the lemon juice to the broth and simmer gently for 10 minutes more.

4. Increase the heat to moderate, and slowly add the beaten eggs to the broth, stirring constantly. Cook, stirring, for 8 minutes, or until the eggs are set but not dry, and most of the liquid is absorbed. Pour the egg mixture into a coarse sieve set over a bowl and allow it to drain for 10 minutes. Discard the drained liquid.

5. Preheat the oven to 400°F. Cut enough phyllo sheets to make sixty 6-inch squares. Carefully wrap and seal the remaining dough. Sandwich the squares between 2 pieces of waxed paper, and cover with a damp kitchen towel. Place 1 square on a work surface and brush with melted butter. Brush 4 more squares with melted butter, placing each one on top of the first square. Sprinkle with 1 tablespoon of the almond mixture, leaving a 1-inch border all around the edges. Top with ¼ cup of the egg mixture. Cover with 2 squares of phyllo, brushing each with melted butter. Add ⅓ cup of the chicken, again leaving a 1-inch border all around. Sprinkle with 1 tablespoon of the almond mixture. Fold the edges up and over to partially cover the top. Place 3 squares of phyllo on the top, brushing each with butter. Fold the top 3 squares down and under to keep the filling from spilling out. Repeat to make 5 more parcels. Place all 6 parcels in a shallow baking pan and bake for 15 minutes, or until golden brown. Sprinkle with confectioners' sugar and cinnamon and serve.

FOUR AND TWENTY BLACKBIRDS . . .

During the Middle Ages, any dish of meat, fowl, or fish with a top crust was called a pie. On special occasions, a nonedible "pie surprise" was sometimes carried to the banquet table. Though this custom is long since forgotten, a reminder persists in the nursery rhyme "Sing a Song of Sixpence," with its 24 blackbirds. Another popular pie of the period had a dwarf springing up out of the piecrust and diving headlong into a bowl of custard. Robert May, a 17th-century cookbook author, concocted a recipe for a pie that concealed live frogs. May wrote that when the pie was opened, the frogs would leap up "and cause the ladies to squeak and hop about."

In restaurants — whether we're talking about an upscale establishment with a pretense of culinary sophistication or a fast-food urban lean-to take-out — bistro-style herb-infused roast chicken is the most popular item served. Here are some spice-laden cross-cultural versions of Henny Penny.

COOK'S NOTES:
TO ROAST THE PERFECT CHICKEN

A. Use a roasting chicken, not a broiler/fryer. Roasting chickens weigh more and are meatier and more succulent.

B. Buy a really good chicken. The best brands are Bell and Evans and Empire Kosher.

C. For the crispiest skin, allow the chicken to dry out by storing it uncovered in the refrigerator overnight.

D. To infuse the most flavor into the chicken, tuck the seasonings under the chicken's skin.

E. For even crispier skin, roast initially at a high temperature (about 450°F), and then lower to a moderate temperature (350°F).

ROAST CHICKEN
WITH LEMONGRASS
Our friend Irene Khin Wong owned the renowned restaurant
Road to Mandalay, located in New York.
This is her spicy Vietnamese rendition of the ubiquitous roast bird.

4 SERVINGS

1 **roasting chicken (4–5 pounds)**	3 **tablespoons vegetable oil**
3 **fresh lemongrass stalks, outer leaves and top half discarded, bottom half chopped**	1 **tablespoon soy sauce**
	1 **tablespoon granulated sugar**
	1 **tablespoon brown sugar**
5 **garlic cloves, minced**	2 **teaspoons freshly ground black pepper**
One **1-inch piece fresh ginger, peeled and thinly sliced**	1 **teaspoon cayenne pepper**
3 **tablespoons Vietnamese fish sauce (nuoc nam)**	**Lemongrass-Mushroom Stuffing, optional (recipe follows)**
	2 **tablespoons honey**

1. Rinse and dry the chicken, and allow to stand uncovered in the refrigerator overnight.

2. In a food processor, combine the lemongrass, garlic, ginger, fish sauce, oil, and soy sauce. Process until pureed. Add the granulated sugar, brown sugar, black pepper, and cayenne pepper and process until well mixed.

3. Preheat the oven to 450°F. Carefully loosen the skin and rub half of the lemongrass paste between the skin and the chicken. Rub the

remaining paste all over the skin and inside the cavity. Fill the cavity lightly with the stuffing, if desired, and skewer and lace the bird closed.

4. Place the chicken on a rack in a roasting pan. Roast for 15 minutes at 450°F. Reduce the oven to 350°F and continue roasting, basting frequently with the pan juices and the honey, for about 1 hour and 20 minutes, or until a leg moves freely in its socket and juices run clear when a thigh is pricked with a fork. (An unstuffed chicken will require about 20 minutes less roasting time.) Allow the chicken to stand for 15 minutes before serving.

LEMONGRASS-MUSHROOM STUFFING
ABOUT 3 CUPS

½ cup dry red wine
2 lemongrass stalks, outer leaves and top half discarded, bottom half chopped
2 large shallots, coarsely chopped
1 garlic clove, quartered
½ cup (1 stick) unsalted butter
¾ pound white mushrooms, thinly sliced

1 chicken liver, coarsely chopped
½ cup plain dried white bread crumbs
¼ cup chopped celery
2 tablespoons chopped fresh parsley
½ teaspoon dried lemon thyme, crumbled
Salt and freshly ground black pepper, to taste

1. Combine ¼ cup of the wine, the lemongrass, shallots, and garlic in a food processor and process until pureed. Set aside.

2. Melt ¼ cup of the butter in a large skillet over medium heat. Add the mushrooms and sauté for 10 minutes, or until softened. Remove to a bowl. Add the remaining ¼ cup of butter to the skillet, heat until hot but not smoking, and add the chicken liver. Sauté for 2 minutes, or until cooked through. Add the lemongrass mixture and cook for 2 minutes more, stirring frequently. Remove to the mushrooms bowl.

continued on next page

FARCED [STUFFED] CHICKENS, COLORED OR GLAZED

They first be blown up and all the flesh within taken out, then filled up with other meat, then coloured or glazed; but there is too much to do, it is not a work for a citizen's cook, nor even for a simple knight's; and therefore I leave it.

THE GOODMAN OF PARIS, 1392

SESAME OIL

Used extensively in China, Japan, and Korea, this amber-colored aromatic oil is made from crushed white sesame seeds. Because of its intense flavor and low burning point, it should be combined with another vegetable oil for deep frying. An even stronger variety is Chinese black sesame oil. Cold-pressed sesame oil sold in health food stores is not a substitute.

3. Pour the remaining ¼ cup of wine into the skillet and cook, stirring to loosen any bits that are stuck to the bottom of the skillet, until the wine is reduced to 1 tablespoon. Remove to the bowl with the chicken liver and mushroom sauce. Add the bread crumbs, celery, parsley, thyme, salt, and pepper and mix well. Allow to cool before stuffing.

CHINESE ROAST CHICKEN
WITH BLACK MUSHROOM AND PORK STUFFING
Oriental flavors will waft through the house, luring your family to the table.

4 SERVINGS

1 roasting chicken (4–5 pounds)	3 tablespoons cracked Szechuan pepper
¼ cup minced fresh ginger	1 tablespoon Five-Spice Powder (page 52)
4 scallions (white and 2 inches of green), minced	1 teaspoon red pepper flakes
2 garlic cloves, minced	½ teaspoon salt
3 tablespoons roasted sesame oil	Black Mushroom and Pork Stuffing, optional (recipe follows)
2 tablespoons soy sauce	

1. Rinse and dry the chicken, and allow it to stand uncovered in the refrigerator overnight.

2. Preheat the oven to 450°F. Combine the ginger, scallions, garlic, roasted sesame oil, and soy sauce in a small bowl and mix well. Carefully loosen the skin and rub the spice paste between the skin and the chicken.

3. In a small bowl, combine the Szechuan pepper, Five-Spice Powder, pepper flakes, and salt, and rub onto the skin of the chicken. Fill the cavity lightly with the stuffing, if desired, and skewer and lace the bird closed.

4. Place the chicken on a rack in a roasting pan. Roast for 15 minutes at 450°F. Reduce the oven to 350°F and continue roasting, basting frequently with the pan juices, for about 1 hour and 20 minutes, or until a leg moves freely in its socket and juices run clear when a thigh is pricked with a fork. (An unstuffed chicken will require about 20 minutes less roasting time.) Allow the chicken to stand for 15 minutes before serving.

BLACK MUSHROOM AND PORK STUFFING

ABOUT 1 CUP

6 dried Chinese black or shiitake mushrooms	2 tablespoons safflower oil
½ cup hot water	2 scallions (white and 2 inches of green), minced
3 tablespoons rice wine or sake	4 garlic cloves, minced
2 tablespoons soy sauce	One 1-inch piece fresh ginger, peeled and minced
1 teaspoon brown sugar	½ cup canned water chestnuts, drained and julienned
½ teaspoon roasted sesame oil	
⅓ pound pork loin, trimmed and cut into medium dice	

1. Soak the mushrooms in the water for 15 minutes. Drain, cut off and discard the tough stems, and cut the caps into julienne. Set aside. Combine 2 tablespoons rice wine, 1 tablespoon soy sauce, and the sugar in a small bowl. Stir until the sugar is dissolved and set aside.

2. Combine the remaining 1 tablespoon rice wine, the remaining 1 tablespoon soy sauce, and the roasted sesame oil in a medium bowl. Add the pork and stir to mix well. In a wok or skillet over medium heat, heat 1 tablespoon of the safflower oil until hot but not smoking. Add the pork mixture and stir-fry for 4–5 minutes, or until the pork is no longer pink. With a slotted spoon, remove the pork and set aside.

3. In the wok, heat the remaining 1 tablespoon of safflower oil until hot but not smoking. Add the mushrooms, scallions, garlic, and ginger. Stir-fry for 30 seconds. Add the water chestnuts and the rice wine mixture and stir-fry for 30 seconds. Add the pork, stir, and remove from heat. Allow to cool before stuffing.

HISTORICAL RECIPE:

ROAST GOOSE

Roast it before a brisk fire but at considerable distance at first. It will require basting, for which purpose a little butter should be used at first, but its own fat will soon begin to drip. Dredge with flour and salt, and see that it is nicely browned all over. A green goose, one that has not attained its full growth, will take from 50 minutes to 1½ hours; a full-grown goose will require nearly or quite 2 hours.

THE HOUSEKEEPER'S GUIDE,
ESTHER COPLEY, 1838

PERUVIAN ROAST CHICKEN

WITH RICE STUFFING WITH SAUSAGE, RAISINS, AND OLIVES

Garlic and paprika contribute to the incredibly bold flavor of this bird.
Serve with a salad and a lusty red wine or microbrewed beer.

4 SERVINGS

1 roasting chicken (4–5 pounds)	1 tablespoon freshly ground black pepper
6 garlic cloves, minced	½ teaspoon ground cayenne pepper
¼ cup red wine vinegar	½ teaspoon ground cinnamon
3 tablespoons red wine	½ teaspoon salt
3 tablespoons olive oil	Rice Stuffing with Sausage, Raisins, and Olives (recipe follows)
3 tablespoons sweet paprika	
1 tablespoon ground cumin	

1. Rinse and dry the chicken, and allow it to stand uncovered in the refrigerator overnight.

2. Combine the garlic, vinegar, wine, oil, paprika, cumin, black pepper, cayenne pepper, cinnamon, and salt in a small bowl. Mix well.

3. Preheat the oven to 450°F. Carefully loosen the skin and rub half of the spice paste between the skin and the chicken. Rub the remaining paste all over the skin and inside the cavity. Fill the cavity lightly with the stuffing, if desired, and skewer and lace the bird closed.

4. Place the chicken on a rack in a roasting pan. Roast for 15 minutes at 450°F. Reduce the oven to 350°F and continue roasting, basting frequently with the pan juices, for about 1 hour and 20 minutes, or until a leg moves freely in its socket and juices run clear when a thigh is pricked with a fork. (An unstuffed chicken will require about 20 minutes less roasting time.) Allow the chicken to stand for 15 minutes before serving.

VARIATIONS

A good-quality annatto paste, homemade or mail-ordered, can be substituted for the rub. Add 1 or 2 tablespoons of fresh orange juice if it needs thinning.

RICE STUFFING WITH SAUSAGE, RAISINS, AND OLIVES

ABOUT 5 CUPS

4 cups chicken stock	1 cup pine nuts, dry-roasted
1 tablespoon unsalted butter	1 cup mixed firm olives, pitted and chopped
2 cups short-grain white rice	½ red bell pepper, diced small
¾ cup golden or dark raisins	Salt and freshly ground black pepper, to taste
1 cup boiling water	1 tablespoon olive oil
3 sweet or hot Italian sausages (about 1 pound)	

1. Bring the chicken stock to a boil in a medium saucepan. Add the butter, stir in the rice, and cover. Reduce the heat and simmer for 12–15 minutes, or until the rice is soft and all the broth is absorbed. Set aside.

2. In a small bowl, soak the raisins in the water for 15 minutes. Drain and set aside. Cook the sausages in a large skillet over medium heat, turning frequently, for 15 minutes, or until lightly browned. Remove from the heat, allow to cool, and slice into 1-inch rounds. Combine the sausage and raisins in a large bowl. Stir in the rice, pine nuts, olives, bell pepper, salt, and black pepper. Add the olive oil and stir to mix well.

HISTORICAL RECIPE:

POACHED FOWL AND BACON WITH "PUDDING"

First stuff your capons with saveray, / With parsley, a little, hissop I say; / Then take the neck, remove the bone; / And make a pudding thereof at once / With an egg and minced bread also / With hacked liver and heart thereto . . . / Then boil the capon, as I they say, / With parsley, sage, hissop, saveray . . . / With slices of bacon embrawded here / And colour your broth with saffron dear . . .

MRS. GROUNDES-PEACE'S OLD COOKERY NOTEBOOK, COMPILED BY ZARA GROUNDES-PEARE, 1971

DUCK, AMERICAN STYLE

Roast rare 2 or more mallard ducks; carve the legs in two, and the fillets in 3 or more slices, keep warm in a covered plate; crack the carcasses, put them in a saucepan with ½ pint of broth, 2 shallots, a bay leaf, a sprig of thyme, 2 cloves and 2 ladlefuls of thick brown gravy; boil ½ hour, strain through a colander, add 2 glasses of port wine and some melted currant jelly; reduce to the desired consistency, skim and press through a napkin, dish up the ducks in a pyramid form, pour the sauce over, and serve with quartered lemon on a plate.

THE FRANCO-AMERICAN COOKERY BOOK,
FELIX J. DÉLIÉE, 1884

You first parents of the human race . . . who ruined yourself for an apple, what might you not have done for a truffled turkey.

*THE PHYSIOLOGY OF TASTE: OR MEDITA-
TIONS ON TRANSCENDNTAL GASTRONOMY,*
JEAN-ANTHELME BRILLAT-SAVARIN, 1825

GARLIC ROAST DUCK
WITH BLACKBERRY SAUCE

Many people shy away from serving or eating duck because they think it's difficult to make, or too fatty. We say nay to all of that: Much of the fat can be removed, and the resulting bird is worth the extra few minutes of preparation. And think of the entertainment value of telling your guests you used a hair dryer to crisp the duck! The overnight seasoning really helps the flavors permeate the duck.

4 SERVINGS

2 ducks (4–5 pounds each), fresh or thoroughly defrosted in the refrigerator or microwave oven
30 garlic cloves
12 juniper berries
6 whole cloves, or ½ teaspoon ground cloves
2 tablespoons freshly ground black pepper
2 teaspoons dried thyme, crumbled
1 bay leaf, crumbled, or 1 teaspoon ground bay leaf
Salt, to taste
Blackberry Sauce (recipe follows)

1. Remove the giblets from the duck body cavities and reserve for another use. Rinse the ducks and pat dry with paper towels. Remove any excess fat from around the neck and cavity. Mince 6 garlic cloves and put in a small bowl. Combine the juniper, cloves, black pepper, thyme, bay leaf, and salt and grind in a spice grinder or with a mortar and pestle until fine. Add to the garlic and mix well. Rub the mixture under the skin, on the skin, and in the cavity of each duck. Put 6 garlic cloves in each duck cavity. Cover and refrigerate the ducks for 12–24 hours, basting occasionally if you're awake. Remove from the refrigerator 1–2 hours before final preparation so they reach room temperature.

2. Preheat the oven to 450°F. With a hair dryer on medium or high, dry the ducks inside and out for 10 minutes. Gently prick the skin all over with a fork, trying not to pierce the flesh.

3. Place each duck, breast-side up, on a V-shaped rack in a roasting

pan and roast at 450°F for 15 minutes. Reduce the heat to 350°F, add 6 garlic cloves to each roasting pan, and roast for 20 minutes more. Baste the ducks and remove accumulated fat drippings while roasting. Turn the ducks over and roast for another 15 minutes. Turn the ducks again and roast, breast-side up, for 10 minutes more, or until the duck is crispy, the meat is slightly pink and still juicy, and a leg is easily moved in its socket. Let rest for 15 minutes before serving. Serve with Blackberry Sauce.

BLACKBERRY SAUCE
ABOUT 1 CUP

½ pint fresh blackberries
¼ cup cranberry juice
1 tablespoon crème de cassis
  or pomegranate molasses
  (optional)

2 teaspoons fresh lemon juice
¼ teaspoon hot Hungarian
  paprika
2 tablespoons finely chopped
  fresh watercress

Push the blackberries through a sieve with a wooden spoon, discarding the seeds. In a small saucepan over low heat, combine the blackberries, cranberry juice, crème de cassis, lemon juice, and paprika and simmer for 15 minutes. Add the watercress, stir to mix, and simmer 1 minute more. Remove from the heat, let cool, and serve.

It is to be regretted that domestication has seriously deteriorated the moral character of the duck. In a wild state, he is a faithful husband . . . but no sooner is he domesticated than he becomes polygamous, and makes nothing of owning ten or a dozen wives at a time.

THE BOOK OF HOUSEHOLD MANAGEMENT,
MRS. ISABELLA BEETON, 1861

SAGE

For centuries, this old gray man of the North Mediterranean coasts was considered one of the most important culinary and medicinal herbs. The bitter, minty, musty flavor of sage can be extremely powerful. Use it judiciously, as the camphorlike overtones can dominate a dish. It goes well with fatty meats and poultry, and is often found in stuffings and sausages.

Italy has a great love for the herb, as it is often added to risotto and Tuscan bread salad. This symbol of wisdom is not limited to meats: Sage jam and blueberry sage tea are quite delicious. Turn on an Italian opera, tuck a sprig of sage into your hair, and show people how smart you can be using sage.

CRISPY DUCK BREASTS
WITH WILD MUSHROOM AND GREEN PEPPERCORN SAUCE

Wild mushrooms and a peppercorn sauce add elegance and sophistication, but this duck dish is still fast food.

4 SERVINGS

4 boneless duck breasts with skin (about 6 ounces each)
Salt and freshly ground black pepper, to taste
1 tablespoon extra-virgin olive oil
¼ cup unsalted butter
2 large shallots, finely chopped
1 pound assorted fresh wild mushrooms (portobello, porcini, chanterelle, oyster, or shiitake), thinly sliced

One 1-inch piece fresh ginger, peeled and minced
½ cup chicken broth
2 tablespoons green peppercorns in brine, drained and crushed
½ teaspoon dried sage, crumbled
½ teaspoon cornstarch dissolved in 1 tablespoon warm water
3 tablespoons chopped fresh chives

1. Trim excess fat from the duck breasts. Season the breasts with salt and pepper. Heat the olive oil in a heavy skillet over high heat until very hot but not smoking. Add the duck breasts, skin-side down. Reduce the heat to medium and cook for 15 minutes, or until the skin is crisp and brown. Remove extra fat from the skillet as it accumulates. Turn the breasts over and cook for 3 minutes, or until pink (medium rare) or done to taste. Transfer the breasts to a serving platter and tent with foil to keep warm.

2. Meanwhile, melt the butter in a large skillet over medium heat. Sauté the shallots for 5 minutes, or until softened. Add the mushrooms and ginger and sauté for 5 minutes, or until the mushrooms are softened. Add the broth, peppercorns, and sage. Stir the cornstarch mixture once or twice and stir into the sauce. Simmer for 5 minutes, or until the liquid is reduced and thickened. Remove from the heat, pour the sauce over the duck, sprinkle with the chives, and serve.

LACQUERED DUCK
WITH SZECHUAN FENNEL-SPICED WINE

This highly glazed bird is similar to Peking Duck, but more aromatic and easier to prepare. The wine needs to steep 2 or 3 days in advance, if possible, and the ducks should marinate overnight.

4 SERVINGS

- **2 ducks (4–5 pounds each), fresh or fully defrosted**
- **8 garlic cloves, minced**
- **½ cup soy sauce**
- **2 tablespoons Szechuan Fennel-Spiced Wine (recipe follows), plus more for serving**
- **2 tablespoons sesame oil**
- **1 teaspoon Five-Spice Powder (page 52)**
- **1 teaspoon freshly ground black pepper**
- **½ teaspoon salt**

1. Remove the giblets from the duck body cavities and reserve for another use. Rinse the ducks and pat dry with paper towels. Remove excess fat from around the neck and cavity. Combine the garlic, soy sauce, wine, sesame oil, Five-Spice Powder, pepper, and salt in a small bowl. Pour the marinade into the cavity of each duck and on the skin, and rub some between skin and flesh. Cover and refrigerate for 12–24 hours, basting occasionally if you're awake. Remove from the refrigerator 1–2 hours before final preparation so they reach room temperature.

2. Preheat the oven to 450°F. With a hair dryer on medium or high, dry the ducks inside and out for 10 minutes. Gently prick the skin all over with a fork, trying not to pierce the flesh.

3. Place each duck, breast-side up, on a V-shaped rack in a roasting pan and roast at 450°F for 15 minutes. Reduce the heat to 350°F and roast for 20 minutes more. Baste the ducks and remove the fat drippings while roasting. Turn the ducks over and roast for another 15 minutes. Turn the ducks again and roast, breast-side up, for 10 minutes more, or until the duck is crispy, the meat is slightly pink and still juicy, and a leg is easily moved in its socket. Let rest for 15 minutes. Drizzle with some of Szechuan Fennel-Spiced Wine and serve.

HISTORICAL RECIPE:
CRANE OR DUCK
(GRUEM VEL ANATEM)

Wash and dress the bird, and put it in a pot. Add water, salt, and anise seed. When the bird is half cooked and the flesh firm, take it out and put it into another saucepan with olive oil and stock and a bouquet of oregano and coriander. When nearly cooked, add a little boiled wine for coloring. Blend pepper, lovage, cumin, coriander, laser root, rue, boiled wine, and honey. Add gravy and vinegar. Stir. Pour the sauce into a saucepan, heat, and thicken with starch. Put onto a platter and pour the sauce on top.

OF CULINARY MATTERS,
MARCUS GARVIUS APICIUS, 14 A.D.

SZECHUAN FENNEL-SPICED WINE

ABOUT 3 CUPS

½ cup Szechuan peppercorns
½ cup fennel seeds
2 cinnamon sticks, preferably
    Ceylon cinnamon
2 teaspoons whole cloves

4 star anise pods
3 cups dry white wine
One 1-inch piece fresh ginger,
    peeled

Dry-roast the Szechuan peppercorns, fennel seeds, cinnamon sticks, cloves, and star anise in a skillet over medium heat for 2 minutes, or until the spices are evenly roasted and fragrant. Let cool and place in a large glass bowl or jar. Add the white wine and ginger and stir to mix. Cover and let stand at room temperature for 2–3 days. Strain. Refrigerated, this wine will keep for about 3 months.

VARIATION

If you're feeling really ambitious, stuff 4 roasted and peeled poblano chiles with the picadillo, instead of using tortillas. Omit the marinara sauce and the cheese. Cover with foil and bake for 15 minutes, or until thoroughly hot. Top with Ancho and Pasilla Cream, page 111.

DUCK PICADILLO ENCHILADAS

Here's a great way to reinvigorate leftover chicken or duck. Combine yesterday's bird with Mexico's authentic — as well as some of my favorite — flavors. Picadillo, a Mexican stuffing whose root means "minced," makes a delicious filling for tacos, chiles (see sidebar), and even Vietnamese rice paper rolls.

4 SERVINGS

¼ cup chicken broth
2 ancho chile peppers
1½ tablespoons duck fat or
    olive oil
½ onion, diced small
2 ripe plum tomatoes, seeded
    and diced small
1 small Granny Smith apple,
    peeled, cored, and diced
    small

¼ cup golden raisins or
    currants
2 tablespoons coarsely
    chopped almonds
1 tablespoon capers, drained
1 teaspoon chili powder
½ teaspoon ground cinnamon
½ teaspoon ground cloves
¼ teaspoon cayenne pepper
    (optional)

1½ cups shredded cooked duck
   or chicken
Salt and freshly ground black
   pepper, to taste

3 cups homemade or
   commercial marinara sauce
   or other prepared tomato
   sauce
8 large flour tortillas
¾ cup grated Monterey Jack
   cheese

1. Heat the chicken broth in a small saucepan over medium heat and pour into a small bowl. Add the chiles and soak for 15–20 minutes, or until softened. Chop the chiles coarsely and return them to the broth.

2. Heat the duck fat in a large skillet over medium heat until hot but not smoking. Add the onion and sauté for 5 minutes, or until softened and translucent. Add the chiles with the broth, the tomatoes, apple, raisins, almonds, capers, chili powder, cinnamon, cloves, and cayenne pepper. Stir to mix well and cook for 3 minutes, or until thoroughly blended. Remove from the heat, stir in the duck or chicken, and season with salt and black pepper.

3. Preheat the oven to 350°F. Pour 1 cup of the marinara sauce into a shallow baking pan, completely covering the bottom. Spoon ¼ cup of the picadillo onto the center of a tortilla. Spread to cover, leaving a 1-inch border all around. Roll up the tortilla and place seam-side down in the marinara sauce. Repeat with the remaining tortillas and picadillo. Pour the remaining 2 cups of marinara sauce over the enchiladas. Sprinkle the cheese on top. Bake for 20 minutes, or until the top is slightly browned and the cheese is melted. Serve.

"What's inside it?" asked the Mole, wriggling with curiosity. "There's cold chicken inside it," replied the Rat briefly; "coldtonguecoldhamcoldbeefpickledgherkinssaladfrenchrollscresssandwidgespottedmeatgingerbeerlemonadesodawater —" "O stop, stop," cried the Mole in ecstasies; "This is too much!" "Do you really think so?" inquired the Rat seriously. "It's only what I always take on these little excursions; and the other animals are always telling me that I'm a mean beast and cut it very fine!"

THE WIND IN THE WILLOWS,
KENNETH GRAHAME, 1908

MEAT

GARLIC FENNEL PRIME RIB

WITH GINGER PORT SAUCE

*This meat is seasoned twice, and so has two separate layers of flavor.
It's well worth the overnight seasoning time.*

6–8 SERVINGS

One 3-bone standing rib roast (about 8 pounds), ribs cracked
¼ cup freshly ground black pepper
8 garlic cloves, minced
2 tablespoons fine sea salt or salt
2 Spanish onions, thinly sliced
2 tablespoons fennel seeds

2 tablespoons ground white pepper
1 tablespoon ground Szechuan pepper
1 tablespoon dried thyme, crumbled
2 teaspoons dry mustard
¾ teaspoon ground cayenne pepper
2 tablespoons olive oil
Ginger Port Sauce (recipe follows)

Roast Beef, Medium, is not only a food. It is a philosophy. Seated at Life's Dining Table, with the menu of Morals before you, your eye wanders a bit over the entrées, *the* hors d'oeuvres, *and the things* à la, *though you know the Roast Beef, Medium, is safe and sane, and sure.*

EDNA FERBER

1. Cut the fat cap off the top of the roast and reserve. Stand the roast on the bones in a large roasting pan. Score the skin lightly all over. Combine the black pepper, garlic, and salt and press evenly all over the top of the meat. Arrange the sliced onions on top of the spice layer. Carefully cover with the reserved fat cap. Refrigerate for 24 hours if you have the time, 8 hours if you don't.

2. Preheat the oven to 500°F. Roast the meat for 30 minutes, or until the fat is dark and crispy on the top. Remove from the oven and let cool. Refrigerate for 2 hours, or until well chilled.

3. Remove and discard the fat cap. Peel off the onions, scrape off the spice layer, and discard. Trim off ¼ inch of the browned meat on both ends of the roast. Stand the roast on one end and slice into 6 or 8 slices with a carving knife.

4. Combine the fennel seeds, white pepper, Szechuan pepper, thyme, mustard, and cayenne pepper in a small bowl and mix well. If you are grilling, rub the olive oil all over the steaks. If you are pan-broiling, save the oil for later.

5. Rub the spice mixture all over the steaks, pressing it into the meat. Let the steaks stand for 30 minutes. Prepare a medium fire for grilling or heat the oil in a large skillet until hot but not smoking. Grill or pan-broil the steaks, turning, 10–12 minutes for rare. Add more oil to the skillet, if necessary. Drizzle each steak with Ginger Port Sauce and serve.

Noncooks think it's silly to invest two hours' work in two minutes' enjoyment; but if cooking is evanescent, well, so is the ballet.

JULIA CHILD

GINGER PORT SAUCE
ABOUT ¾ CUP

1	tablespoon olive oil	1	cup ruby port
2	large shallots, minced		Salt and freshly ground black
1	garlic clove, minced		pepper, to taste
1½	tablespoons fincly chopped fresh ginger	1½	tablespoons unsalted butter, cut into pieces

Heat the olive oil in a small skillet over medium heat until hot but not smoking. Add the shallots and garlic and sauté for 4–5 minutes, or until softened and translucent. Add the ginger and sauté for 1 minute. Add the port and bring to a boil. Boil, stirring frequently, for 5 minutes, or until the liquid is reduced to a thin syrup. Remove from the heat, strain, and discard the solids. Return the syrup to the skillet and continue cooking over medium heat until the syrup reaches the boiling point. Boil for 2 minutes, or until the syrup is thickened. Remove from heat and swirl in the butter.

STWED BEEFF.

Take faire Ribbes of ffresh beef, And (if thou wilt) roste hit til hit be nygh ynowe; then put hit in a faire possenet; caste ther-to parcely and oynons mynced, reysons of corauns, powder peper, canel, clowes, saundres, safferon, and salt; then caste there-to wyn and a litull vynegre; sette a lyd on the potte, and let hit boile sokingly on a fair charcole til hit be ynogh; then lay the fflesh, in disshes, and the strippe there-upon, And serve it forth.

TWO FIFTEENTH CENTURY COOK BOOKS,
THOMAS AUSTIN, ED.

HEARTY LEMON–SCENTED BEEF STEW
WITH ASIAN AIOLI

Flavors from Thailand and China combine beautifully with those from Europe. Think of this as a Southeast Asian answer to Boeuf Bourguignon.

6 SERVINGS

2 fresh lemongrass stalks, outer leaves and top half discarded
¼ cup roasted sesame oil
3 tablespoons vegetable oil
2 small Spanish onions, finely chopped
10 small white onions, peeled
5 garlic cloves, minced
3 tablespoons all-purpose flour
3 pounds boneless chuck eye roast or other stewing beef, cut into 1½-inch cubes
2 cups beef broth

1 cup red wine
⅓ cup yellow bean sauce
½ teaspoon ground cayenne pepper
½ teaspoon asafetida
4 star anise pods
One 3-inch cinnamon stick, preferably Ceylon cinnamon
1 teaspoon whole black peppercorns, preferably Tellicherry
2 tablespoons palm sugar or brown sugar
Asian Aioli (recipe follows)

1. Cut the lemongrass into 2-inch sections, crush, and set aside. Combine the roasted sesame oil and the vegetable oil in a small bowl and stir to mix.

2. Heat 3 tablespoons of the oil mixture in a small skillet over medium heat until hot but not smoking. Add the Spanish onions, small white onions, and garlic and sauté for 3 minutes. Add the lemongrass and sauté, stirring frequently, for 5 minutes more, or until the white onions are slightly browned. Stir in the flour and cook, stirring, until the flour is lightly colored. Remove from the heat. Transfer the small white onions to a bowl and set aside.

3. Heat the remaining oil mixture in a large heavy casserole over high heat until hot but not smoking. Add as many beef cubes as can be placed in 1 layer in the casserole and cook, turning frequently, for

3–5 minutes, or until browned all over. With a slotted spoon, transfer the beef to a bowl. Brown the remaining beef in the same way.

4. Return all of the beef cubes to the casserole. Reduce the heat to medium and add the lemongrass mixture, beef broth, and wine. Mash the yellow bean sauce in a small bowl and combine with the cayenne pepper, asafetida, star anise, cinnamon, black peppercorns, and palm sugar. Stir to mix well and add to the beef stew. Bring the stew to a boil, stirring frequently. Cover, reduce the heat to low, and simmer for 1½ hours. Add the white onions, stir once, and simmer for 15 minutes more. Raise the heat to medium and cook, uncovered, for 30 minutes, or until the sauce has thickened and the meat is tender. Skim off the fat, ladle into soup bowls, and serve with dollops of Asian Aioli.

Talk of joy: There may be things better than beef stew and baked potatoes and home-made bread — there may be.

DAVID GRAYSON

ASIAN AIOLI
ABOUT 2 CUPS

1 **lemongrass stalk, outer leaves and top half discarded, bottom half coarsely chopped**	1 **teaspoon soy sauce**
5 **garlic cloves, smashed**	2 **large egg yolks**
	2 **cups extra-virgin olive oil**
	2 **tablespoons fresh lemon juice**

In a food processor, combine the lemongrass, garlic, and soy sauce and process until pureed. Add the egg yolks and process to blend. With the motor running, gradually drizzle in the olive oil; the emulsion will become very thick. Gradually add the lemon juice and pulse to blend.

Drunken Chipotle Pepper Chili
with Cheddar Cream

This is one of those dishes where tasting is a hazard, not an advantage; if you taste this chili too often, you may be asleep by dinnertime. Our guests' first clue that something's out of whack is the loud singing that emanates from the kitchen.

6 SERVINGS

3 ancho chile peppers, stemmed and seeded
2 tablespoons olive oil
1 Spanish onion, diced small
4 garlic cloves, minced
1 pound chuck, cut into ¾-inch cubes
1 pound boneless pork shoulder, cut into ¾-inch cubes
1 cup beef broth
1 cup water
¾ cup good beer, preferably microbrewed
1 tablespoon tarragon vinegar
1 small hot red or green chili pepper, seeded and minced

2 tablespoons chopped canned chipotle chiles in adobo sauce
1 tablespoon chili powder
1 teaspoon ground cumin
¾ teaspoon dried Mexican oregano, crumbled
Salt and freshly ground pepper, to taste
1 cup canned tomatoes, chopped, with their juice
2 red onions, chopped
1 cup finely chopped fresh coriander
1 cup sour cream
Cheddar Cream (recipe follows)

1. Heat a skillet over medium heat. Press the ancho chiles into the hot skillet with a metal spatula. Dry-roast them for a few seconds until they crackle and change color. Flip them over and dry-roast the other sides. Remove from the heat and set aside.

2. Bring 1 quart of water to a boil in a medium saucepan over medium heat. Add the ancho chiles, remove from the heat, and weigh the chiles down with a plate so they stay submerged. Soak for 1 hour, or until the skins are loosened. Remove as much skin as possible and discard. Set the chiles aside.

3. Heat the olive oil in a large stockpot over medium heat until hot but not smoking. Add the Spanish onion and garlic and sauté, stirring frequently, for 5 minutes, or until the onion is softened and translucent. Add the chuck and pork and cook, stirring, for 10 minutes or until the meat is browned all over. Add the broth, water, beer, and vinegar and bring to a simmer. Add the ancho chiles, the minced chili, chipotle chiles, chili powder, cumin, oregano, salt, and pepper. Simmer over medium heat, uncovered and stirring occasionally, for 1 hour.

4. Add the tomatoes and simmer for 15 minutes, or until the sauce is reduced and thickened. Serve in individual soup bowls and pass the red onions, coriander, sour cream, and Cheddar Cream separately.

CHEDDAR CREAM
ABOUT 3 CUPS

1 cup grated cheddar cheese   **2 cups crème fraîche**

Melt the cheddar cheese in a small saucepan over medium heat. Whip the crème fraîche until thick and stiff peaks have formed. Gradually swirl the cheddar into the crème fraîche.

So y'all, hear . . . me . . . good. It's them poisons in all the fast eatin that's caused this lack of pride, idle-handedness, and general no-count. It ain't the Fat. An, if I'm standin here as Aunt Doe Rae Dollar, I betcha ninety percent of them rapers, robbers and killers is skinny, skinny. An it ain't two of 'em that has ever said the blessin an eat on the ground.

SINKIN SPELLS, HOT FLASHES,
FITS AND CRAVINGS,
ERNEST MATTHEW MICKLER, 1988

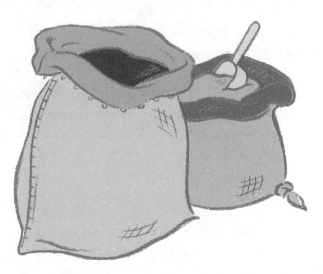

Magnificent Spice-Filled Meat Loaf
with Down-Home Hot Gravy

This is comfort food with a capital C. Serve this up to your family with mashed potatoes and your kids will never leave home (only joking).

6 SERVINGS

- 2 bay leaves
- 1½ teaspoons freshly ground black pepper
- 1 teaspoon sea salt or salt
- ¾ teaspoon ground cayenne pepper
- ½ teaspoon ground cumin
- ½ teaspoon ground mace
- ¼ cup (½ stick) unsalted butter
- 1 onion, finely chopped
- 1 celery stalk, finely chopped
- ½ red bell pepper, finely chopped
- 4 scallions (white and 2 inches of green), finely chopped
- 4 garlic cloves, minced
- 1 tablespoon hot sauce, preferably Inner Beauty or Melinda's
- 1 tablespoon Worcestershire sauce
- ½ cup plain yogurt
- ½ cup ketchup
- 1 pound ground chuck
- ½ pound ground pork
- ½ pound ground veal
- 2 eggs, lightly beaten
- 1 cup very fine dried bread crumbs
- **Down-Home Hot Gravy (recipe follows)**

1. Combine the bay leaves, black pepper, salt, cayenne pepper, cumin, and mace in a small bowl and mix well. Melt the butter in a saucepan over medium heat. Add the spice mixture, onion, celery, bell pepper, scallions, garlic, hot sauce, and Worcestershire. Cook, stirring, for 5 minutes, or until the mixture begins to stick to the bottom of the saucepan. Scrape up any browned bits from the bottom of the saucepan and add the yogurt and ketchup. Stir well to blend and cook for 2 minutes more, or until thoroughly hot and well blended. Remove from heat, discard the bay leaves, and let cool.

2. Preheat the oven to 350°F. Combine the beef, pork, and veal in a large bowl and mix well. Add the onion mixture, eggs, and bread crumbs. Mix well with a fork or wet hands until thoroughly blended.

3. Turn the meat mixture onto a work surface. With wet hands, pat the mixture into an approximately 10 x 5-inch loaf, and place in a foil-lined shallow roasting pan. Bake, uncovered, at 350°F for 25 minutes. Raise the heat to 400°F and cook for 30 minutes more, or until cooked through. Serve with Down-Home Hot Gravy.

DOWN-HOME HOT GRAVY
ABOUT 3 CUPS

¼ cup vegetable oil
¼ cup all-purpose flour
1 onion, finely chopped
½ red bell pepper, finely chopped
½ celery stalk, finely chopped
2 garlic cloves, minced
1 bay leaf

1 tablespoon minced red or green chili pepper
1 teaspoon coarsely ground black pepper
½ teaspoon ground cayenne pepper
2 cups beef broth
1 cup water

1. Heat the oil in a saucepan over medium-low heat until hot but not smoking. Make a roux by gradually adding the flour, stirring constantly, until smooth. Cook, always stirring, for 2 minutes, or until the roux is light brown. (Don't be deterred by the idea of making a roux from scratch, but commercially prepared roux is available in gourmet shops and by mail.)

2. Reduce the heat to low and add the onion, bell pepper, celery, garlic, bay leaf, chili pepper, black pepper, and cayenne pepper. Cook for 1 minute, stirring constantly. Remove from the heat and set aside.

3. Bring the broth and water to a boil in a saucepan over medium heat. Gradually add the roux to the boiling broth, stirring constantly. Reduce the heat to low and simmer for 15 minutes, or until thickened. Skim off any oil, remove and discard the bay leaf, and serve.

One cannot think well, love well, sleep well, if one has not dined well.

VIRGINIA WOOLF

WHEN IS STEAK DONE?

Test for doneness by poking the meat with your finger. Meat is rare when it is as cushy as the soft spot between the base of your thumb and your index finger when your hand is open. It's medium rare if it has the same resiliency as the cushiony part of your palm midway between your wrist and the base of your little finger. It's medium if it's as solid as the pad of your palm at the base of your thumb. Practice this method or — simplicity itself — make a little cut in the meat and look at it.

COLORFUL STEAK AU POIVRE
WITH PEPPERCORN-MUSTARD SAUCE

Every now and again I dream of a steak as big as a Volkswagen. Here, then, covered with a crust of peppers, is the ultimate steak experience. — R. Z.

2 SERVINGS

3 tablespoons drained green peppercorns
3 tablespoons Dijon mustard
2 tablespoons butter, softened
1 tablespoon all-purpose flour
1 tablespoon black peppercorns, preferably Tellicherry
1 teaspoon grains of paradise (melegueta) peppercorns
1 teaspoon pink peppercorns
1 teaspoon dried green peppercorns
1 teaspoon white peppercorns
1 teaspoon red pepper flakes
1½ tablespoons olive oil
One 1½-inch-thick T-bone or porterhouse steak or two 1¼-inch-thick top sirloin steaks
½ cup beef broth
¼ cup heavy cream

1. Mash the green peppercorns in a small bowl. Add the mustard, butter, and flour and mix well. Set aside. Coarsely grind the black, melegueta, pink, dried green, and white peppercorns with a spice grinder or in a mortar and pestle. Add the red pepper flakes and mix well.

2. If you are grilling, rub olive oil all over both sides of the steak.

3. Rub the pepper blend all over the steak. Prepare the grill for a hot fire or heat the olive oil in a large skillet over high heat. Grill or pan-broil the steak, turning, about 15 minutes for rare (10–12 minutes for the smaller steaks). Transfer to a plate, letting the browned bits and steak juices in the skillet stand.

4. Combine the broth and cream in a clean skillet over medium heat. Add 1 teaspoon of juice and browned bits from the steak crust (or from the bottom of the steak skillet, if you've pan-broiled). Heat to the boiling point and cook, stirring constantly, for 3 minutes, or until it thickens enough to coat a spoon. Add the peppercorn-and-mustard mixture and cook for 1 minute more, whisking constantly. Slice the steak, pour the sauce over, and serve.

Sweet and Savory Lamb Shanks
with Currants and Mint

Woodsy herbal flavors, slow-cooked lamb, bright mint,
and honey — all reminiscent of a perfect spring day.

4 SERVINGS

4 lamb shanks (about 1 pound each)	2 tablespoons pomegranate molasses
2 tablespoons Ras el Hanout	6 garlic cloves, minced
3 tablespoons extra-virgin olive oil	Two 3-inch cinnamon sticks
1 onion, diced small	4 fresh sage leaves
1 large carrot, diced small	3 ripe plum tomatoes, seeded and coarsely chopped
1 cup beef broth	1 cup dried currants
1 cup dry red wine	¼ cup chopped fresh mint

1. Preheat the oven to 350°F. Rub the lamb shanks with the Ras el Hanout. Heat 2 tablespoons of the olive oil in a large heavy casserole over medium heat until hot but not smoking. Add the lamb shanks and cook, turning, for 12–15 minutes, or until evenly browned. Remove the lamb and discard the fat.

2. Reduce the heat to low and add the remaining 1 tablespoon of olive oil to the casserole. Add the onion and carrot and cook, stirring occasionally, for 10 minutes, or until the onion is softened and translucent. Increase the heat to medium and add the broth, wine, pomegranate molasses, garlic, cinnamon, and sage. Bring to a boil, stirring frequently.

3. Add the lamb to the casserole, cover, and bake, stirring occasionally, for 1 hour, or until tender. Stir in the tomatoes and currants and bake, covered, for 30 minutes, or until the lamb is almost falling off the bone. Garnish with the mint and serve.

Cookery cannot be done like pharmacy: the Pharmacist is obliged to weigh every ingredient that he employs, as he does not like to taste it; the Cook, on the contrary, must taste often, as the reduction increases the flavour. It would be blind work, indeed, without tasting: the very best soups or entrées, in which you have omitted to put salt, are entirely without flavour; seasoning is in Cookery what chords are in music; the best instrument, in the hand of the best professor, without its being in tune, is insipid.

THE FRENCH COOK,
LOUIS EUSTACHE UDE, 1813

Grilled Spice-Rubbed Leg of Lamb

with Citrus Olive Salsa

Lemon, sweet spices, and thyme enhance this spicy lamb.
Use the spice blend below, or one of your own devising.

8 SERVINGS

In roasting butchers' meat,
be careful not to run the spit
through the nice parts.

THE VIRGINIA HOUSEWIFE
OR, METHODICAL COOK,
MARY RANDOLPH, 1824

2 tablespoons coriander seeds
2 tablespoons cumin seeds
6 large garlic cloves, minced
½ cup red wine
2 tablespoons ground aleppo pepper or sweet paprika
2 tablespoons ground cinnamon
1 tablespoon ground thyme
1 tablespoon ground allspice
1 tablespoon ground ginger

1 tablespoon preserved lemon pulp or lemon juice (Preserved Lemons recipe follows)
1 teaspoon cayenne pepper
1 teaspoon ground cloves
1 boneless butterflied leg of lamb (4–5 pounds)
Citrus Olive Salsa (recipe follows)

1. Dry-roast the coriander seeds and cumin seeds in a small skillet over medium heat for 1 minute, or until fragrant. Let cool. In a food processor, combine the coriander seeds, cumin seeds, garlic, wine, aleppo pepper, cinnamon, thyme, allspice, ginger, preserved lemon, cayenne pepper, and cloves. Process until well mixed and pureed. Rub the paste all over the leg of lamb.

2. Prepare a hot fire for grilling, building the coals on one side of the grill. Grill the lamb over the coals for 4 minutes, or until seared and well browned.

3. Transfer the lamb to the noncoal side of the grill, cover, and cook, turning once, 15 minutes for medium rare. Check for doneness with the finger-poking method or the cut-and-peek technique (page 144). Remove the lamb from the grill and let rest for 10 minutes before slicing. Serve with Citrus Olive Salsa on the side.

CITRUS OLIVE SALSA

½ cup chopped pitted
  Kalamata olives
½ cup chopped pitted firm
  green olives
½ cup chopped pine nuts
3 tablespoons minced fresh
  parsley
1 tablespoon minced fresh
  thyme

2 teaspoons freshly grated
  Parmesan cheese
2 garlic cloves, minced
1 teaspoon capers
1 oil-packed anchovy fillet,
  chopped
Finely grated zest of 1 lemon
1½ tablespoons extra-virgin
  olive oil

Combine all of the ingredients, mixing well.

PRESERVED LEMONS

One of the essential ingredients in Moroccan cuisine, preserved lemons are used in lamb and vegetable stews, soups, and salads. Use them whenever you want a silky-textured, piquant citrus flavor. Preserved lemons are available through mail order, or you can make your own.

6 thin-skinned lemons, well
  scrubbed
¼ cup coarse sea salt
2 cinnamon sticks
1 teaspoon cloves

1 teaspoon coriander seeds
1 teaspoon black peppercorns
1 bay leaf
Fresh lemon juice

You must reflect carefully beforehand with whom you are to eat and drink, rather than what you are to eat and drink. For a dinner of meats without the company of a friend is like the life of a lion or a wolf.

EPICURUS

1. Quarter the lemons from the top to within ¼ inch of the bottom. Sprinkle salt on the lemon pulp and reshape the fruit.

2. Place 1 tablespoon of the salt on the bottom of a sterile 1-quart mason jar. Pack in the lemons, adding the remaining salt and spices between them. Add lemon juice to cover. Tightly seal the jar and let stand for 30 days, shaking each day to distribute the spices. To use, rinse the lemons, removing any of the harmless lacy white substance, and add the pulp and/or rind to your dish in progress. Preserved lemons will keep for up to 1 year.

MINT

There at six hundred species of mint, and those are just the ones with names. The two most popular flavorings used in cooking are spearmint and peppermint. The sweetish-sharp flavor of mint is much loved because it blends so well with pungent spices. Though fresh mint is usually prefered, dried mint works extremely well in Middle Eastern yogurt dishes, with vegetables, and in salads. It should be added to tomato sauces at the last minute, since acidic sauces will turn it black. In India, mint is used in curries, chutneys, and as a garnish for highly spiced food. A sprig of fresh mint makes a Vietnamese rice paper role sublime. Mint is continually undervalued in the United States. Sure, it's dragged out with the spring lamb, and a sprig or two is languidly dropped into iced tea on hot humid days, but it deserves better.

SOY SAUCE LAMB CHOPS
WITH GINGER MINT PESTO

*The saltiness of the soy sauce complements the sweetness of the lamb.
Tradition is upheld by the mint in the pesto.*

4 SERVINGS

3 tablespoons sesame oil
Eight 1-inch-thick lamb chops
    (about ½ pound each)
8 scallions, finely chopped
4 garlic cloves, minced
¼ cup soy sauce
¼ cup hoisin sauce

2 tablespoons rice vinegar
1 tablespoon Sambal Oelek,
    (page 55)
One 1-inch piece fresh ginger,
    peeled and minced
Ginger Mint Pesto (recipe
    follows)

1. Heat the roasted sesame oil in a large skillet over medium heat until hot but not smoking. Add the chops and cook, turning once, for 6 minutes, or until browned lightly. Remove the chops from the skillet and drain on paper towels.

2. Add the scallions and garlic to the skillet and sauté for 10 minutes, or until softened. Add the soy sauce, hoisin sauce, vinegar, Sambal Oelek, and ginger and simmer for 3 minutes, stirring constantly.

3. Return the chops to the skillet and reduce the heat to low. Cover and cook, turning once, for 5 minutes, or until cooked through. Pour the Ginger Mint Pesto into a plastic mustard dispenser and squiggle a design on each of 4 plates. Top with the lamb chops, drizzle with the pan juices, and serve.

GINGER MINT PESTO
ABOUT 1 CUP

3 cups fresh mint leaves
One 2-inch piece fresh ginger,
    peeled and chopped

½ cup pine nuts
½ cup extra-virgin olive oil
1 garlic clove, minced

Combine all of the ingredients in a food processor and process until smooth.

SEARINGLY HOT ETHIOPIAN LAMB STEW
WITH BERBERE CREAM

Rachel Yohannes, producer of a delicious Ethiopian condiment called Afri-Q and contributor of this recipe, may have a different sense of "hot" than you or I, but she knows what "good" is. Before serving this torrid stew, assess your dinner guests: Do they like really hot food? Taste a tiny, tiny bit of the berbere to gauge its strength, and be moderate in the amount used if you ever want to see your guests again — outside of the courtroom.

4 SERVINGS

¼ cup olive oil
2 pounds boneless lamb, preferably from the leg, cut into 1½-inch cubes
1 large red onion, chopped
3 garlic cloves, minced
1 red bell pepper, coarsely chopped
¼ cup chicken broth

1–2 tablespoons plus 1 teaspoon berbere
½ teaspoon minced fresh ginger
1 ripe tomato, seeded and chopped
Salt, to taste
1 cup crème fraîche
Pomegranate seeds, for garnish
Fresh coriander, for garnish

1. Heat the olive oil in a large heavy skillet over medium heat until hot but not smoking. Add the lamb and cook, turning frequently, until browned all over. Transfer the lamb to a bowl and set aside.

2. Add the onion and garlic to the skillet and sauté, stirring constantly, for 6–8 minutes, or until softened and lightly browned. Add the bell pepper, broth, 1–2 tablespoons berbere, and ginger and cook, stirring frequently, for 10 minutes, or until the sauce thickens slightly. Reduce the heat to low, add the lamb, and cover. Simmer for 30 minutes, or until the lamb is tender. Stir in the tomato, taste, and add salt if needed.

3. To make Berbere Cream, whip the crème fraîche until stiff peaks form. Fold in 1 teaspoon berbere. Ladle the stew into bowls and garnish with dollops of Berbere Cream, pomegranate seeds, and coriander.

HISTORICAL RECIPE:

ROAST LAMB IN A MEADOW OF SPINACHES

Choose a thick and fat leg of lamb; pare the knucklebone; salt and roast rather well for about an hour. Pick and wash enough spinach; cook uncovered and at the last moment, in plenty of salted boiling water; drain thoroughly without cooling; chop it a little, season it with the surface of the lamb drippings; put the lamb on a dish, surround with the spinach, put a white-paper ruffle on the bone, and serve the rest of the drippings in a sauce bowl. Add croutons, for garnish.

THE FRANCO-AMERICAN COOKERY BOOK,
FELIX J. DÉLIÉE, 1884

COUSCOUS

Couscous, a semolina pasta, is available in a variety of sizes in Middle Eastern markets, health food stores, and supermarkets. The fine-grain, precooked couscous is the most commonly used. Authentic couscous is steamed in the top of a couscousière, but it may be boiled in water as any pasta.

LAMB AND ARTICHOKES IN PHYLLO
WITH SUN-DRIED TOMATO PESTO

Once you've used delicate, light phyllo dough and discovered how easily you can transform the mundane into something elegant, you'll want to use it all the time. Prepare this dish with the stuffing below, try it with Duck Picadillo (page 134), or devise your own filling.

4 SERVINGS

1 pound lean ground lamb
1 onion, chopped
¾ cup beef broth
1 teaspoon ground cumin
½ teaspoon ground coriander
½ teaspoon ground cinnamon
¼ teaspoon ground cayenne pepper
Salt and freshly ground black pepper, to taste

½ cup couscous
8 sheets phyllo dough, thawed according to package directions
1 cup unsalted butter, melted
¾ cup drained marinated artichoke hearts, chopped
Sun-Dried Tomato Pesto (recipe follows)

1. Cook the lamb and onion in a large skillet over medium heat for 5 minutes, or until the lamb is browned and the onions are soft and translucent. Drain off and discard the fat. Add the broth, cumin, coriander, cinnamon, cayenne pepper, salt, and pepper. Bring to a boil. Cover, reduce the heat to low, and simmer for 5 minutes. Stir in the couscous, remove from heat, stir again, and let stand for 5 minutes.

2. Preheat the oven to 350°F. Sandwich the phyllo between 2 pieces of waxed paper and cover with a very clean, damp kitchen towel. Place 1 sheet of phyllo on a barely damp towel on a work surface and brush with melted butter. Take a second sheet of phyllo, place it directly over the first, and brush with melted butter. Continue until all of the sheets are stacked one on top of the other, each brushed with butter. Cover the top sheet with plastic wrap and press down to bond all of the sheets together. Remove and discard the plastic wrap.

3. Lightly butter a lipped baking sheet. Add the artichoke hearts to the lamb mixture and stir to mix. Spoon the mixture along 1 long edge

of the phyllo, leaving a 2-inch border on 3 sides. Fold over the short edges to cover 2 inches of the lamb mixture on each short end.

4. Starting at the long end with the lamb mixture, carefully and gently roll up the lamb and phyllo like a carpet by lifting the edge of the towel. Place the roll, seam-side down, on the prepared baking sheet. Make diagonal cuts about ⅜ inch deep on the top of the roll. Brush with 1 tablespoon of the melted butter (discard any remaining butter). Bake for 30 minutes, or until golden brown. Cut into slices and serve with Sun-Dried Tomato Pesto.

SUN-DRIED TOMATO PESTO
ABOUT 3 CUPS

1½ cups drained sun-dried tomatoes in oil, plus 1 tablespoon of the oil
½ cup pitted black olives
½ cup packed chopped Italian parsley

½ cup pine nuts
7 tablespoons olive oil
3 garlic cloves, minced
1 teaspoon capers, drained
1 anchovy fillet, drained and chopped

Place all of the ingredients in a food processor and process until coarsely chopped and well blended.

There is no question that Rumanian Jewish food is heavy. One meal is equal in heaviness, I would guess, to eight or nine years of steady mung-bean eating. Following the Rumanian tradition, garlic is used in excess to keep the vampires away; following the Jewish tradition, a dispenser of schmaltz (liquid chicken fat) is kept on the table to give vampires heartburn if they get through the garlic defense.

CALVIN TRILLIN

Fried Pork and Peanuts

with Cumberland Sauce

It's wonderful when something so exotic can be prepared in a flash.

4 SERVINGS

2 pounds boneless loin of
pork, cut into 1-inch cubes
½ cup soy sauce
½ cup packed brown sugar
½ cup all-purpose flour
1 teaspoon ajowan

Salt and freshly ground
pepper, to taste
½ cup vegetable oil
1 cup blanched peanuts
Cumberland Sauce (recipe
follows)

Combine the pork, soy sauce, sugar, flour, ajowan, salt, and pepper in a large bowl. Heat the oil in a skillet over medium heat until hot but not smoking. Add the pork mixture and cook, stirring, for 10 minutes, or until the meat is brown and crusty. With a slotted spoon, remove the pork. Add the peanuts to the skillet and sauté for 5 minutes, or until lightly browned. Return the pork to the skillet, scrape up any browned bits from the bottom of the skillet, and stir. Drain off the fat and serve with Cumberland Sauce.

Pork is an unwholesome meat, and should never be eaten by children, or people with weak digestion, nor, indeed, by any one except in cold weather.

MRS. LINCOLN'S BOSTON COOK BOOK,
MRS. D. A. LINCOLN, 1884

Cumberland Sauce

A favored condiment throughout the British Isles, Cumberland sauce is a sweet jelly, with a hint of heat from either mustard or horseradish. Find it in gourmet shops or by mail, or make your own.

ABOUT 2 CUPS

2 cups red currant jelly
½ cup ruby port
½ cup finely chopped shallots
Grated zest and juice of 2
lemons and 1 orange

1 tablespoon dry mustard
1 teaspoon coarsely ground
black pepper
½ teaspoon salt

Combine all of the ingredients in a saucepan over medium heat. Cook, stirring constantly, for 5 minutes, or until the jelly has melted. Remove from the heat and let cool. Refrigerate for 2 hours or until firm.

Marinated Spice-Rubbed Spareribs

The best spareribs we have ever tasted come from Cendrillon, a Filipino-and Asian-influenced restaurant in Manhattan. Chef-owner Romy Dorotan shares his recipe. The overnight marination allows flavor to develop.

4–6 SERVINGS

1 cup soy sauce
½ cup rice wine
½ cup fresh lime juice
½ cup honey
One 4-inch piece fresh ginger, peeled and thinly sliced
10 garlic cloves, minced
2 racks spareribs
¼ cup black peppercorns
2 tablespoons coriander seeds
2 tablespoons Szechuan peppercorns

2 tablespoons yellow mustard seeds
2 tablespoons cumin seeds
2 teaspoons whole cloves
2 teaspoons cardamom seeds
2 teaspoons red pepper flakes
4 star anise pods
4 cinnamon sticks, preferably Ceylon cinnamon
½ cup packed brown sugar
¼ cup sweet Hungarian paprika
2 tablespoons salt

1. Combine the soy sauce, rice wine, lime juice, honey, ginger, and garlic in a shallow roasting pan. Stir to mix well. Place the spareribs in the pan and brush all over with the soy sauce mixture. Cover with plastic wrap and refrigerate overnight, turning and basting once or twice if you're awake.

2. In a small skillet over low heat, combine the black peppercorns, coriander, Szechuan peppercorns, mustard, cumin, cloves, cardamom, red pepper flakes, star anise, and cinnamon. Dry-roast, stirring, for 1 minute, or until aromatic. Remove from the heat and let cool.

3. Preheat the oven to 300°F. With a spice grinder or mortar and pestle, grind the spices to a medium consistency. Transfer to a small bowl and add the brown sugar, paprika, and salt. Stir to mix well.

4. Remove the spareribs from the marinade, drain well, and pat dry with paper towels. Discard the marinade. Rub the ribs with the spice mixture, place on a rack, and roast for 1½–2 hours, or until tender. Cut between each rib and serve with plenty of paper napkins.

THE ORIGINS OF ROAST PORK

According to an ancient Chinese folk tale, Bo-Bo, a clumsy adolescent peasant boy, discovered the joys of roast pork when he accidentally burned down his father's pigsty. As Charles Lamb relates in "Dissertation Upon Roast Pig," "Imitators were soon building and burning down pigsties at a terrifying rate."

Portuguese Pork and Shellfish Stew
with Avocado Cream

Portugal, one of the tiniest countries, produces food with some of the biggest, boldest flavors. Overnight marination enhances the flavor of this stew. Serve with crusty bread and a Spanish Rioja wine.

8 SERVINGS

2 cups dry red Rioja wine
6 garlic cloves, minced
1 teaspoon red pepper flakes
3½ pounds boneless pork shoulder, cut into 2-inch pieces
1 teaspoon caraway seeds
1 teaspoon sweet paprika, plus more for garnish
1 teaspoon sea salt
1 teaspoon coarsely ground black pepper

1 avocado, pitted and peeled
1 cup crème fraîche
One 28-ounce can tomatoes, drained and chopped
One 8-ounce can tomato sauce
½ cup pitted Kalamata olives
1½ pounds jumbo shrimp, shelled and deveined
1½ dozen littleneck clams, soaked and scrubbed
¼ cup chopped fresh parsley, for garnish

1. Combine the wine, garlic, and red pepper flakes in a large bowl. Add the pork and mix to blend. Cover and refrigerate overnight.

2. Combine the pork mixture, caraway, paprika, salt, and black pepper in a large saucepan over medium heat. Bring to a boil, reduce the heat to low, cover, and cook for 1½ hours, or until tender.

3. Meanwhile, to make the Avocado Cream, process the avocado in a food processor until smooth. Whip the crème fraîche until stiff peaks form. Fold the avocado into the crème fraîche.

4. Add the tomatoes, sauce, olives, shrimp, and clams to the stew and raise the heat. Cover and simmer for 3 minutes, or until the shrimp are firm and opaque. Remove the shrimp. Simmer the stew for 3 more minutes. Discard any clams that do not open. Return the shrimp to the stew, stir once, and ladle into bowls. Put a dollop of Avocado Cream on each serving and garnish with paprika and parsley.

Do any of you, or can any of you, remember when Nuvell was just Raenelle's twin-sister, plain ol, and not some skimpy kinda French cookin. I mean, last year at our dinner, I saw a three bean salad that consisted of egxactly that! Three beans, and a sprig of somethin that looked everbit like dogfennel to me. They a-fiddlin with our fat. That's what they doin. Now, I ain't advocatin un-healthy food but what can you say against Miss Lyddie's fried pork chops, she et 'em for 96 years. And she ain't never robbed, raped er murdered nobody. She did die, but it weren't her pork chops. She simply wore out.

SINKIN SPELLS, HOT FLASHES,
FITS AND CRAVINGS,
ERNEST MATTHEW MICKLER, 1988

VEGETABLES

HOT AND SPICY GREEN BEANS
WITH FERMENTED BLACK BEANS

These green beans are more addictive than potato chips.

4 SERVINGS

1 pound fresh green beans, trimmed

3 tablespoons peanut or vegetable oil

8 scallions (white and 2 inches of green), chopped

4 garlic cloves, minced

1 fresh hot red or green chili pepper, seeded and minced

One 1-inch piece fresh ginger, peeled and minced

2 tablespoons fermented black beans

¼ cup rice vinegar

3 tablespoons dry sherry

2 tablespoons soy sauce

½ teaspoon packed brown sugar

1½ teaspoons cornstarch dissolved in 1 tablespoon warm water

1. Blanch the green beans in a large pot of boiling water for 2 minutes; drain and set aside. Heat the oil in a large skillet until hot but not smoking. Add the scallions, garlic, chili, ginger, and fermented black beans and stir-fry for 1 minute. Add the green beans and stir-fry for 3 minutes, or until the beans are almost tender.

2. Add the rice vinegar, sherry, soy sauce, and brown sugar and stir to mix. Stir the cornstarch mixture once or twice and stir into the skillet. Cook for 1 minute, or until the beans are well coated. Serve.

GARNISH

Chop red, green, yellow, purple, and orange bell peppers into small dice and sprinkle all over the beans. If you have the time, cook up some white rice as a "go with."

Most people spoil garden things by overboiling them. All things that are green should have a little crispness, for if they are overboiled they neither have any sweetness or beauty.

THE ART OF COOKERY
MADE PLAIN & EASY,
MRS. HANNAH GLASSE, 1747

ASPARAGUS

Set a stew-pan with plenty of water on the fire, sprinkle a handful of salt in it, let it boil, and skim it; then put in the asparagus prepared thus; scrape all the stalks till they are perfectly clean; throw them into a pan of cold water as you scrape them; when they are all done, tie them in little bundles, of a quarter of a hundred each, with bass, if you can get it, or tape; cut off the stalks at the bottom, that they may be all of a length; when they are tender at the stalk, which will be in from twenty to thirty minutes, they are done enough.

THE VIRGINIA HOUSEWIFE OR, METHODICAL COOK,
MARY RANDOLPH, 1824

SAUTÉED ASPARAGUS
WITH BLACK-PEPPERED PESTO
Asparagus fulfills my need for spring all year round.

4 SERVINGS

2 tablespoons extra-virgin olive oil	Sea salt and freshly ground black pepper, to taste
1 garlic clove, minced	Black-Peppered Pesto (recipe follows)
1 pound thin asparagus	
½ teaspoon sweet paprika	

Heat the olive oil in a skillet over low heat until hot. Add the garlic and sauté for about 3 minutes, or until barely golden. Add the asparagus and sauté, turning frequently, for 15 minutes, or until almost tender. Add the paprika, salt, and pepper and stir to mix well. Drizzle with Black-Peppered Pesto and serve.

BLACK-PEPPERED PESTO
ABOUT ¾ CUP

¼ cup blanched almonds	2 teaspoons coarsely ground black pepper
1½ cups packed fresh basil	¼ cup freshly grated Pecorino Romano cheese
½ cup fresh Italian parsley	
¾ cup extra-virgin olive oil	
2 garlic cloves	

Dry-roast the almonds in a small skillet over medium heat, stirring frequently, for 4 minutes, or until just golden and fragrant. Chop coarsely. Bruise the basil and parsley by rolling with a rolling pin or bottle. In a food processor, combine the almonds, basil, parsley, olive oil, garlic, and pepper and process until well mixed and coarsely ground. Transfer to a small bowl and stir in the cheese.

Grilled Corn on the Cob

with Chile Citrus Butter

*There are some hot summer nights when what would normally
be 6 servings actually serves just 1 or 2.*

6 SERVINGS

6 tablespoons unsalted butter
1 tablespoon ground ancho
   chile
1 tablespoon fresh orange
   juice
1 tablespoon fresh lemon
   juice

1 teaspoon honey
½ teaspoon ground cumin
½ teaspoon freshly ground
   black pepper
¼ teaspoon ground cayenne
   pepper
6 ears fresh corn, with husks

1. Prepare a medium fire for grilling or preheat the oven to 350°F.
Combine the butter, ground chile, orange juice, lemon juice, honey,
cumin, black pepper, and cayenne pepper in a small saucepan over
low heat. Heat, stirring to blend well, for 3 minutes, or until the
butter melts.

2. Shuck the corn and brush with the seasoned butter. Wrap each
ear well in foil and grill, turning frequently, or bake for 15 minutes.
Remove the foil and serve.

VARIATION:

GRILLED CORN WITH CORIANDER AND LIME BUTTER

For a milder, citrusy corn treat,
melt the 6 tablespoons butter with
¼ cup chopped fresh coriander, 1
teaspoon fresh lime juice, and ½
teaspoon grated lime zest. Continue with the recipe at step 2.

Minted Pomegranate Eggplant

Eggplant and tomato always work well together,
so serve this with fresh tomato salsa.

6 SERVINGS

Vegetables in the Middle East do not play second fiddle as do the "two veg" to meat in England. They hold a dignified, sometimes splendid position in the hierarchy of food.

A BOOK OF MIDDLE EASTERN FOOD,
CLAUDIA RODEN, 1968

4 slender eggplants (about ½ pound each)
1 cup coarse sea salt
3 tablespoons extra-virgin olive oil
3 tablespoons pomegranate molasses
1 tablespoon fresh orange juice

1 teaspoon ground sumac
1 teaspoon packed brown sugar
1 garlic clove, minced
3 tablespoons chopped fresh mint
3 tablespoons fresh pomegranate seeds

1. Remove the stem from each eggplant. Slice them on the bias into ½-inch-thick elongated ovals. Sprinkle generously with the salt and let stand in a colander for 1 hour. Rinse off the salt and pat dry with paper towels.

2. Combine 1 tablespoon of the olive oil, the pomegranate molasses, orange juice, sumac, brown sugar, and garlic. Mix well and set aside. Preheat the oven to 400°F. Brush both sides of the eggplant slices sparingly with the remaining 2 tablespoons of olive oil and place in a single layer on a baking sheet. Bake, turning once, for 20 minutes, or until golden brown.

3. Brush the eggplant slices with half of the pomegranate molasses mixture and bake for 2 minutes. Turn the slices and brush with the remaining pomegranate mixture. Bake for 2 minutes more, or until the eggplant is soft but not mushy. Transfer to a serving bowl, garnish with mint and pomegranate seeds, and serve.

Spicy Mushrooms

with Fenugreek and Lemon

*Mushrooms win the congeniality award, taking on any flavor
you toss them with. Here they become slightly Indian,
as they share the skillet with cumin and fenugreek.*

4 SERVINGS

1 teaspoon cumin seeds
¾ teaspoon fenugreek seeds
3 tablespoons peanut oil
1 medium onion, diced
One 2-inch piece fresh ginger,
   peeled and minced
2 garlic cloves, minced
1 fresh hot green or red chili
   pepper, seeded and minced

1½ pounds portobello or large
   white mushrooms,
   stemmed and cut into
   1-inch pieces
½ teaspoon Szechuan pepper
Salt, to taste
1 teaspoon lemon juice

1. Dry-roast the cumin and fenugreek seeds in a small skillet over medium heat for 2 minutes, or until aromatic. Grind the seeds with a spice grinder or mortar and pestle and set aside.

2. Heat the oil in a wok or skillet over medium heat until hot but not smoking. Add the onion and sauté for 5 minutes, or until softened and translucent. Add the ginger, garlic, and chili and cook, stirring constantly, for 2 minutes.

3. Add the mushrooms, Szechuan pepper, and salt and cook, stirring frequently, for 15 minutes, or until all the liquid has evaporated. Reduce the heat to low and add the cumin and fenugreek seeds and the lemon juice. Stir to mix thoroughly and cook for 3 minutes, or until the lemon juice is absorbed. Serve.

VARIATION

You can serve this versatile fungus dish as is, or stir into plain cooked rice or baked butternut squash. If you're feeling extremely creative, try enveloping the mushrooms in Vietnamese rice paper wrappers.

HISTORICAL RECIPE:
MUSHROOMS IN CREAM

Pour a 2-pound can of mushrooms in a saucepan with their juice and boil a while. Place the saucepan on a corner of the range and add 2 yolks mixed in a bowl with 1 tablespoonful cornstarch, 1 glassful cream and some chopped parsley. Heat. Serve as a garnish for fine dinners.

LA CUISINE FRANÇAISE,
FRANÇOIS TANTY, 1894

GARNISH

Decorate the spinach with a small still life of cardamom pods, cinnamon sticks, and red chili peppers in one corner of the serving platter.

Spinach. Great care must be used in washing and picking it clean; drain it, and throw it into boiling water — a few minutes will boil it sufficiently: press out all the water, put it in a stew pan with a piece of butter, some pepper and salt — chop it continually with a spoon till it is quite dry: serve it with poached eggs or without, as you please.

THE VIRGINIA HOUSEWIFE
OR, METHODICAL COOK,
MARY RANDOLPH, 1824

SAUTÉED SPINACH AND ONIONS

WITH CARDAMOM AND FENNEL SEEDS

*Spinach moves out of the realm of the ordinary
with this robustly flavored dish.*

6 SERVINGS

2 tablespoons vegetable oil
2 tablespoons unsalted butter
1 teaspoon fennel seeds
4 brown or green cardamom pods
1 cinnamon stick
3 onions, thinly sliced into half-rings
One 2-inch piece fresh ginger, peeled and julienned
1 garlic clove, minced
3 pounds spinach, rinsed and stemmed
½ teaspoon salt
¼ teaspoon ground cayenne pepper
½ teaspoon Garam Masala (page 50)

1. Heat the oil and butter in a large saucepan over medium heat until hot but not smoking. Add the fennel, cardamom, and cinnamon and stir. Add the onions and sauté for 10 minutes, or until they turn a light brown. Add the ginger and garlic and cook, stirring, for about 15 minutes, until the onions are golden brown. Be careful not to burn them.

2. Stir in the spinach, cover, and reduce the heat to low. Cook, stirring occasionally, for 5 minutes, or until the spinach is thoroughly wilted. Add the salt and cayenne pepper, cover, and cook, stirring occasionally, for 20 minutes. Stir in the Garam Masala and cook for 5 minutes more. Remove and discard the cinnamon stick. Serve.

Pilaf-Stuffed Onions

WITH SUMAC AND NUTMEG

*Stuffed vegetables are doubly delightful or doubly despicable,
depending on how you feel about vegetables. If you fall to
the despicable side, don't think of these onions as vegetables,
but rather as pearly white orbs holding hidden treasure.*

6 SERVINGS

5 cups chicken broth or water	1 cinnamon stick
1½ cups basmati, jasmine, or long-grain rice	3 garlic cloves, minced
	6 Spanish onions, unpeeled
1¾ teaspoons ground sumac	3 tablespoons unsalted butter
½ teaspoon freshly ground black pepper	½ cup blanched almonds, coarsely chopped
½ teaspoon grated nutmeg	3 tablespoons lemon juice

1. Bring 3 cups of the broth to a boil in a saucepan over medium heat. Stir in the rice, ¾ teaspoon of the sumac, the pepper, nutmeg, cinnamon, and one-third of the garlic and mix well. Cover, reduce the heat to low, and simmer for 12 minutes, or until all of the liquid has been absorbed and the rice is tender. Set aside.

2. Meanwhile, blanch the onions in a large pot of boiling water for 10 minutes. Drain and cool. For each onion, remove the thin outer skin, cut off the root, and cut a ½-inch slice off the top, reserving the "cap." With a sharp knife, remove the inner core of each onion, keeping the 3 outermost layers intact. Finely chop the inner cores. Arrange the onion shells in a shallow baking dish.

3. Preheat the oven to 350°F. Melt the butter in a small skillet over medium heat. Add the chopped onion and sauté for 10 minutes, or until barely browned. Add to the rice along with the almonds; mix well. Spoon the rice mixture into the onion shells and place the onion caps on top.

4. Pour the remaining broth around the onions in the baking dish, add the remaining sumac and garlic, and the lemon juice. Bake for 30 minutes, basting occasionally, or until the onions are tender. Serve.

Our ration that winter had been one pound of onions per person. I opened several cupboards and drawers, and in one I found a whole heap of shallots. Knowing that Caitlin and Dylan had been in Sussex, I thought they must have brought them up with them. I peeled, sliced and cooked them, made a magnificent dish and proudly bore it in. We all fell on it and then seconds later started to feel not only odd, but sick. Caitlin questioned me as to where I had found the shallots: "In that drawer." Her reply was terse and to the point. "You've taken my bloody tulip bulbs for the window-boxes."

WITH LOVE,
THEODORA FITZGIBBON, 1982

The juice of onions annointed upon a bald head in the sun bringeth the haire againe very speedily.

THE HERBAL OR GENERAL
HISTORY OF PLANTS,
JOHN GERARD, 1633

Vanilla Sweet Potato and Carrot Mousse

with Cardamom Mint Cream

Although variations of this dish are traditionally served at Thanksgiving, please don't feel that you can only serve this vegetable confection on holidays. It works quite well on normal rainy Wednesdays, too.

6 SERVINGS

[Sweet potatoes are] the most delicate rootes that may be eaten, and doe farre exceed our passeneps or carets.

RICHARD HAKLUYT,
HISTORIAN, 1584

6 carrots, thickly sliced
4 medium sweet potatoes, peeled and cubed
½ cup (1 stick) unsalted butter
2 vanilla beans, split and scraped, pods reserved for another use

½ teaspoon ground cardamom
Coarse sea salt and freshly ground black pepper, to taste
Cardamom Mint Cream (recipe follows)

Place the sweet potatoes and carrots in a large saucepan, add water to cover, and bring to a boil. Cook over medium heat for 15 minutes, or until tender. Drain, combine with the butter in a food processor, and process until pureed. Add the vanilla scrapings, cardamom, salt, and pepper and pulse to mix. Mound on a plate and serve with dollops of Cardamom Mint Cream.

Cardamom Mint Cream

ABOUT ⅔ CUP

1 tablespoon dry white wine
1 teaspoon minced fresh mint

½ teaspoon ground cardamom
⅔ cup heavy cream

Combine the wine, mint, and cardamom in a small bowl. Whip the heavy cream until thick and stiff peaks form. Fold in the wine mixture. Serve.

Spicy Smashed Potatoes

with Garam Masala

Usually the meat, poultry, or seafood part of a meal is the most enticingly spiced, with the vegetables playing a supporting role. We've turned the roles around with these potatoes. Serve this spicy cloud with a subtly spiced meat or chicken dish.

6 SERVINGS

3 pounds Idaho potatoes, peeled and quartered
1 tablespoon butter ghee or vegetable oil
½ teaspoon black or yellow mustard seeds
1 small onion, finely chopped
1 fresh hot green chili pepper, seeded and finely chopped

1 teaspoon Garam Masala (page 50)
½ teaspoon chili powder
½ teaspoon ground ginger
½ teaspoon ground turmeric
½ teaspoon salt
1 tablespoon lemon juice

What I say is that, if a fellow really likes potatoes, he must be a pretty decent sort of fellow.

A. A. MILNE

1. Place the potatoes in a large saucepan, add water to cover, and bring to a boil. Cook over medium heat for 30 minutes, or until very tender. Mash, set aside, and keep warm.

2. Meanwhile, heat the ghee in a saucepan over medium heat until hot. Add the mustard seeds and sauté for 1 minute, or until they begin to pop. Add the onion and chili pepper and sauté, stirring frequently, for 5 minutes, or until the onion is softened and barely browned. Add the Garam Masala, chili powder, ginger, turmeric, and salt. Stir in the lemon juice. Add to the potatoes and mix well to blend. Serve.

Pasta and Rice

Ten years ago, when she and
Harvey had first moved to
Mill Valley and started making
the scene, it was easy; if you had
people to dinner, you just cooked
yourself blind. Kate and all her
women friends competed with
each other to serve the first
really authentic couscous or the
first Mongolian Hotpot, complete
with those little mesh dippers
from Cost Plus you passed
around so each guest could
fish out his own individual
bits of bok choy.

THE SERIAL,
CYRA MCFADDEN, 1976

Ginger Citrus Couscous
with Minted Red Pepper Harissa

*The piquant flavors of lime, orange, and ginger stand up well to
that drizzle of harissa on the plate. For a festive look,
serve the couscous in hollowed-out orange or grapefruit halves.*

4 SERVINGS

One 1-inch piece ginger,
   peeled and thinly sliced
2 tablespoons safflower oil
2¼ cups water
¾ cup fresh orange juice
½ teaspoon coarse sea salt
   or salt
2 cups couscous
1 teaspoon fresh lime juice

2 scallions (white and 2 inches
   of green), thinly sliced
½ cup canned mandarin
   orange slices, chopped
Salt and freshly ground black
   pepper, to taste
Minted Red Pepper Harissa
   (recipe follows)

1. Combine the ginger and oil in a small saucepan and heat thoroughly over low heat. Let stand for 1 hour if you have the time. Strain out and discard the ginger.

2. Combine the water, orange juice, and salt in a saucepan over medium heat and bring to a boil. Stir in the couscous, remove from the heat, cover, and let stand for 5 minutes.

3. Combine the ginger oil and lime juice in a small bowl. Stir to mix and then add to the couscous while fluffing it with a fork. Stir in the

scallions, oranges, salt, and pepper. Pour the Minted Red Pepper
Harissa into a plastic mustard dispenser and squiggle a design on each
of 4 plates. Spoon couscous onto each plate and serve.

MINTED RED PEPPER HARISSA
ABOUT ½ CUP

12 small dried hot red chili
    peppers, stemmed and
    seeded
6 garlic cloves, minced

3 tablespoons olive oil
3 tablespoons minced fresh
    mint

Soak the chilies in hot water to cover for 1 hour. Drain and mince.
In a food processor, combine the chilies, garlic, olive oil, and mint and
process until blended.

SINGAPORE RICE VERMICELLI
WITH HOT AND SPICY NUTS

*In Singapore, noodles are stir-fried with curry powder, though it is not a
predominant flavor. Instead, the crunchy textures stand out.*

4 SERVINGS

½ pound rice vermicelli
4 tablespoons peanut oil
1 onion, sliced into thin
    half-rings
1 tablespoon curry powder
¼ teaspoon ground cayenne
    pepper
1 red bell pepper, seeded and
    julienned

1 pound medium shrimp,
    shelled and deveined
2 cups fresh mung bean
    sprouts
2 scallions (white and 2 inches
    of green), thinly sliced
Hot and Spicy Nuts (recipe
    follows)
¼ cup fresh coriander, finely
    chopped

RICE NOODLES

The most widely available Asian
noodles are called rice sticks, and
the thinnest of these is rice vermicelli. Made from rice flour, these
light noodles are delectable in soups
and sauced dishes. Fried in hot oil
for a few seconds, rice vermicelli
will puff up.

continued on next page

1. Soak the rice vermicelli in warm water to cover for 1 hour, or until softened. Drain well. In a large pot of boiling water, add 1 tablespoon of the oil and the vermicelli. Cook for 1 minute, or until just tender. Rinse with cold water and drain well. Set aside.

2. Heat the remaining 3 tablespoons of oil in a wok or skillet over medium heat until hot but not smoking. Add the onion and sauté for 3 minutes, or until softened and translucent. Add the curry powder and cayenne pepper and cook, stirring, for 1 minute. Add the bell pepper and cook, stirring constantly, for 2 minutes, or until softened.

3. Stir in the shrimp and sauté for 3 minutes, or until firm and opaque. Add the bean sprouts, scallions, and vermicelli, stirring well. Sprinkle with Hot and Spicy Nuts and coriander and serve.

HOT AND SPICY NUTS

ABOUT 1½ CUPS

2 tablespoons unsalted butter	½ teaspoon dried thyme, crumbled
1 tablespoon oyster sauce	½ teaspoon fine sea salt or salt
1 teaspoon fresh lemon juice	1½ cups unsalted macadamia nuts, Brazil nuts, or hazelnuts
½ teaspoon Cajun Seasoning (page 60)	
½ teaspoon garlic powder	
½ teaspoon Szechuan pepper	

Preheat the oven to 350°F. Melt the butter in a small saucepan over low heat. Add the oyster sauce, lemon juice, Cajun Seasoning, garlic powder, Szechuan pepper, thyme, and salt. Simmer for 2 minutes. Add the nuts and stir to coat thoroughly. Spread the nuts on a baking sheet and bake for 10 minutes, or until heated through.

Fettuccine with Lobster and Avocado
with Basil Vanilla Cream

I love the soft colors of this dish. If possible, buy saffron or other pale-colored fettucine. The vanilla enhances the Chardonnay. — R. M.

6 SERVINGS

2 live lobsters (about 2 pounds each)
1 pound thin saffron or egg fettuccine
3 tablespoons extra-virgin olive oil
3 shallots, minced
¼ cup Chardonnay
1¼ cups heavy cream
¼ vanilla bean, split in half

One 1-inch piece fresh ginger, peeled and minced
3 cups lightly packed fresh basil leaves
½ cup (1 stick) unsalted butter, in pieces
2 avocados, peeled and sliced
Fine sea salt and freshly ground black pepper, to taste

1. Blanch the lobsters in a large pot of boiling water for 3 minutes. Remove and rinse under cold water until cool. Remove the lobster meat from the shells and cut into ¼-inch slices.

2. In a fresh pot of salted boiling water, cook the pasta until al dente, 7–8 minutes or according to package instructions. Drain, transfer to a large serving bowl, and toss with 1 tablespoon of the olive oil. Set aside and keep warm.

3. Meanwhile, heat the remaining 2 tablespoons olive oil in a large skillet over medium heat until hot but not smoking. Add the lobster meat and the shallots and cook, stirring frequently, for 2 minutes, or until the shallots are softened. Transfer the lobster to a plate with tongs.

4. Add the Chardonnay, cream, and vanilla bean to the skillet and bring to a boil. Reduce the heat to low and simmer for 3 minutes. Add the ginger and basil and simmer for 1 minute more. Add the butter and lobster and stir to mix well. Add the avocados, salt, and pepper and cook, stirring, until thoroughly warmed. Remove and discard the vanilla bean. Add the sauce to the pasta, toss thoroughly, and serve.

Matters of taste must be felt, not dogmatized about. A large crayfish or lobster rearing itself menacingly on its tail seems quite at home on the sideboard of a Brighton hotel-de-luxe, but will intimidate a shy guest at a small dinner party.

KITCHEN ESSAYS,
LADY JEKYLL, 1922

HISTORICAL RECIPE:

TO MAKE VERMICELLI

Beat two or three fresh eggs quite light, make them into a stiff paste with flour, knead it well, and roll it out very thin, cut it in narrow strips, give them a twist, and dry them quickly on tin sheets. It is an excellent ingredient in most soups, particularly those that are thin. Noodles are made in the same manner, only instead of strips they should be cut in tiny squares and dried. They are also good in soups.

THE VIRGINIA HOUSEWIFE OR, METHODICAL COOK,
MARY RANDOLPH, 1824

SAFFRON RISOTTO

WITH THYME AND FRESH FIGS

We don't think there's a food in the world that's as versatile as rice.
If you've never used Arborio rice you're in for a treat. Add some thyme,
Parmesan, and figs, and serve with roast lamb or chicken.

6 SERVINGS

½ cup sugar
½ cup water
¼ cup rice vinegar
1 lemon slice
1 cinnamon stick
¾ cup fresh figs or drained
    bottled figs
¼ cup (½ stick) unsalted
    butter
1 onion, finely chopped
1 teaspoon saffron threads,
    crumbled

2 cups Arborio rice
1 cup dry white wine
6 cups chicken broth,
    simmering
1 cup freshly grated Parmesan
    cheese
1 teaspoon fresh thyme leaves,
    bruised, or ½ teaspoon
    dried thyme, crumbled
Freshly ground black pepper,
    to taste

1. Combine the sugar, water, vinegar, lemon, and cinnamon in a saucepan over medium heat. Bring to a boil, reduce the heat to low, and simmer for 5 minutes. Add the figs and simmer for 10 minutes more. Cover and let stand for 1 hour. Drain the figs, discarding the lemon and cinnamon, and coarsely chop. Set aside.

2. Melt the butter in a skillet over medium heat. Add the onion and sauté for 5 minutes, or until softened. Stir in the saffron and cook for 1 minute, stirring frequently. Add the rice and mix well to coat.

3. Add the wine and cook, stirring, until it is absorbed. Add 1 cup of the broth and cook, stirring constantly, until the broth is absorbed. Continue adding broth, ½ cup at a time, stirring constantly. As each half-cup of broth becomes absorbed, add the next half-cup, continuing to stir and cook, until the rice is tender and creamy looking, but still al dente. This should take about 30 minutes.

4. Stir in the figs, Parmesan, thyme, and pepper and cook until thoroughly heated. Serve immediately.

ARBORIO RICE

Named for the village in the humid Piedmont region of Italy where it is grown, this pearly short-grain rice has a creamy texture that makes it the best choice for risotto. Use it in desserts as well.

Fragrant Rice

with Coconut Milk and Sweet Spices

Coconut milk adds just the right amount of creaminess to balance the spices.

6 SERVINGS

- 4 cups unsweetened coconut milk
- 4 slices fresh or dried galangal or 2 slices fresh ginger
- 1 fresh lemongrass stalk or 1 teaspoon finely grated lemon zest
- 1 teaspoon salt
- ½ teaspoon freshly ground black pepper
- ½ teaspoon freshly grated nutmeg
- ½ teaspoon ground cloves
- 2 cups jasmine or long-grain rice

Combine the coconut milk, galangal, lemongrass, salt, pepper, nutmeg, and cloves in a saucepan and bring to a boil over medium heat. Stir in the rice and return to a boil. Cover, reduce the heat to low, and simmer for 12 minutes. Uncover, mix in any coconut milk that has not been absorbed, replace the lid, and cook for another 5 minutes, or until all of the liquid has been absorbed and the rice is tender. Remove the lemongrass stalk and serve.

The rice is pregnant, It swells past its old transparency. Hard, translucent worlds inside the grains open like fans. It is raining rice! The peasants stand under oiled rice paper umbrellas cheering.

FRUITS AND VEGETABLES,
ERICA JONG, 1971

ALLSPICE PILAF
LAYERED WITH PHYLLO

*Rice pilaf studded with dried apricots, dates, currants, and slivered
almonds is splendid on its own. Phyllo adds drama.*

8 SERVINGS

¾ cup slivered blanched
  almonds
¼ cup (½ stick) unsalted
  butter, plus 6 tablespoons,
  melted
1 onion, minced
1½ cups basmati rice, preferably
  Indian Dehraduni
8 dried apricots, diced small

6 dried dates, preferably
  Medjool, pitted and diced
  small
3 tablespoons dried currants
3 cups chicken broth
1 teaspoon ground allspice
½ teaspoon almond extract
Fine sea salt and freshly ground
  black pepper, to taste
7 large sheets phyllo dough,
  thawed according to
  package instructions

1. Dry-roast the almonds in a small skillet over low heat for 2–3
minutes, or until fragrant and barely colored. Set aside. Melt the ¼
cup of butter in a heavy saucepan over medium heat. Add the onion
and sauté for 5 minutes, or until soft and translucent. Add the rice
and sauté for 2 minutes, stirring constantly to mix well.

2. Stir in the apricots, dates, and currants. Add the broth, allspice,
almond extract, salt, and pepper and bring to a boil. Cover, reduce the
heat to low, and simmer for 12 minutes, or until all of the liquid has
been absorbed and the rice is tender. Keep in mind that it is better to
peek at the pilaf than to burn it. Remove from the heat and let stand
for 30 minutes. Stir the almonds into the pilaf and fluff with a fork.

3. Preheat the oven to 375°F. Brush melted butter on the bottom
and sides of a 9 x 11-inch baking dish. Fit 1 sheet of phyllo into the
baking dish, centering it so that the ends hang over the dish. Brush
with melted butter. Place 4 more sheets directly on top of the first,
brushing each with melted butter.

4. Spoon the pilaf evenly onto the phyllo. Cut the 2 remaining sheets of phyllo to exactly fit the baking dish. Place 1 sheet over the pilaf and brush with melted butter. Neatly fold all of the overhanging phyllo toward the center. Cover with the remaining sheet of phyllo and drizzle with the remaining melted butter.

5. Bake the pilaf for 30 minutes, or until the phyllo is golden brown. Let stand for 10 minutes, cut into squares with a sharp knife, and serve.

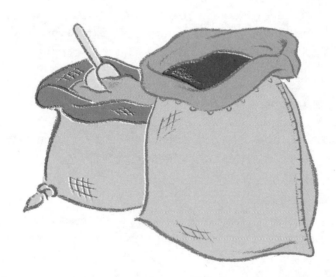

SPICED PILAF WITH CARDAMOM, FRUIT, AND NUTS
GARNISHED WITH EDIBLE SILVER

*Imagine the fuss this rice will make, with its shiny flakes of edible silver or —
if spending the entire food budget on one dish of rice is appealing — gold.*

4 SERVINGS

VARAK

Varak is gossamer-thin, beaten silver or gold that is sold in specialty Indian stores and by mail. It is used throughout India, most often at celebrations, to lavishly decorate pilafs, sweetmeats, and special dishes. Tasteless and odorless, it is perfectly safe to eat. To use, remove the top protective sheet, press the varak directly on the dish to be garnished, and gently peel away the paper. Varak will remain on the food. Store varak wrapped tightly in plastic wrap. Since it's silver, it will tarnish if left out, just like Grandma's silver candy dish.

¾ teaspoon saffron threads
3 cups plus 2 tablespoons boiling water
2 tablespoons butter ghee or 1 tablespoon olive oil plus 1 tablespoon butter
6 brown or green cardamom pods, bruised
6 cloves
1 cinnamon stick
¾ teaspoon black peppercorns

2½ cups jasmine or long-grain rice
Finely grated zest of 1 orange
1 cup fresh orange juice
1 teaspoon salt
2 tablespoons golden raisins
2 tablespoons sliced blanched almonds
2 tablespoons halved blanched pistachios
1 sheet edible silver (varak)

1. Soak the saffron in 2 tablespoons of the boiling water for 10 minutes. (Allow the remaining water to cool slightly.)

2. Heat the ghee in a heavy saucepan over medium heat. Add the cardamom, cloves, cinnamon, and peppercorns and sauté for 2 minutes, or until fragrant. Add the rice and sauté for 2 minutes, stirring constantly to mix well. Add the remaining 3 cups of hot water, the orange zest, orange juice, salt, and saffron and saffron water. Stir well and bring to a boil. Cover, reduce the heat to low, and cook for 12 minutes, or until the liquid has been absorbed and the rice is tender. Scatter the raisins over the rice, cover, and cook for 2 minutes more. Carefully spoon onto a serving plate, top with the almonds, pistachios, and edible silver, and serve.

Garnish with the cucumber and serve.

ain.
out
e.

rown

awed
eeled,
ped
2 inches
liced
thinly

return
tes, or
Remove

he garlic
r-fry for
gar and
paque.
seconds.

CURRIED RICE

"It is Extremely Filling,'" says Miss Gibbons. "It's cheap, and men love it."

Method: Fry a clove of garlic in margarine until it is brown. Then put into the pan a breakfast-cupful of cooked rice that has been washed before cooking (more rice can be used if you want more, of course) and keep on stirring it until it has absorbed the fat. Then put curry powder to taste, the pulp and seeds of three tomatoes, and a third of a cupful of currants and sultanas (well washed of course). A dash of salt, pepper and lemon-juice improves it. (You need to be careful and choice with the seasoning, or there is a risk of the dish being merely rich and sticky.)

If the average housewife is scared of garlic she can use onion. The dish goes well with a plain salad of lettuce leaves dressed sharply with vinegar and salt (but you might as well say a plain salad of gold leaf with the price lettuces can be during wartme).

A KITCHEN GOES TO WAR.
A RATION-TIME COOKERY BOOK
WITH 150 RECIPES CONTRIBUTED
BY FAMOUS PEOPLE, 1940

While I was in school in London, I became so intoxicated with the fragrance of jasmine tea that I dumped a pound of it into the bathtub and took one of the most interesting baths of my life. The hot, perfumed air and the water teeming with the seaweedlike tea created a tropical environment. Unfortunately, the old porcelain tub was very porous, and by the end of the bath both it and I were luridly green. Jasmine Tea Rice provides the same extraordinary fragrance — but without the consequences. — R. Z.

4 SERVINGS

RICE LORE

In Java, Shiva, a Hindu god, pined for the goddess Retna Dumila. She agreed to be his, but only after he created the perfect food. He failed. She died, and was buried by her grieving suitor. The perfect food grew from her tomb: rice.

2 teaspoons sesame seeds	½ pound fresh snow peas, trimmed
4 teaspoons loose jasmine tea	4 scallions (white and 2 inches of green), thinly sliced
4 cups boiling water	½ carrot, minced
2 cups jasmine rice or long-grain rice	2 tablespoons seasoned rice vinegar
½ teaspoon salt	

1. Dry-roast the sesame seeds in a small skillet over low heat for 2 minutes, or until aromatic. Set aside. Combine the tea and boiling water in a Pyrex bowl, cover, and steep for 5 minutes. Strain the tea into a saucepan. Add the rice and salt and bring to a boil over medium heat, stirring once. Cover, reduce the heat to low, and cook for 12 minutes, or until all the liquid has been absorbed and the rice is tender. Uncover and let stand until cooled.

2. Steam the snow peas in a vegetable steamer set over gently boiling water for 3 minutes, or until tender but still crisp. Rinse with cold water and cut into ¼-inch diagonal slices.

3. Combine the rice, snow peas, scallions, and carrot in a large serving bowl and mix well. Drizzle with the vinegar and toss to coat. Sprinkle with the sesame seeds and serve.

SALADS

ASSORTED SALAD GREENS
WITH GINGER AND SOY DRESSING
*Pick your salad greens, as at a salad bar,
and add this wonderfully pungent dressing.*

6 SERVINGS

VEGETABLES
(choose 3 of the following):
- 1 romaine lettuce head, leaves separated, washed, and dried
- 1 watercress bunch, stemmed, washed, and dried
- 4 tomatoes, each cut into 6 wedges
- 1 cucumber, peeled, halved lengthwise, seeded, and sliced
- 2 arugula bunches, stemmed, washed, and dried
- 3 endive heads, trimmed and cut into ¼-inch rounds

DRESSING:
- ½ small onion, finely chopped
- One 1½-inch piece ginger, peeled and chopped
- ⅓ cup peanut oil
- 2 tablespoons rice vinegar
- 2 tablespoons water
- 1½ tablespoons chopped celery
- 1½ tablespoons soy sauce
- 1 teaspoon fresh lemon juice
- 1 teaspoon tomato paste

Combine all the vegetables in a large salad bowl. Combine all the dressing ingredients in a food processor and process until smooth. Pour the dressing over the salad, toss, and serve.

*Lettuce is divine, although I'm
not sure it's really a food.*

DIANA VREELAND

HISTORICAL RECIPE:
SALAT

Parsley, sage, garlic, chibolls [small onions], onons, leek, borage, mint, porrette [greens], fennel and cresses, rue, rosemary, purslene. Lave and wash them clean, pick them, pluck them small with thine hand and mingle them well with raw oil, lay on vinegar and salt and serve it forth.

THE FORME OF CURY [COOKERY],
WRITTEN IN 1390,
EDITED BY SAMUEL PEGGE, LONDON, 1780

VARIATION

You can use any leftover dressing to top nachos, dip corn chips, or stir into chili. You may want to add some sour cream to tone it down.

I made a new dressing with olive oil, eggs, capers, anchovies, garlic, and Quatre Épices to go with the fennel. And did a new shrimp pâté of chopped shrimp added to whipped butter, with mace, Pernod and parsley. . . . Good food is so sexy in its way.

LOVE & KISSES & A HALO OF TRUFFLES:
LETTERS TO HELEN EVANS BROWN,
JAMES BEARD, 1994

CAESAR SALAD
WITH CHIPOTLE CHILE DRESSING

Don't think of this as an improvement on Caesar salad. A classic Caesar salad is perfect just the way it is. This is an alternative to Caesar salad, when your meal requires more robust flavor.

6 SERVINGS

¼ cup unsalted butter
3 garlic cloves, 1 sliced, 2 minced
1 cup sourdough bread cubes (¾-inch cubes)
1 canned chipotle chile in adobo sauce
1 tablespoon pomegranate molasses or honey
1 tablespoon balsamic vinegar
1 tablespoon fresh lime juice

1 tablespoon Dijon mustard
3 anchovy fillets
1 scallion (white and 2 inches of green), finely minced
½ cup corn oil
¼ cup extra-virgin olive oil
2 romaine lettuce heads, torn into bite-size pieces
Freshly grated Parmesan cheese, to taste

1. Melt the butter in a skillet over moderate heat. Add the sliced garlic and sauté for 2 minutes, or until fragrant. Add the bread cubes and sauté, stirring and tossing frequently, for 5 minutes, or until golden brown. Drain the croutons on paper towels and set aside.

2. In a food processor, combine the minced garlic, the chile, pomegranate molasses, vinegar, lime juice, mustard, anchovies, and scallions. Process until pureed. With the motor running, gradually drizzle in both oils.

3. Toss the lettuce in a large serving bowl with enough dressing to coat. Add the croutons and toss again. Sprinkle with the Parmesan and serve.

Burmese Ginger and Cabbage Salad

with Coconut and Sesame Seeds

When I owned Adriana's Bazaar, one of the dishes sold daily was this astonishing salad supplied by Irene Khin Wong from her restaurant, Road to Mandalay. Find young ginger if at all possible, and note that it needs to soak for 3 days to mellow the ginger bite. – R. Z.

6 SERVINGS

½ pound fresh young ginger, peeled and julienned
1½ cups fresh lemon juice
½ cup yellow split peas
1 cup corn oil
½ cup shredded fresh coconut
12 large garlic cloves, thinly sliced
½ cup chickpea flour (besan)

½ cup sesame seeds
2 cups thinly shredded cabbage
½ cup halved roasted peanuts
6 tablespoons Thai fish sauce (nam pla), preferably Tiparos
¼ cup peanut oil

1. Combine the ginger and lemon juice in a glass bowl, cover, and refrigerate for 3 days to soften the ginger and mellow the flavor.

2. Soak the split peas in cold water to cover for 6 hours; drain and set aside.

3. Drain the ginger, squeeze out the lemon juice, and set aside. Heat the corn oil in a wok or skillet over low heat. Add the split peas and cook for 1 minute. Remove with a sieve or slotted spoon, drain on paper towels, and set aside. Add the coconut to the oil and cook for 1 minute. Remove with a sieve or slotted spoon, drain on paper towels, and set aside. Add the garlic to the oil and cook for 5 minutes, or until lightly browned. Remove with a sieve or slotted spoon, drain on paper towels, and set aside. Discard the corn oil in the skillet.

4. Dry-roast the chickpea flour and sesame seeds in a small skillet over medium heat for 1 minute. Transfer to a small bowl.

5. Combine the ginger, split peas, coconut, garlic, chickpea flour and sesame seeds, cabbage, peanuts, fish sauce, and peanut oil in a large serving bowl. Toss well and serve.

VARIATION

For a zingy appetizer, enclose ½-cup portions in Vietnamese rice paper wrappers.

CHICKPEA FLOUR

Also called besan, or gram flour, chickpea flour is made from dried chickpeas. It is used extensively in Indian vegetarian cooking to make batter, pastry, dumplings, and noodles. It is available at Indian specialty stores and by mail.

Anise-Flavored Beet and Onion Salad

with Pink Peppercorn Mayonnaise

If you like your food to be color coordinated, then this salad's for you.

4 SERVINGS

2 medium fresh beets, stems trimmed

6 tablespoons extra-virgin olive oil

3 tablespoons red wine vinegar

Salt and freshly ground white pepper, to taste

½ medium red onion, thinly sliced, each slice quartered

1 teaspoon crushed anise seeds

Pink Peppercorn Mayonnaise (recipe follows)

1 tablespoon pink peppercorns, for garnish

1. Place the beets in a large saucepan, add water to cover, and bring to a boil. Reduce the heat to low and simmer, covered, for 1 hour, or until tender. Drain, cool, peel, and cut into ½-inch slices. Quarter each slice.

2. Combine the olive oil, vinegar, salt, and white pepper in a large bowl and mix well. Add the beets, onion, and anise seeds and toss gently.

3. Pour the Pink Peppercorn Mayonnaise into a plastic mustard dispenser and squiggle a design on each of 4 plates. Top with salad, squirt more mayonnaise on top, and garnish with the pink peppercorns. Serve.

PINK PEPPERCORN MAYONNAISE

1 CUP

1 cup homemade or prepared mayonnaise

1 tablespoon tomato paste

1 tablespoon pink peppercorns

Combine the mayonnaise, tomato paste, and pink peppercorns in a processor and process until well mixed.

You English are even worse; after washing the salad heaven knows how, you put the vinegar in the dish first, and enough of that for a footbath for Morgante, and serve it up, unstirred, with neither oil nor salt, which you are supposed to add at table. By this time some of the leaves are so saturated with vinegar that they cannot take the oil, while the rest are quite naked and fit only for chicken food.

THE FRUIT, HERBS, AND VEGETABLES OF ITALY, GIACOMO CASTELVETRO, TRANSLATED BY GILLIAN RILEY, 1989

DEVILISHLY HOT FRUIT SALAD

Serve this adult fruit salad with curries, in place of chutney, or with traditional desserts, like melon or ice cream, to wake them up. We've included our favorite fruits and vegetables; feel free to choose your favorites, altering the recipe based on what you like and availability.

6 SERVINGS

FRUIT
(choose 4 of the following):
- 1 banana, sliced
- 1 small cantaloupe, cubed
- 1 small cucumber, seeded and thinly sliced
- 1 small honeydew melon, cubed
- ½ jicama, thinly sliced
- 1 cup fresh, shelled litchis or drained canned litchis
- 1 mango, peeled, pitted, and sliced
- 1 small ripe papaya, cubed
- 1 Asian pear, cubed
- 1 Fuyu persimmon, cubed
- ½ fresh pineapple, skinned, cored, and cubed
- 1 starfruit (carambola), thinly sliced

DRESSING:
- ¼ cup dry-roasted peanuts
- 1 fresh hot red chili pepper, seeded and sliced
- One 1-inch piece fresh ginger, peeled and sliced
- ½ cup palm sugar or packed brown sugar
- ¼ cup fresh orange juice
- 1 tablespoon tamarind concentrate or pulp
- 1 tablespoon fresh lime juice
- 1 tablespoon rice vinegar
- Mint leaves, for garnish

Combine all the fruit in a large bowl. Place the peanuts in a food processor and process until finely chopped. Add the chili, ginger, sugar, orange juice, and tamarind and process until well mixed. Add the lime juice and vinegar and pulse. Pour the dressing over the fruit and toss to blend. Garnish with mint leaves and serve.

JICAMA

Sometime referred to as the Mexican potato, *jicama* is a large root vegetable, eaten raw or cooked, with a crunchy texture and a nutty flavor. You can find it in Mexican markets and most large supermarkets.

LITCHIS

Native to Southeast Asia, the *litchi* is one of China's most cherished fruits. About the size of a walnut, it has a thin, dark, red shell protecting a luscious, sweet, white fruit, and is available in the summer wherever exotic produce is sold. Canned and dried litchis are available year-round in Chinese specialty stores and by mail.

FUYU PERSIMMON

The Fuyu persimmon looks like a tangerine-colored tomato. The fruit is sweet, with a firm, crunchy, applelike texture even when ripe. Persimmons are available in the winter and spring months at exotic produce stores.

To Citizeness Boilleau, Rue
Révolutionnaire, former Saint-
Louis, at Paris, this 4 Floréal

My dear friend,
I beg you to do your utmost to
bring a well-seasoned lettuce
salad or rather the materials for
making one, we have bowls; but
try to make sure that it is fresh
and in good condition. If you
have no money, try to get hold of
some for this advance. As I am
writing to you by the small post,
I don't want to send it to you, but
I shall get it to you later. Don't
forget the oil and vinegar. If you
cannot get money to do this, take
the trouble to come and see me
and I shall give you what you
need to buy what is necessary.
We have salt, but bring a little
pepper. Try to do this for us
today, if at all possible, I shall be
very obliged to you, and bring as
much oil as you can. I shall
be very obliged to you and
embrace you with all my heart
Your husband Boilleau.

LAST LETTERS: PRISONS AND PRISONERS
OF THE FRENCH REVOLUTION, 1793–4,
OLIVIER BLANC, ED.,
TRANSLATED BY ALAN SHERIDAN, 1987

FLAGEOLET SALAD
WITH OLIVES, CAPERS, AND FRESH BASIL

Celebrate the herbs and flavors of Tuscany with this piquant salad.
Flageolets, delicate pale green kidney beans from Brittany and central
France, are seldom sold fresh, but can usually be found canned or dried in
specialty food shops. Dried beans require soaking overnight.

4 SERVINGS

1½ cups dried flageolets
2 cups chicken broth
½ cup chopped pitted black olives
½ cup chopped drained canned artichoke hearts
2 tablespoons capers
1 tablespoon finely chopped fresh parsley
⅓ cup extra-virgin olive oil

2 tablespoons white wine vinegar
2 garlic cloves, minced
2 tablespoons chopped fresh basil
Salt and freshly ground black pepper, to taste
Thinly shaved Parmigiano-Reggiano cheese, for garnish

1. Rinse the flageolets, place in a large bowl with 6 cups of water, and soak overnight.

2. Drain the beans, rinse well, and place in a large saucepan. Cover with 8 cups of water and the chicken broth. Bring to a boil over medium heat, reduce the heat to low, and simmer, partially covered, for 1½ hours, or until the beans are tender but not mushy. Drain.

3. Combine the flageolets with the olives, artichokes, capers, and parsley in a large serving bowl. In a small bowl, combine the olive oil, vinegar, garlic, basil, salt, and pepper. Whisk to blend well, pour over the beans, and toss to combine. Garnish with the Parmesan shavings and serve.

BEEF SALAD
WITH SUMAC AND LEMONGRASS

*Although this tart and tangy salad can be created in the kitchen,
in the summer it's nice to grill the beef on the barbecue.*

4 SERVINGS

2 teaspoons safflower oil
1 pound lean boneless beef
   sirloin
3 fresh lemongrass stalks
½ cup fresh lime juice
2 tablespoons Thai fish sauce
   (nam pla), preferably
   Tiparos
1 fresh red Thai chili pepper,
   seeded and chopped
4 garlic cloves, minced
½ teaspoon ground sumac

1 small red onion, very thinly
   sliced
½ cup finely chopped fresh
   Thai basil or basil
4 scallions (white and 2 inches
   of green), thinly sliced
1 seedless cucumber, diced
   small
Freshly cracked black pepper,
   to taste
Mint leaves, for garnish

1. Heat the oil in a skillet over medium heat until hot but not
smoking. Add the beef and cook, turning, for about 16 minutes, or
until well browned all over and medium rare in the center. Slit with a
knife to check the center. Allow to cool. Cut the beef across the grain
into thin slices and place in a large bowl.

2. Remove and discard the outer leaves and upper half of the lemongrass stalks. Coarsely chop the bottom half. In a food processor, combine the lemongrass, lime juice, fish sauce, chili, garlic, and sumac.
Process until well blended. Add the red onion, stir to mix, and add to
the beef.

3. Add the basil, scallions, cucumber, and black pepper and toss to
mix well. Garnish with mint leaves and serve.

*A cucumber should be well
sliced, and dressed with pepper
and vinegar, and then thrown
out, as good for nothing.*

SAMUEL JOHNSON

Stir-Fried Chicken Salad

with Black Mushrooms

This lively stir-fried salad works equally well for parties and picnics.

6 SERVINGS

Chicken salad has a certain glamour about it. Like the little black dress, it is chic and adaptable anywhere.

LAURIE COLWIN

1 cup dried Chinese black mushrooms
3 endive heads
6 scallions
1 cucumber, peeled
3 skinless boneless chicken breasts (about ½ pound each)
3 cups chicken broth
1 teaspoon chili oil
1 small fresh red chili pepper, seeded and halved
One 2-inch piece fresh ginger, peeled and sliced

2 tablespoons roasted sesame oil
4 garlic cloves, minced
¾ cup peanuts, chopped
3 tablespoons sesame seeds
1 teaspoon ground Szechuan pepper
1 cup drained canned straw mushrooms
2 tablespoons soy sauce
¼ cup peanut oil
2 tablespoons rice vinegar
1 bunch fresh coriander, stemmed and chopped, for garnish

1. Soak the black mushrooms in hot water to cover for 20 minutes, or until soft. Drain, press out the water, and trim and discard any tough stems. Slice into thin strips and set aside.

2. Cut off the bases of the endive heads, cut in half lengthwise, and then cut into ⅛-inch slices. Cut the scallion bulbs into thin rounds and the greens into ⅛-inch slices, the same size as the endive. Cut the cucumber in quarters, then into ⅛-inch slices, the same size as the endive. With your knife parallel to the working surface, cut each chicken breast in half. Then cut into ¼-inch strips, no more than 2 inches long.

3. Combine the broth, chili oil, chili, and ginger in a wok or skillet over medium heat. Bring to a boil, reduce the heat to low, and simmer for 5 minutes. Add the chicken and cook, stirring constantly, for 2 minutes, or until cooked through. Transfer the chicken with a slotted spoon to a bowl and transfer the cooking liquid to another bowl; allow to cool. Dry the wok. Remove the ginger from the cooking liquid and julienne.

4. Heat the roasted sesame oil in the wok over medium heat until hot but not smoking. Add the garlic and stir-fry for 1 minute, or until barely browned. Add the peanuts and stir-fry for 1 minute, or until barely browned. Add the sesame seeds and stir-fry for 30 seconds, or until barely browned. Add the black mushrooms, julienned ginger, and Szechuan pepper and stir to mix. Stir in the straw mushrooms. Add the soy sauce and ¼ cup of the reserved cooking liquid. Stir-fry for 4–5 minutes, or until the liquid is almost completely evaporated. Add the scallion greens and whites and stir-fry for 2 minutes more, or until wilted. Add the endive and cucumber and stir-fry for 30 seconds. Remove from the heat.

5. Stir in the chicken, another ¼ cup of reserved cooking liquid, the peanut oil, and the rice vinegar. Stir to mix well. Allow to cool, garnish with coriander leaves, and serve.

Some great Master having given us Rules in that Art so strangely odd and fantastical, that 'tis hard to say, whether the Reading has given more Sport and Diversion, or the Practice more Vexation and Chagrin, in spoiling us many a good Dish, by following their directions. But so it is, that a Poor Woman must be laugh'd at for only sugaring a Mess of Beans; whilst a Great Name must be had in Admiration, for Contriving Relishes a thousand times more Distasteful to the palate.

COLLECTION OF SOME
THREE HUNDRED RECEIPTS,
MARY KETTILBY, 1728

Squid and Black Bean Salad

with Chorizo and Fresh Coriander

*Once again the "shall we soak or shall we cheat?"
dilemma raises its ugly head. There is no question that dried beans
are better than canned beans. The question is: How much better?
The ideal solution would be to try it both ways, and then make an
educated decision for subsequent offerings of this dish.*

6 SERVINGS

1½ cups dried black beans or
   canned black beans
1 pound cleaned squid, cut
   into rings
1 onion, peeled
2 tablespoons sherry vinegar
¼ cup chopped fresh coriander
   leaves, stems reserved
Salt and freshly ground black
   pepper, to taste
4 tablespoons olive oil

3 chorizos, cases removed and
   discarded, sausage
   crumbled
8 scallions (white and 2 inches
   of green), finely chopped
2 red, yellow, or orange bell
   peppers, stemmed, seeded,
   and chopped
1 tablespoon lemon juice
1½ teaspoons ground cumin
¼ teaspoon ground cayenne
   pepper

1. Wash and rinse the dried beans. Soak overnight in cold water
to cover.

2. Drain and rinse the beans, place in a saucepan with water to
cover, and bring to a simmer. Reduce the heat to low and cook, partially covered, for 1 hour, or until tender but not mushy. Drain and
set aside. If using canned beans, drain, rinse, and set aside.

3. Combine the squid, whole onion, vinegar, reserved coriander
stems, salt, and pepper in a saucepan and add water to cover. Bring to
a boil over medium heat, reduce the heat to low, and simmer for 25
minutes, or until the squid is tender. Leave the squid in the stock to
cool. Transfer the squid to a large bowl with a slotted spoon.

4. Heat 1 tablespoon of the olive oil in a skillet over medium heat until hot but not smoking. Add the chorizos and sauté, turning frequently, for 10 minutes, or until no longer pink. Remove the chorizos with a slotted spoon, drain, and set aside.

5. Add the black beans, chorizos, scallions, and bell peppers to the squid. Whisk the remaining 3 tablespoons of olive oil, the lemon juice, cumin, and cayenne pepper in a small bowl. Add to the squid mixture and toss to mix well. Garnish with the coriander leaves and serve.

The kitchen, reasonably enough, was the scene of my first gastronomic adventure. I was on all fours. I crawled into the vegetable bin, settled on a giant onion, and ate it, skin and all. It must have marked me for life, for I have never ceased to love the hearty flavor of raw onions.

JAMES BEARD

Desserts and Beverages

Baked Asian Pears
with Nutmeg Crème Brûlée

My first really exotic cooking utensil was an electric salamander, used exclusively to melt brown sugar on crème brûlée. One episode ended badly when the salamander heated the wrought-iron trivet and the trivet proceeded to burn a hole in the kitchen table. Now I use a propane torch for our crème brûlée, and I am much happier. – R. Z.

4 SERVINGS

4 large Asian pears or baking apples
1 tablespoon unsalted butter
½ cup water
½ cup dark brown sugar
2 cups heavy cream

2 tablespoons granulated sugar
4 large egg yolks
1 teaspoon vanilla extract
½ teaspoon ground nutmeg
Pinch salt

1. Preheat the oven to 350°F. Core the pears, keeping the bottoms intact, and pare a 1-inch strip from around each top. Butter a baking dish large enough to hold the pears, and place the pears in it.

2. Bring the water to a boil and add ¼ cup of the brown sugar, stirring until the sugar has dissolved. Pour the sugar water over the pears and bake, uncovered and basting occasionally, for 30 minutes, or until the pears are tender and their skins begin to crack. Allow to cool.

3. Reduce the oven temperature to 275°F. Heat the heavy cream in the top of a double boiler over simmering water, add the granulated sugar, and stir until dissolved. Do not allow the cream to boil. Beat the egg yolks in a medium bowl and add the vanilla, nutmeg, and salt. Stir in the hot cream. Pour the mixture into a 9 x 4-inch loaf pan. Place the pan in a larger baking dish and pour boiling water around it to a depth of 1½ inches.

4. Bake the custard for 1 hour, or until set. Allow to cool slightly. Fill the pears with custard, reserving the leftover custard. Sprinkle with the remaining brown sugar. Melt the sugar with a propane torch or salamander, or under a hot broiler. Cool slightly, put out all the fires, and serve with the remaining custard.

HOT AND SPICY ICE CREAM

If you like spicy food and adore ice cream, satisfy both your cravings here.

1 QUART

1½ cups heavy cream	½ teaspoon freshly grated
½ cup milk	nutmeg
1 teaspoon ground cinnamon	¼ teaspoon ground cayenne
1 teaspoon ground ginger	pepper
½ teaspoon ground cardamom	¾ cup sugar
	6 egg yolks, beaten

1. Combine the cream, milk, spices, and half of the sugar in a saucepan over medium heat. Mix well, bring to a boil, and remove from heat. Stir the remaining sugar into the yolks.

2. Add the cream mixture in a stream to the egg yolk mixture, stirring constantly, and pour the mixture back into the saucepan. Cook over low heat, stirring constantly, until the mixture coats the back of a spoon. Cool, pour into an ice cream maker, and freeze according to the manufacturer's directions.

HISTORICAL RECIPE:

Pare, stone, and scald twelve ripe Apricots, beat them fine in a Marble Mortar, put to them six Ounces of double refined Sugar, a Pint of scalding Cream. Work it through a Hair Sieve, then put it into a Tin which has a close Cover, set it in a Tub of Ice broken small, and a large quantity of Salt put amongst it. When you see your Cream grow thick around the Edges of your Tin, stir it and set it in again 'till it all grows quite thick

When your Cream is all froze up, take it out of your Tin, and put it in the Mould you intend it to get turned out of. Then put on the Lid, and have ready another Tub with Ice and Salt in as before. Put your Mould in the Middle, and lay your Ice under and over it. Let it stand for five Hours. Dip your Tin in warm Water when you turn it out. If it be Summer, you must not turn it out 'till the Moment you want it.

You may use any Sort of Fruit if you have not Apricots, only observe to work it fine.

*THE EXPERIENCED ENGLISH HOUSE-KEEPER,
FOR THE USE AND EASE OF LADIES,
HOUSE-KEEPERS, COOKS, & C.
WROTE PURELY FROM PRACTICE,*
ELIZABETH RAFFALD, 1769

Jamaican Gingerbread

A touch of cayenne adds an element of surprise.
Serve this Caribbean specialty for dessert, or as a side dish,
or maybe even as a main course — only kidding.

8 SERVINGS

½ cup (1 stick) unsalted butter, softened
¾ cup molasses
½ cup packed dark brown sugar
3 large eggs
½ cup sour cream
1 tablespoon finely grated lemon zest
1 teaspoon vanilla extract
2 cups all-purpose flour
1 teaspoon baking soda

1½ teaspoons ground cinnamon
¾ teaspoon ground allspice
½ teaspoon salt
¼ teaspoon ground cayenne pepper
¼ teaspoon ground cloves
¼ teaspoon freshly grated nutmeg
One 2-inch piece fresh ginger, peeled and minced
2 tablespoons finely chopped crystallized ginger

1. Butter a 9 x 4-inch loaf pan with 1 tablespoon of the butter. Line the bottom of the pan with a piece of parchment or waxed paper and butter the paper. Dust the pan with flour, shaking out the excess. Preheat the oven to 350°F.

2. Combine the remaining 7 tablespoons of butter, the molasses, and the sugar in a large bowl and mix with an electric mixer until smooth. Add the eggs one at a time, mixing constantly. Add the sour cream, lemon zest, and vanilla and mix well.

3. Sift together the flour, baking soda, cinnamon, allspice, salt, cayenne, cloves, and nutmeg in a medium bowl. Stir the dry ingredients into the batter. Add the fresh ginger and crystallized ginger and mix well. Spoon the batter into the prepared pan and bake for 50 minutes, or until a cake tester inserted in the center comes out clean. Remove from the oven and let stand on a wire rack for 15 minutes. Remove from the pan, peel off the paper, and cool. Cut into slices and serve.

CHAI

At sunrise, in India, the ritual brewing of Chai —
a soothing blend of exotic spices, black tea, and milk — begins,
just as it has every day for the last 5,000 years.

4 SERVINGS

4 cups water	8 cloves
1 cinnamon stick	1 teaspoon coriander seeds
One 1-inch piece ginger,	4 teaspoons black tea leaves
peeled and cut into 4 slices	1 cup milk
12 green cardamom pods	Honey, to taste
8 allspice berries	

Combine the water, cinnamon, ginger, cardamom, allspice, cloves, and coriander seeds in a saucepan over medium heat and bring to a boil. Reduce the heat to low, cover, and simmer for 20 minutes. Add the tea and milk and simmer for 3 more minutes. Sweeten with honey, strain through a fine sieve, and serve.

CARIBBEAN SORREL DRINK

Made from sepals of the hibiscus flower,
sorrel is a traditional Christmas drink in Trinidad.

2 QUARTS

2 cups sugar	2 cinnamon sticks
2 tablespoons dried Carribean	1 teaspoon cloves
sorrel	2 quarts boiling water
One 3 x 1-inch piece dried	½ cup medium dark rum
orange peel	

Combine the sugar, sorrel, orange peel, cinnamon, and cloves in a large jar and pour the boiling water over them. Cool, cover loosely, and leave for 3 days at room temperature. Add the rum, strain through a sieve lined with cheesecloth, and serve.

Sometimes they brought him [Montezuma] in cups of pure gold a drink made from the cocoa-plant, which they said he took before visiting his wives. We did not take much notice of this at the time though I saw them bring in a good fifty large jugs of this chocolate, all frothed up, of which he would drink a little.

THE CONQUEST OF NEW SPAIN,
BERNAL DÍAZ,
TRANSLATED BY J. M. COHEN, 1963

I feel the end approaching. Quick, bring me my dessert, coffee, and liqueur.

JEAN-ANTHELME BRILLAT SAVARIN

RAS EL HANOUT
FOR COFFEE

Peppery and sweet spices add a warm, mysterious flavor to coffee. This Ras el Hanout is milder than the blends used for cooking, but is still pungent.

ABOUT ⅓ CUP

4 teaspoons freshly grated nutmeg
1 tablespoon ground ginger
1 tablespoon sesame seeds
2 teaspoons green cardamom pods
2 teaspoons dried rosebuds
1 teaspoon anise seeds
1 teaspoon ground cinnamon

1 teaspoon whole cloves
1 teaspoon fennel seeds
2 slices dried galangal
¾ teaspoon pink peppercorns
½ teaspoon allspice berries
½ teaspoon dried lavender flowers
½ teaspoon ground mace

Grind all the spices in a spice grinder or blender. Sift and store in a tightly sealed glass jar. Add a pinch of the Ras el Hanout for each tablespoon of ground coffee and brew the coffee as usual.

SPICED GINGER BEER

Another great Caribbean-inspired drink is ginger beer.

5 QUARTS

½ pound fresh ginger, peeled and grated
2 limes, thinly sliced
2 tablespoons cream of tartar

4 cups sugar
5 quarts water
1 tablespoon dried yeast

Combine the ginger, lime, cream of tartar, and sugar in a large jar. Warm 1 cup of the water and pour over the yeast. Set aside. Boil the remaining water and pour over the ginger mixture. Let cool to luke-warm. Whisk the yeast and stir into the ginger mixture. Cover and let stand for 2 days. Strain and bottle. The ginger beer will keep for up to 1 week in the refrigerator.

SOURCES

ADRIANA'S CARAVAN

Free mail-order catalog of over 1,500 spices,
condiments, and exotic ingredients from
every corner of the world
409 Vanderbilt Street, Brooklyn, NY 11218,
(800) 316-0820; in New York (718) 436-8565;
fax (718) 436-8565 #96; e-mail Adriana@AOL.com

BALDUCCI'S

Large gourmet shop of very high-quality fruits, vegetables, and meats, with emphasis on Italian products
424 Sixth Avenue, New York, NY 10011,
(212)673-2600 or (800) 225-3822

BANGKOK MARKET

A small, crowded store specializing in
Southeast Asian condiments
106 Mosco Street, New York, NY 10013,
(212) 349-1979

DEAN & DELUCA

Chic food emporium and mail-order catalog
560 Broadway, New York, NY 10012, (800) 221-7714;
in New York (212) 431-1619

FRIEDA'S BY MAIL

Fresh exotic produce
P.O. Box 58488, Los Angeles, CA 90058,
(213) 627-2981

KATAGIRI & COMPANY

Specialists in Japanese condiments
224 East 59th Street, New York, NY 10022,
(212) 755-3566

KALUSTYAN

An international grocery with
emphasis on Indian products
123 Lexington Avenue,
New York, NY 10016, (212) 685-3451

KAM KUO FOOD CORPORATION

Asian supermarket with large selection of
Chinese and Japanese condiments
7 Mott Street, New York, NY 10013, (212) 571-0330

MO'HOTTA, MO'BETTA

Nothing but hot stuff, by mail, to torture your palate
P.O. Box 4136, San Luis Obispo, CA 93403,
(800) 462-3220

PENZEYS, LTD.

A family-owned spice company famous
for its carefully mixed custom blends
P. O. Box 1448, Waukesha, WI 53187,
(414) 574-0277

RAFAL SPICE COMPANY

A large selection of spices and blends.
2521 Russell Street, Detroit, MI 48207,
(800) 228-4276; in Michigan (313) 259-6373

SAHADI IMPORTING COMPANY, INC.

A wonderful family-owned business specializing
in Middle Eastern spices and condiments
187 Atlantic Avenue, Brooklyn, NY 11201,
(718) 624-4550

BIBLIOGRAPHY AND SUGGESTED READING

American Trade Association. *A Treasury of Spices*. Baltimore: Pridemark Press, 1956.

Apicius, Marcus Garvius. *The Roman Cookery of Apicius*. Translated and Adapted for the Modern Kitchen by John Edwards. Emmaus: Rodale Press, 1984.

Beard, James. *Love & Kisses & a Halo of Truffles: Letters to Helen Evans Brown*. Edited by John Ferrone. New York: Arcade, 1994.

Beston, Henry R. *Herbs & the Earth*. Boston: David R. Godine, 1990.

Black, Maggie. *The Medieval Cookbook*. New York: Thames and Hudson, 1993. Published by arrangement with the British Museum Press.

Brears, Peter, Maggie Black, Gill Corbishley, Jennifer Renfrew, and Jennifer Stead. *A Taste of History: 10,000 Years of Food in Britain*. London: British Museum Press, 1993.

Clarkson, Rosetta E. *Magic Gardens*. New York: Macmillan, Collier Books, 1939.

Cosman, Madeleine Pelner. *Fabulous Feasts*. New York: George Braziller, 1976.

Del Conte, Anna. *Gastronomy of Italy*. New York: Prentice Hall, 1988.

Farmer, Fannie Merritt. *The Original Boston Cooking School Cook Book,* 1896. Reprint, New York: The New American Library, 1974.

Freeman, Margaret B. *Herbs for the Mediaeval Household*. 1943. Reprint, New York: The Metropolitan Museum of Art, 1979.

Garland, Sarah. *The Complete Book of Herbs & Spices,* 1979. London: Frances Lincoln, 1989.

Gerard, John. *The Herbal or General History of Plants*. Reprint of the complete 1633 edition as revised and enlarged by Thomas Johnson. New York: Dover, 1975.

Grieve, Mrs. M. *A Modern Herbal*. 1931. Reprint, New York: Dover, 1971.

Hale, William Harlan, and the editors of *Horizon Magazine. The Horizon Cookbook*. New York: American Heritage, 1968.

Herbst, Sharon Tyler. *Food Lover's Companion*. Hauppauge, NY: Barron's Educational Series, 1990.

Lincoln, Mrs. D. A. *Mrs. Lincoln's Boston Cook Book,* 1884. Reprint, Mineola, NY: Dover, 1993.

Makay, Ian, ed. *Food for Thought*. Freedom, CA: The Crossing Press, 1995.

Norman, Jill. *The Complete Book of Spices*. New York: Viking Studio, 1995.

Ortiz, Elisabeth Lambert. *The Encyclopedia of Herbs, Spices, & Flavorings*. New York: Dorling Kindersley, 1994.

Oster, Maggie, and Sal Gilbertie. *The Herbal Palate Cookbook*. Pownal, VT: Storey Communications, 1996.

Oster, Maggie. *Herbal Vinegar*. Pownal, VT: Storey Communications, 1995.

Passmore, Jacki. *The Encyclopedia of Asian Food and Cooking*. New York: William Morrow, 1991.

Peterson, T. Sarah. *Acquired Taste*. Ithaca, NY: Cornell University Press, 1994.

Randolph, Mary. *The Virginia Housewife Or, Methodical Cook,* 1824. New York: Dover, 1993.

Robbins, Maria Polushkin, ed. *A Cook's Alphabet of Quotations*. New York: Penguin Group, 1991.

Rosengarten, F. Jr. *The Book of Spices*. Wynwood: Livingston Publishing Co., 1969.

Shapiro, Anna. *A Feast of Words*. New York: W. W. Norton, 1996.

Skelly, Carole J. *Dictionary of Herbs, Spices, Seasonings, and Natural Flavorings*. New York: Garland Publishing, 1994.

Spencer, Colin, and Claire Clifton, eds. *The Faber Book of Food*. London: Faber and Faber, 1993.

Stobart, Tom. *Herbs, Spices, and Flavorings*. Woodstock, NY: The Overlook Press, 1982.

Swahn, J. O. *The Lore of Spices*. New York: Crescent Books, 1995.

Tannahill, Reay. *Food in History*. New York: Crown Publishers, 1995.

Toussaint-Samat, Maguelonne. *The History of Food, 1987*. Translated from the French by Anthea Bell. Cambridge, MA: Blackwell Publishers, 1992.

Trager, James. *The Food Chronology*. New York: Henry Holt, 1995.

Von Welanetz, Diana & Paul. *The Von Welanetz Guide to Ethnic Ingredients*. New York: Warner Books, 1987.

Whitman, Joan, and Dolores Simon. *Recipes into Type*. New York: HarperCollins, 1993.

Wolfe, Linda. *The Literary Gourmet*. New York: Simon & Schuster, 1989.

HISTORICAL COOKBOOKS

14 A.D. *Of Culinary Matters* (De Re Coquinaria), by Marcus Garvius Apicius

1226 *Baghdad Cookery Book,* by Muhammad ibn al-Hasam ibn Muhammad ibn al-Karim al Katib al-Baghdadi

1375 *Le Viandier,* by Guillaume Tirel aka Taillevent

1392 *The Goodman of Paris* (Le Ménagier de Paris)

1467 *A Noble Boke of Cookry for a Prynce Houssolde or Eny Other Estately Houssolde*

1485 *Master of the Kitchen,* printed anonymously at Nuremberg

1587 *The Good Huswife's Jewell,* by Thomas Dawson

1651 *Le Cuisiner Francais,* by Franç Pierre de la Varenne

1660 *The Accomplisht Cook, or, The Art and Mystery of Cooking. Wherein the Whole Art is Revealed in a More Easie and More Perfect Method, Than Hath Been Publist in Any Language,* by Robert May

1680 *Acetaria, a book about Sallets ,* by John Evelyn

1742 *The Compleat Housewife, or, Accomplish'd Gentlewoman's Companion,* by Elizabeth Smith

1747 *The Art of Cookery Made Plain & Easy,* by Mrs. Hannah Glasse

1759 *A Complete System of Cookery,* by William Verral

1792 *New Art of Cookery,* by Richard Briggs

1796 *American Cookery, or the Art of Dressing Viands, Fish, Poultry, and Vegetables, and the Best Modes of Making Pastes, Puffs, Pies, Tarts, Puddings, Custards, & Preserves, and all Kinds of Cakes, from the imperial Plumb to plain Cake adapted to This Country & All Grades of Life,* by Amelia Simmons, An American Orphan.

1804 *The Very Newest Cookbook for Meat and Fast Days by Maria Anna Busswald, Former Cook of Her Excellency Rosalia, Countess von Attems.*

1814 *L'Art du Cuisinier,* by Beauvilliers

1824 *The Virginia Housewife Or, Methodical Cook,* by Mary Randolph

1825 *Physiology of Taste* (Physilogie du Gaîby) by Jean-Anthelme Brillat-Savarin

1828 *The French Cook,* by Louis Eustache Ude

1832 *The Frugal Housewife, Dedicated to Those Who Are Not Ashamed of Economy,* by Lydia Maria Child

1838 *The Housekeeper's Guide or a Plain and Practical System of Domestic Cookery,* by Esther Copley

1845 *Modern Cookery In All Its Branches Reduced to a System of Easy Practice for the Use of Private Families,* by Eliza Acton

1846 *Miss Beecher's Domestic Receipt Book*

1863 *What to Eat and How to Cook It,* by Pierre Blot

1873 *Dictionary of Cuisine* (Grand Dictionnaire de Cuisine), by Alexander Dumas

1882 *336 Menus and 1200 Recipes,* by Baron Brisse

1884 *Mrs. Lincoln's Boston Cook Book: What to Do and What Not to Do in Cooking,* by Mrs. D. A. Lincoln

1884 *The Franco-American Cookery Book,* by Felix J. Déliée

1885 *La Cuisine Creole,* Lafcadio Hearn

1886 *French Dishes for American Tables,* by Pierre Caron

1896 *The Original Boston Cooking School Cook Book,* by Fannie Merritt Farmer

1899. *The Hostess of To-day,* by Linda Hull Larnned

Converting Recipe Measurements to Metric

Use the following formulas for converting U.S. measurements to metric. Since the conversions are not exact, it's important to convert the measurements for all of the ingredients to maintain the same proportions as the original recipe.

WHEN THE MEASUREMENT GIVEN IS	MULTIPLY IT BY	TO CONVERT TO
teaspoons	4.93	milliliters
tablespoons	14.79	milliliters
fluid ounces	29.57	milliliters
cups (liquid)	236.59	milliliters
cups (liquid)	.236	liters
cups (dry)	275.31	milliliters
cups (dry)	.275	liters
pints (liquid)	473.18	milliliters
pints (liquid)	.473	liters
pints (dry)	550.61	milliliters
pints (dry)	.551	liters
quarts (liquid)	946.36	milliliters
quarts (liquid)	.946	liters
quarts (dry)	1101.22	milliliters
quarts (dry)	1.101	liters
gallons	3.785	liters
ounces	28.35	grams
pounds	.454	kilograms
inches	2.54	centimeters
degrees Fahrenheit	$\frac{5}{9}$ (temperature − 32)	degrees Celsius (Centigrade)

While standard metric measurements for dry ingredients are given as units of mass, U.S. measurements are given as units of volume. Therefore, the conversions listed above for dry ingredients are given in the metric equivalent of volume.

Index

Note: Page numbers in *italics* indicate historical recipes or remedies

OTHER STOREY TITLES YOU WILL ENJOY

Growing & Using Herbs Successfully, by Betty E. M. Jacobs. This helpful guide teaches how to plant, propagate, harvest, dry, freeze, and store sixty-four popular herbs. 240 pages. Paperback. ISBN #0-88266-249-X.

The Herbal Palate Cookbook: Delicious Recipes That Showcase the Versatility and Magic of Fresh Herbs, by Maggie Oster & Sal Gilbertie. Through more than 130 recipes, this book creates an innovative palate for fresh herbs. From appetizers to desserts, each recipe offers an informative sidebar on one of the herbs used. Full-color illustrations and photos also teach readers how to cultivate herbs in small spaces and containers for fresh herbs year-round. 176 pages. Hardcover. ISBN #0-88266-915-X.

The Herbal Tea Garden: Planning, Planting, Harvesting & Brewing, by Marietta Marshall Marcin. Herbal tea lovers will learn how to select, grow, and create their own special brews from seventy specific herbal tea plants. It includes the history of tea, how to plan and cultivate herb gardens, and how to dry, freeze, and store herbs. 224 pages. Paperback. ISBN #0-88266-827-7.

Herbal Vinegar, by Maggie Oster. This book begins with dozens of ideas for making and flavoring inexpensive and easy herb, spice, vegetable, and flower vinegars. It continues with more than 100 recipes for using flavored vinegars in everything from appetizers, soups, and salsas to pastas, vegetables, and entrées. In addition, this book includes instructions for growing herbs indoors and out and more than 100 vinegar-based personal and household uses and hints. 176 pages. Paperback. ISBN #0-88266-843-9. Hardcover. ISBN #0-88266-876-5.

Herbed-Wine Cuisine: Creating & Cooking with Herb-Infused Wines, by Janice Mancuso. This first-of-its-kind recipe book unveils a simple method that turns ordinary wine into a magical cooking ingredient. Now cooks, herb gardeners, and winemakers can try Mancuso's imaginative techniques for changing store-bought or homemade wines into a wide range of savory cooking wines. As simple as making herbal vinegar, this unique process flavors wines with herbs, flowers, fruits, and spices. More than 100 easy-to-make recipes using the wines are included. 160 pages. Hardcover. ISBN #0-88266-967-2.

The Herb Gardener: A Guide for All Seasons, by Susan McClure. For the home and garden, this book provides complete instructions on every conceivable aspect of herbs so that the reader can successfully grow and use seventy-five different herbs all year long. It also includes more than 100 color photos, charts, and tables. 240 pages. Paperback. ISBN #0-88266-873-0. Hardcover. ISBN #0-88266-910-9.

Herb Mixtures & Spicy Blends, edited by Deborah Balmuth. This book is an essential guide to dozens of easy-to-make recipes that use herb mixtures and spice blends to create healthy, tasty dishes without a lot of added salt or fat. It also includes a listing and brief profiles of the growers who developed the blends, as well as advice on how best to use them, instructions for drying and storing, and time-saving tips for bottling and labeling. 160 pages. Paperback. ISBN # 0-88266-918-4. Hardcover. ISBN #0-88266-919-2.

These books and other Storey books are available from your bookstore, farm store, garden center, or directly from Storey Publishing, Schoolhouse Road, Pownal, Vermont 05261, or by calling 1-800-441-5700. www.storey.com